Perspectives on Asian Tourism

Series Editors
Catheryn Khoo, Griffith University, Nathan, QLD, Australia
Paolo Mura, Zayed University, Abu Dhabi, United Arab Emirates

While a conspicuous body of knowledge about tourism in Asia is emerging, Western academic ontologies and epistemologies still represent the dominant voice within tourism circles. This series provides a platform to support Asian scholarly production and reveals the different aspects of Asian tourism and its intricate economic and socio-cultural trends.

The books in this series are aimed to pave the way for a more integrated and multifaceted body of knowledge about Asian tourism. By doing so, they contribute to the idea that tourism, as both phenomenon and field of studies, should be more inclusive and disentangled from dominant (mainly Western) ways of knowing.

More specifically, the series will fill gaps in knowledge with regard to:

- the ontological, epistemological, and methodological assumptions behind Asian tourism research;
- specific segments of the Asian tourist population, such as Asian women, Asian backpackers, Asian young tourists, Asian gay tourists, etc;
- specific types of tourism in Asia, such as film-induced tourism, adventure tourism, beauty tourism, religious tourism, etc;
- Asian tourists' experiences, patterns of behaviour, and constraints to travel;
- Asian values that underpin operational, management, and marketing decisions in and/or on Asia (travel);
- external factors that add to the complexities of Asian tourism studies.

Richard S. Aquino • Brooke A. Porter
Editors

Tourism in the Philippines

Communities, Hosts and Guests

Editors
Richard S. Aquino
University of Canterbury
Christchurch, Canterbury, New Zealand

Brooke A. Porter
Auckland University of Technology
Auckland, Auckland, New Zealand

ISSN 2509-4203　　　　　　ISSN 2509-4211　(electronic)
Perspectives on Asian Tourism
ISBN 978-981-19-4012-5　　　ISBN 978-981-19-4013-2　(eBook)
https://doi.org/10.1007/978-981-19-4013-2

© Springer Nature Singapore Pte Ltd. 2022
This work is subject to copyright. All rights are reserved by the Publisher, whether the whole or part of the material is concerned, specifically the rights of translation, reprinting, reuse of illustrations, recitation, broadcasting, reproduction on microfilms or in any other physical way, and transmission or information storage and retrieval, electronic adaptation, computer software, or by similar or dissimilar methodology now known or hereafter developed.
The use of general descriptive names, registered names, trademarks, service marks, etc. in this publication does not imply, even in the absence of a specific statement, that such names are exempt from the relevant protective laws and regulations and therefore free for general use.
The publisher, the authors, and the editors are safe to assume that the advice and information in this book are believed to be true and accurate at the date of publication. Neither the publisher nor the authors or the editors give a warranty, expressed or implied, with respect to the material contained herein or for any errors or omissions that may have been made. The publisher remains neutral with regard to jurisdictional claims in published maps and institutional affiliations.

This Springer imprint is published by the registered company Springer Nature Singapore Pte Ltd.
The registered company address is: 152 Beach Road, #21-01/04 Gateway East, Singapore 189721, Singapore

Acknowledgments

Mabuhay!

The completion of this book project would have not been possible without the following individuals. We sincerely thank Prof. Catheryn Khoo and Assoc. Prof. Paolo Mura, the series editors of Perspectives on Asian Tourism, for their outmost support and encouragement throughout this project. Most especially to Catheryn, thank you for inviting us to edit not just one but two books about Philippine tourism.

We'd also like to thank the coordinators of this publication: Lucie Bartonek, Marielle Klijn, Neelofar Yasmeen, and Arunsanthosh Kannan. We thank you for your understanding as we faced extraordinary circumstances in editing this volume. We appreciate your consistent support to us in this journey.

Finally, and most importantly, our huge appreciation goes to all chapter contributors. Thank you for putting all the hard work and patience in crafting your chapter manuscripts, and sharing your knowledge through this platform. It has been a pleasure collaborating with you all.

Maraming Salamat po!

Contents

Part I Introduction

Tourism in the Philippines Through the Gaze of Communities, Hosts and Guests... 3
Richard S. Aquino and Brooke A. Porter

Part II The Host Gaze

Exploring Residents' Perceptions of Tourism in a Pilgrimage Destination: The Case of Our Lady of Peñafrancia in Naga City, Philippines 17
Anne Marie F. Bagadion and Robert Charles G. Capistrano

Community-Based Tourism: An Analysis of Ugong Rock Adventures Stakeholders' Social Capital in Facilitating Community Participation 35
Patricia Alace E. Delas Alas, Anne Marie M. Pagador, and Robert Charles G. Capistrano

Part III The Tourist Gaze

Strolling Between Shanties: Tourists' Perceptions and Experiences of Manila's Slums............................. 59
Jonna C. Baquillas and Brian C. Gozun

Home Away from Home: Foreign Vloggers' Gaze of the Philippines during the COVID-19 Pandemic................. 79
Maria Criselda G. Badilla, Adrian Lawrence Carvajal, Carl Francis Castro, and Maria Paz Castro

The Traveling Filipina in Periodicals (1898–1938)................. 93
Katherine G. Lacson and Brian C. Gozun

Part IV The Researcher's (Reflexive) Gaze

Significance of the Carabaos in Harvest Festivals in the Philippines.. 113
Peter Jerome B. Del Rosario

Interpreting the Meanings of Carabao Festivals in the Philippines: A Multi-method Study 129
Peter Jerome B. Del Rosario, Anna Reylene J. Montes, and Liza G. Battad

Researching Luzon Island's Pancit Culinary Heritage: Cultural Mapping and Stakeholders' Perspective................... 151
Jame Monren T. Mercado and Avi Ben P. Andalecio

Tourism in the Philippine Society: Conclusions and Looking Forward............................... 171
Richard S. Aquino and Brooke A. Porter

Editors and Contributors

About the Editors

Richard S. Aquino is a Lecturer in Tourism and Marketing at the UC Business School, University of Canterbury in Christchurch, New Zealand. He holds a Doctor of Philosophy from the Auckland University of Technology in New Zealand, where he also obtained his master's degree in international tourism management, and a Bachelor of Science in Tourism from the University of Santo Tomas in Manila, Philippines. His doctoral research focused on how the adoption of social entrepreneurship through tourism changes host communities in the Philippines. His other research interests include sustainable tourism planning and development, geotourism, tourist behavior, and, recently, the decolonization of tourism knowledge production. Currently, he serves as the research notes editor of *Tourism in Marine Environments* and an editor of the *Advances in Southeast-East Asian Studies*. Apart from academic work, he has been actively involved in tourism planning consultancy projects in the Philippines and New Zealand.

Brooke A. Porter works in knowledge management as an instructional designer with international aid agencies. Brooke holds a Doctor of Philosophy from the Auckland University of Technology in New Zealand; a master's in education from Chaminade University in Honolulu, Hawai'i; and a Bachelor of Science in Marine Biology from the Florida Institute of Technology in Melbourne, Florida. Some of her current works investigate tourism as a development and conservation strategy as well as the role of gender. Her doctoral research explored marine tourism as a supplemental livelihood for fisheries-based communities in the Philippines. Brooke also serves as an honorary research fellow at Auckland University of Technology in New Zealand, and as scientific adviser to The Coral Triangle Conservancy, an NGO in the Philippines.

Contributors

Avi Ben P. Andalecio College of Tourism and Hospitality Management & The Graduate School, University of Santo Tomas, City of Manila, Philippines

Maria Criselda G. Badilla University of the Philippines – Diliman, Quezon City, Philippines

Anne Marie F. Bagadion College of Business and Accountancy, Ateneo de Naga University, Naga City, Philippines

Jonna C. Baquillas Management and Organization Department, De La Salle University, Manila, Philippines

Liza G. Battad Philippine Council for Agriculture and Fisheries, Department of Agriculture, Quezon City, Philippines

Robert Charles G. Capistrano School of Community Resources and Development, Arizona State University, Phoenix, AZ, USA
Hainan University – Arizona State University Joint International Tourism College, Haikou, Hainan, China

Adrian Lawrence Carvajal Chanthology Limited, Camberley, United Kingdom

Carl Francis Castro La Consolacion College Manila, Manila, Philippines

Maria Paz Castro Our Lady of Fatima University, Quezon City, Philippines

Peter Jerome B. Del Rosario Department of Social Forestry and Forest Governance, College of Forestry and Natural Resources, University of the Philippines Los Baños (UPLB), Los Baños, Laguna, Philippines

Patricia Alace E. Delas Alas Asian Institute of Tourism, University of the Philippines – Diliman, Quezon City, Philippines

Brian C. Gozun (Deceased) Decision Sciences and Innovation, De La Salle University, Manila, Philippines

Katherine G. Lacson Department of History, Ateneo de Manila University, Quezon City, Philippines

Jame Monren T. Mercado College of Tourism and Hospitality Management, Research Center for Social Sciences and Education, The Graduate School – Center for Conservation of Cultural Property and Environment in the Tropics, University of Santo Tomas, City of Manila, Philippines

Anna Reylene J. Montes Philippine Carabao Center, University of the Philippines Los Baños (UPLB), Los Baños, Laguna, Philippines

Anne Marie M. Pagador Asian Institute of Tourism, University of the Philippines – Diliman, Quezon City, Philippines

Abbreviations

BASECO	Bataan Shipping and Engineering Company
CBT	Community-based tourism
CLUP	Comprehensive land use plan
DILG	Department of the Interior and Local Government
ICOMOS	International Council on Monuments and Sites
LGBTQI	Lesbian, gay, bisexual, transgender, queer, and intersexed
LGU	Local government unit
MTE	Memorable tourism experience
NCCA	National Commission for Culture and the Arts
NGO	Nongovernmental organization
OFW	Overseas Filipino worker
PCC	Philippine Carabao Center
PCSD	Palawan Council for Sustainable Development
PDP	Provincial development plan
PHP	Philippine Peso
PPT	Pro-poor tourism
PSA	Philippine Statistics Authority
SDGs	Sustainable Development Goals
SEP	Socio-economic plan
TURSCO	Tagabinet Ugong Rock Service Cooperative
UN	United Nations
UNESCO	United Nations Educational, Scientific and Cultural Organization
UNWTO	United Nations World Tourism Organization
US	United States
USD	United States Dollar
vlog	Video blog
vlogger	Video blogger
WCED	World Commission on Environment and Development

Part I
Introduction

Tourism in the Philippines Through the Gaze of Communities, Hosts and Guests

Richard S. Aquino and Brooke A. Porter

Abstract This introductory chapter presents an overview of Filipino culture and tourism in the contemporary Filipino society. This chapter situates the diversity of Filipino culture, complexity of the Filipino society, and the role of tourism in host communities in the Philippines. The chapter presents the theming of the edited book, mainly drawn from the concepts of the host gaze, tourist gaze, and researcher's gaze. Related studies about tourism and tourists in the Philippines are presented as the parts of the book are introduced. The chapter ends by outlining the contents of the book.

Keywords Culture · Society · Tourism · Philippines · Communities · Tourist gaze · Host gaze

1 Introduction

The first volume (*Tourism in the Philippines: Applied Management Perspectives*) of this two-part title on Philippine tourism, introduces an overview of the geographical characteristics, major tourist destinations, and key tourism statistics of the country (see Aquino & Porter, 2022). These insights establish the importance of tourism in the country's economy, as well as its contemporary tourism management issues. Such introductions are necessary because the first volume's contributions are aimed at proposing management recommendations to make the Philippine tourism industry more economically beneficial and sustainable. An overview of the Filipino

R. S. Aquino (✉)
University of Canterbury, Christchurch, Canterbury, New Zealand
e-mail: richard.aquino@canterbury.ac.nz

B. A. Porter
Auckland University of Technology, Auckland, Auckland, New Zealand

Coral Triangle Conservancy, Taguig, Philippines
e-mail: bporter@aut.ac.nz

© Springer Nature Singapore Pte Ltd. 2022
R. S. Aquino, B. A. Porter (eds.), *Tourism in the Philippines*, Perspectives on Asian Tourism, https://doi.org/10.1007/978-981-19-4013-2_1

culture and society serves as the backdrop of the tourism phenomena explored in the second volume this series.

The Philippines is a country with a diverse culture and society. Its 109.04 million[1] people are characterized by at least 77 ethnolinguistic groups that originate from different geographical locations (Peralta, 2000). A total of 78 languages and 500 dialects are spoken in the country, with its population coming from eight major language groups namely, "Tagalog, Visayan, Ilocano, Hiligaynon (also known as Ilonggo), Bicol, Waray, Pampango, and Pangasinense" (Abinales & Amoroso, 2017, p. 17). Although commonalities exist in their grammatical structures, Philippine languages vary a lot in terms of vocabulary making it difficult for its people to communicate with each other (Boquet, 2017). As Peralta (2000) documented, each ethnolinguistic group in the Philippines possesses a culture shaped by its geography, ecology, traditions, language, and history. Furthermore, there are about 110 groups of indigenous people across the Philippines (National Commission on Indigenous Peoples, 2013). These ethnic groups are the descendants of the first inhabitants of the archipelago, having their own dialects, traditions, and cultures, and have resisted the influence of colonization (see Boquet, 2017). The ethnic and linguistic diversity of the Philippines does not only shape the diversity of Filipino culture; it also makes the Philippines a pluralistic society (Bernad, 1971). For instance, a Filipino tourist from Pampanga (who speaks Pampango or Kapampangan) travelling to Cebu, an island province where Visayan is the main language, would not be able to communicate with their hosts, unless they converse in *Filipino* – the national language that is derived from Tagalog, spoken by the majority, and taught in schools – or in English, especially in more formal settings (e.g., hospitality establishments). While conversing in *Filipino* seems plausible, not all Filipino peoples' first language and culture is Tagalog (e.g., Llamzon, 1968).

From an essentialist perspective,[2] culture in society is founded on history (Ooi, 2019). Prior to colonization, the Philippine capital, Manila, was a Muslim kingdom and its the inhabitants have long trading history with the Chinese, Arabs, Indians, and Malay. The long Philippine colonial history spanned 333 years under the Spanish and 50 years under the US imperialist rule (Agoncillo, 1974), founding the country's national origins (Mulder, 2013). The country's name came from a colonial rule – named after King Philip II during its Spanish colonization. In the same era, Roman Catholicism spread widely across the archipelago, making it the country's main religion (82.9% of the population according to Abinales & Amoroso, 2017). The country's institutions were shaped according to the systems placed by its former colonizers. For example, the US established its public education system in English. As a result, English is now one of the Philippines' official languages and the primary language of instruction in colleges and universities. Although an

---

[1] As of May 2020, according to the Philippine Statistics Authority (2021).

[2] "Culture is seen as the software of society, so that members of society are wired to share and communicate in accepted ways" (Ooi, 2019, p. 15).

outcome of colonialism, English is considered an asset in today's globalized world, and more specifically in the industry of tourism.

Given the lengthy colonial history, describing Filipino culture is challenging. Geert Hofstede's popular framework proposes six dimensions for explaining national cultures (Hofstede, 2022). Applying this framework, Filipinos are collectivistic, masculine, tend to avoid uncertainty, more normative than pragmatic, and do not put much emphasis on pursuing leisure (see Hofstede Insights, 2022). While some of these may hold true, these generalizations may be limited, given the complexity of the origins of Filipino society and history. One of the most prominent Filipino historians, Teodoro A. Agoncillo, posits that the Filipino culture is an amalgamation of indigenous/native and foreign cultures (Agoncillo, 1974). Hence, a better approach to framing the Filipino culture is the one that is functional and negotiated (e.g., Ooi, 2019), meaning that the blanket terms, "The Philippines" and "Filipino", while essential for labelling place and nationality/nationhood, are not sufficient in capturing the cultural diversity of this Southeast Asian archipelago. Such terms fail to recognize the complexity of the Filipino culture and the plurality of the Filipino society.

Although foreshadowed by its natural attractions (e.g., Alejandria-Gonzalez, 2016), the Filipino culture is a fundamental asset showcased in promoting Philippine tourism products and experiences. The tangible manifestations of Filipino culture, which also serve as important tourism resources, illustrate its cultural complexity. For instance, some of the country's World Heritage Sites inscribed by UNESCO include cultural structures made pre-colonization, such the Rice Terraces of the Philippine Cordilleras created by the Ifugao people, while others show its Spanish colonial heritage namely, the Baroque Churches of the Philippines and the Historic City of Vigan (UNESCO World Heritage Convention, 2022; see chapter "Significance of the Carabaos in Harvest Festivals in the Philippines"). Further, fiestas and festivals, most of which have been introduced through Catholicism (see chapter "Exploring Residents' Perceptions of Tourism in a Pilgrimage Destination: The Case of Our Lady of Peñafrancia in Naga City, Philippines") and now have been appropriated and owned by Filipinos (Wendt, 1998), are popular events that draw tourists to regions and provinces. For example, the Sinulog Festival in Cebu held every third Sunday of January to commemorate the conversion of Cebuanos into Catholicism and honor Santo Niño – the Holy Child Jesus – is known for its grand street parade and dances (Oracion, 2012); attracting around 223,000 tourists in 2019 (Galarpe, 2019). Diversity is also manifested in the Filipino culinary heritage (see chapter "Researching Luzon Island's Pancit Culinary Heritage: Cultural Mapping and Stakeholders' Perspective"), which has been attributed to the blending of local and regional and foreign cuisines (Mercado & Andalecio, 2020). Conversely, an intangible aspect of the Filipino culture, one that can only be experienced through social interactions between hosts and guests, is the Filipino hospitality (see chapter "Home Away from Home: Foreign Vloggers' Gaze of the Philippines During the COVID-19 Pandemic"). Kajiwara (1994) analyzes Filipino hospitality as:

> ...not only a touristic gimmick but a password for the national-cultural character. In this notion of hospitality, Filipinos are expected or believed to play a role of being a host. However, this hospitality cannot escape from a [sic] implied set of hierarchical relation between the host and the guest. Looking back at several historical watersheds, those hosts appear to be subjugative to their guests more often than they should be. In Philippine culture, generosity and good behaviour as a host are no mere matter of personal preference, but are part of fundamental conviction about the nature of human relationship which facilitate smooth functioning of the social universe. (Kajiwara, 1994, p. 173)

While the hospitableness of the Filipino people has been identified as an important factor in foreign tourists' perceptions of the country (de Guzman et al., 2012), in-depth explorations of how this trait is extended in touristic spaces are needed. Of course, hospitality is not only extended to foreign guests but also to visiting friends and family, and to strangers more generally. As a cultural norm and obligation, Filipino hosts generally accommodate visiting friends and provide hospitality as a way of maintaining harmony, which is also central to the value of *pakikipagkapwa* associated with the notions of connection and reciprocity (Capistrano & Weaver, 2018). Given the importance of such hospitable traits in the tourism sector, there is a need to further understand how the Filipino culture and society is showcased in, and to some extent created through, contemporary tourism phenomena. This edited book presents a collection of scholarly inquiry into tourism through a largely Filipino lens. Collectively, the chapters present tourism as a social phenomenon in the Philippines, through the perspectives of local communities, individual hosts, and guests – both Filipino and foreign.

2 Intention and Structure of the Book

This edited volume serves as the second instalment of a two-part title that explores contemporary issues and perspectives on tourism in the Philippines. Drawn from a range of disciplinary backgrounds and geographical scales (national, regional, and local), this book presents a critical investigation of issues surrounding Philippine host communities and tourists to and within the country. Tourism is an essential aspect of the Filipino society today. Alongside already existing tourism developments, is the emergence of associated issues that are challenging host communities, individuals, and the society at large. A recent critical accounting of academic works on Philippine tourism showed important gaps in the literature, which included exploration on life in Philippine host communities and conceptualisations of Filipino travellers' perspectives (Aquino, 2019). To protect the stakeholders and the sustainability of the sector, such issues for those involved in tourism, as well as how communities and individuals give meaning to these phenomena, require critical exploration.

As in the first edited volume, this book aims to create a platform for engaging with Filipino scholars allowing them to present their academic works and perspectives on a range of local tourism issues. The chapters in this book are written by

Filipino academics based in the Philippines and in diaspora. This platform supports the cultivation of a "culture of research" in the Philippine tourism and hospitality academia. Like the complex constellation of cultural elements that form Filipino culture and society, the chapter contributions are drawn from a mixture of non-indigenous theoretical approaches and place/culture-based concepts. These scholarly works are informed by a diverse set of social science disciplines and subdisciplines, including sociology, anthropology, mass communications, feminist and gender studies, cultural studies, history, and tourism and hospitality studies. Given this diversity in disciplinary background and training, the contributions were written in different academic writing styles.

The contributions have employed qualitative methodologies and case study research approaches, drawn from a range of primary and secondary data collection techniques, as well as visual research methods. While the chapters examine various topics situated in different socio-cultural and tourism contexts, the contributions have been themed by the role/type of study participants that add insights to such issues.

2.1 Part II: The Host Gaze

Themed under the notion of the *host gaze*, the contributions in Part II examine the host communities and individuals' perceptions of tourism and tourists in various contexts. In this edited book, the host gaze encapsulates residents and communities' attitudes towards tourism, which are shaped by their backgrounds, relationships with tourism, and multiple encounters with and subjective experiences of tourism (Maoz, 2006; Moufakkir, 2011). Understanding the social impacts of tourism, as perceived by residents, has prevailed since the advent of tourism studies (e.g., Deery et al., 2012). Exploring host community perceptions is an essential undertaking in tourism studies, as these should be central to tourism development (Aquino et al., 2018a; Higgins-Desbiolles et al., 2019). Like in many low-income countries, tourism is advocated as a tool for sustainable community development in the Philippines (Okazaki, 2008; Porter & Orams, 2014; Porter et al., 2015).

Given tourism's theoretical role as an alternative and supplemental form of livelihood, communities perceive the economic benefits of tourism in the form of income and job creation, as evident in the Filipino coastal communities explored by Gier et al. (2017) and Quevedo et al. (2021). The positive contribution of tourism to nature conservation, infrastructure development, socio-cultural development, and human capital development has also been recognized by Filipino communities involved in tourism. One of the most notable consequences has been the impact of tourism on individual hosts' self-esteem and collective identity (e.g., Aquino et al., 2021; Zahra & McGehee, 2013). In the context of volunteer tourism, Zahra and McGehee (2013) found that residents developed a form of "personal capital," from interactions with tourists that resulted in feelings of empowerment and a sense of pride in individual hosts. In the case of Culion Island – the country's largest former leper colony – residents communicated that after a century of isolation, a positive image of the community has been developed through their interactions with tourists (Aquino et al., 2021). As with many communities benefiting from tourism, those who have seen and experienced the economic and social benefits of tourism are found to support the industry (Quevedo et al., 2021).

Although tourism can create positive social change, it has also been the cause of an array of social issues. For example, local leaders and residents of a remote coastal community in Bohol Island were happy to welcome foreign investors that could provide them with electricity to better deliver tourism activities; however, this service was found to be costly for residents and resulted in the loss of local control over this basic infrastructure (Gier et al., 2017). In the same locality, negative social outcomes were revealed by local informants, such as the rise of drug trafficking and sex tourism (Gier et al., 2017). In an analysis of panel data gathered throughout the Philippines, regions that receive more foreign tourists are shown to experience more crimes, such as theft and robbery (Palanca-Tan et al., 2015). Such negative consequences of tourism, though not isolated to the Philippines, are known as inhibitors of residents' support for tourism.

The works included in part are informed by the gaze of Filipino host communities. This part starts with Anne Marie Bagadion and Robert Charles Capistrano's exploration of residents' perceptions of tourism in a Catholic pilgrimage destination (chapter "Exploring Residents' Perceptions of Tourism in a Pilgrimage Destination: The Case of Our Lady of Peñafrancia in Naga City, Philippines"). Situated in the context of the Our Lady of Peñafrancia festivities, the authors interviewed residents and stakeholders about their views towards pilgrimage tourism development, and analyzed these insights through the lens of social exchange theory. Following this chapter is Patricia Alace Delas Alas, Anne Marie Pagador, and Robert Charles Capistrano's examination of community-based tourism development using social capital theory (chapter "Community-Based Tourism: An Analysis of Ugong Rock Adventures Stakeholders' Social Capital in Facilitating Community Participation"). Particularly, this chapter investigates the role of trust, norms, and networks in the community-based tourism initiative.

2.2 Part III: The Tourist Gaze

The third part of this book is founded on the *tourist gaze*. The tourist gaze (Urry, 1990, 2002) is one of the popular theoretical frameworks in tourism studies, used in interpreting tourist perceptions and experiences. The tourist gaze is subjective and shaped by environmental forces, social factors, personal factors, and tourism contexts (Urry, 1990, 2002), influencing the creation of tourist experiences.

Previous studies have linked aspects of a hospitable experience to Filipino culture (e.g., Capistrano & Weaver, 2017, 2018). For example, in a study of Australian tourists travelling throughout the Philippines, de Guzman et al. (2012) identified that the common pre- and post-images of these tourists include positive aspects such as the friendliness and hospitality of the people, and value for money for food and accommodation, and negative images such as bad traffic and pollution. In a study of cultural tourism in Palawan (Alejandria-Gonzalez, 2016, p. 509), tourists attributed the island to having an exotic image, as evidenced by their use of the descriptors, "tribal" and "ethnic." Tourists visiting Mount Pinatubo, a volcanic tourism destination known for its destructive eruption in 1991, emphasized the socio-cultural dimension of their experiences by narrating their awe, not only towards the landscape, but also towards the resilience of the host communities living on the volcano (Aquino et al., 2018b). In the same study, a stronger sense of place and people attachment was shown by Filipino domestic tourists (Aquino et al., 2018b).

Conversely, there is a limited understanding of Filipino tourist behaviour and perspectives (Aquino, 2019). Unlike some of its Asian neighbours (e.g., China, Japan, and India), the Philippines is not considered a key tourist market (Chang, 2015). Filipinos travel internationally for various reasons other than for leisure, such as for working overseas. For Filipinos who have migrated to other countries, visiting friends and relatives is a popular form of travel (Capistrano & Weaver, 2017). Other Filipinos, however, face various constraints from undertaking leisure travel. Unlike most populations from Western countries where OE (overseas experience) has been popularized (e.g., New Zealand), in the Philippines there is an expectation for young adults to help out at home financially, making it difficult for them to pursue international tourism experiences (Lacson, 2020). Perhaps, this is one explanation why Filipinos in general score low in Hofstede's "indulgence" dimension (Hofstede Insights, 2022). It is expected that such personal and socio-cultural circumstances affect Filipino tourists' gaze, when they travel for leisure.

The chapters themed under Part III provide insights into the gaze of foreign and Filipino travellers. Authored by Jonna Baquillas and the late, Brian Gozun, chapter "Strolling Between Shanties: Tourists' Perceptions and Experiences of Manila's Slums" uncovers the perceptions and experiences of tourists who have participated in slum tours. Applying concepts of destination image and memorable tourism experience formation, this chapter analyzes online user-generated information posted about the slum tours in Manila. In chapter "Home Away from Home: Foreign Vloggers' Gaze of the Philippines During the COVID-19 Pandemic", authors Maria Criselda G. Badilla, Adrian Lawrence Carvajal, Carl Francis Castro, and Maria Paz Castro, examine online content in the form of vlogs (video blogs) by foreign travel vloggers. Adopting the tourist gaze (Urry, 1990, 2002), the authors thematically analyzed the images of the Philippines and Filipinos that were presented by the vloggers quarantined in the Philippines during COVID-19 lockdown. The last chapter of Part III is dedicated to tracing the voyage of Filipina travellers from 1898 until 1938 (chapter "The Traveling Filipina in Periodicals (1898–1938)"). In this chapter, Katherine Lacson and the late, Brian Gozun, employ historical research methods in uncovering the ways that the Filipina engaged in travel during the early twentieth century.

2.3 Part IV: The Researchers' (Reflexive) Gaze

In the past decade, there has been a call for pursuing critical tourism scholarship in Asia, as few studies about tourism in Asia have employed local, place-based, and culture-based methodologies (Yang & Ong, 2020). As emphasized by Chang (2015, p. 97), the Asian tourism wave should be "understood on its own terms rather than under the gaze of Western eyes.[3]" In proposing the adoption of cultural complexity as a framework in understanding Asian tourist behaviour, Ooi (2019) argues that, "Asian tourist behaviour must be understood in context; Asian societies are heterogeneous." The same contextual conditions are highlighted by Dela Santa and Tiatco (2019) who proposed critical ethnography in examining cultural heritage and tourism using cases from the Philippines. Sharing a similar goal, Aquino (2019) suggested a framework for decolonizing Philippines tourism and hospitality scholarship, stressing the importance of researcher positionality and reflexivity in tourism-focused inquiries.

The chapters under Part IV – The Researchers' (Reflexive) Gaze contribute towards the agenda pursued by the aforementioned scholars, by reflecting on their perspectives and positionalities in undertaking research about Filipino festivals and culinary heritage. In chapter "Significance of the Carabaos in Harvest Festivals in the Philippines", Peter Jerome Del Rosario analyzes the significance of the carabao in harvest festivals in the Philippines. In chapter "Interpreting the Meanings of Carabao Festivals in the Philippines: A Multi-method Study", Peter Jerome Del Rosario, Anna Reylene Montes, and Liza Battad conduct reflexive field observations combined with visual and archival research, in delineating the meanings of selected carabao festivals. Jame Monren Mercado and Avi Ben Andalecio reflect on their experiences and methodological approaches during a culinary mapping project of Pancit performed throughout the provinces of Luzon (chapter "Researching Luzon Island's Pancit Culinary Heritage: Cultural Mapping and Stakeholders' Perspective"). Finally, we present a concluding chapter that synthesizes the theoretical and practical implications of the contributions (chapter "Tourism in the Philippine Society: Conclusions and Looking Forward"). In the same chapter, we identify areas of research that can be focused on to further our understanding of tourism in the Filipino culture and society.

References

Abinales, P. N., & Amoroso, D. J. (2017). *State and society in the Philippines* (2nd ed.). Rowman & Littlefield.

Agoncillo, T. A. (1974). *Introduction to Filipino history*. Garotech Publishing.

---

[3] From the co-editor's (Brooke Porter) cultural outsider perspective, the pride of place is apparent in the contributions. The authors positive outlooks on the potential for the tourism sector are evident, even if not directly stated.

Alejandria-Gonzalez, M. C. P. (2016). Cultural tourism development in the Philippines: An analysis of challenges and orientations. *Journal of Quality Assurance in Hospitality & Tourism, 17*(4), 496–515. https://doi.org/10.1080/1528008X.2015.1127194

Aquino, R. S. (2019). Towards decolonising tourism and hospitality research in the Philippines. *Tourism Management Perspectives, 31*, 72–84. https://doi.org/10.1016/j.tmp.2019.03.014

Aquino, R. S., & Porter, B. A. (2022). Contemporary issues in tourism management in the Philippines. In R. S. Aquino & B. A. Porter (Eds.), *Tourism in the Philippines: Applied management perspectives*. Springer.

Aquino, R. S., Lück, M., & Schänzel, H. A. (2018a). A conceptual framework of tourism social entrepreneurship for sustainable community development. *Journal of Hospitality and Tourism Management, 37*, 23–32. https://doi.org/10.1016/j.jhtm.2018.09.001

Aquino, R. S., Lück, M., & Schänzel, H. A. (2021). Mapping the outcomes of social entrepreneurship and tourism on host communities: A three-dimensional approach. *Journal of Sustainable Tourism*, 1–22. https://doi.org/10.1080/09669582.2021.1986515

Aquino, R. S., Schänzel, H. A., & Hyde, K. F. (2018b). Unearthing the geotourism experience: Geotourist perspectives at Mount Pinatubo, Philippines. *Tourist Studies, 18*(1), 41–62. https://doi.org/10.1177/1468797617717465

Bernad, M. A. (1971). Philippine culture and the Filipino identity. *Philippine Studies, 19*(4), 573–592.

Boquet, Y. (2017). *The Philippine archipelago*. Springer. https://doi.org/10.1007/978-3-319-51926-5

Capistrano, R. C., & Weaver, A. (2017). Host-guest interactions between first-generation immigrants and their visiting relatives: Social exchange, relations of care and travel. *International Journal of Culture, Tourism and Hospitality Research, 11*(3), 406–420. https://doi.org/10.1108/IJCTHR-11-2016-0115

Capistrano, R. C., & Weaver, A. (2018). That's what friends are for: Emotional solidarity, friendship and social interactions between first-generation immigrants and their visiting friends. *Journal of Hospitality and Tourism Management, 36*, 57–66. https://doi.org/10.1016/j.jhtm.2018.07.003

Chang, T. C. (2015). The Asian wave and critical tourism scholarship. *International Journal of Asia-Pacific Studies, 11*(1), 83–101.

de Guzman, A. B., de Castro, B. V., Calanog, J. F. V., Taguinin, A., Afalla, J., Aldover, A., & Gotangco, M. (2012). The Australian tourists' travel motivation and pre-and post-images of the Philippines as their destination. *Asia-Pacific Journal of Innovation in Hospitality and Tourism, 1*(2), 143–164.

Deery, M., Jago, L., & Fredline, L. (2012). Rethinking social impacts of tourism research: A new research agenda. *Tourism Management, 33*(1), 64–73. https://doi.org/10.1016/j.tourman.2011.01.026

Dela Santa, E., & Tiatco, S. A. (2019). Tourism, heritage and cultural performance: Developing a modality of heritage tourism. *Tourism Management Perspectives, 31*, 301–309. https://doi.org/10.1016/j.tmp.2019.06.001

Galarpe, L. (2019, January 8). Tourist arrivals for Sinulog to jump by 4 percent: Airport exec. *Philippine News Agency*. https://www.pna.gov.ph/articles/1058297

Gier, L., Christie, P., & Amolo, R. (2017). Community perceptions of scuba dive tourism development in Bien Unido, Bohol Island, Philippines. *Journal of Coastal Conservation, 21*(1), 153–166.

Higgins-Desbiolles, F., Carnicelli, S., Krolikowski, C., Wijesinghe, G., & Boluk, K. (2019). Degrowing tourism: Rethinking tourism. *Journal of Sustainable Tourism, 27*(12), 1926–1944. https://doi.org/10.1080/09669582.2019.1601732

Hofstede, G. (2022). *The 6D model of national culture*. Retrieved March 22, 2022, https://geerthofstede.com/culture-geert-hofstede-gert-jan-hofstede/6d-model-of-national-culture/

Hofstede Insights. (2022). *What about the Philippines?* Retrieved March 22, 2022, https://www.hofstede-insights.com/country/the-philippines/

Kajiwara, K. (1994). Philippine democracy: A form of resistance against the common good? 年報 人間科学, 15, 163–174. https://doi.org/10.18910/9587

Lacson, F. N. (2020). *The solo Filipina traveller: From the insights of travel bloggers* [Masters, Auckland University of Technology]. http://hdl.handle.net/10292/13267

Llamzon, T. A. (1968). On Tagalog as dominant language. *Philippine Studies, 16*(4), 729–749.

Maoz, D. (2006). The mutual gaze. *Annals of Tourism Research, 33*(1), 221–239. https://doi.org/10.1016/j.annals.2005.10.010

Mercado, J. M. T., & Andalecio, A. B. P. (2020). Ysla de panciteria: A preliminary study on the culinary heritage significance of pancit using the heritage documentation approach—The case of Luzon Island, Philippines. *Journal of Ethnic Foods, 7*(1), 19. https://doi.org/10.1186/s42779-020-00057-1

Moufakkir, O. (2011). The role of cultural distance in mediating the host gaze. *Tourist Studies, 11*(1), 73–89. https://doi.org/10.1177/1468797611412065

Mulder, N. (2013). Filipino identity: The haunting question. *Journal of Current Southeast Asian Affairs, 32*(1), 55–80. https://doi.org/10.1177/186810341303200103

National Commission on Indigenous Peoples. (2013). *Indigenous peoples of the Philippines*. Retrieved March 22, 2022, https://web.archive.org/web/20131028074053/http://ncipro67.com.ph/indigenous-peoples-of-the-philippines/

Okazaki, E. (2008). A community-based tourism model: Its conception and use. *Journal of Sustainable Tourism, 16*(5), 511–529. https://doi.org/10.1080/09669580802159594

Ooi, C.-S. (2019). Asian tourists and cultural complexity: Implications for practice and the Asianisation of tourism scholarship. *Tourism Management Perspectives, 31*, 14–23. https://doi.org/10.1016/j.tmp.2019.03.007

Oracion, E. G. (2012). The Sinulog festival of overseas Filipino workers in Hong Kong: Meanings and contexts. *Asian Anthropology, 11*(1), 107–127. https://doi.org/10.1080/1683478X.2012.10600859

Palanca-Tan, R., Garces, L. P. D. M., Purisiman, A. N. C., & Zaratan, A. C. L. (2015). Tourism and crime: Evidence from the Philippines. *Southeast Asian Studies, 4*(3), 565–580. https://doi.org/10.20495/seas.4.3_565

Peralta, J. T. (2000). *Glimpses: Peoples of the Philippines*. National Commission for Culture and the Arts. https://issuu.com/ncca0/docs/glimpses-peoples_of_the_philippines

Philippine Statistics Authority. (2021). *2020 census of population and housing (2020 CPH) population counts declared official by the president*. https://psa.gov.ph/content/2020-census-population-andhousing-2020-cph-population counts-declared-official-president

Porter, B. A., & Orams, M. B. (2014). Exploring tourism as a potential development strategy for an artisanal fishing community in the Philippines: The case of Barangay Victory in Bolinao. *Tourism in Marine Environments, 10*(1–2), 49–70. https://doi.org/10.3727/154427314X14056884441743

Porter, B. A., Orams, M. B., & Lück, M. (2015). Surf-riding tourism in coastal fishing communities: A comparative case study of two projects from the Philippines. *Ocean & Coastal Management, 116*, 169–176. https://doi.org/10.1016/j.ocecoaman.2015.07.015

Quevedo, J. M. D., Uchiyama, Y., & Kohsaka, R. (2021). Linking blue carbon ecosystems with sustainable tourism: Dichotomy of urban–rural local perspectives from the Philippines. *Regional Studies in Marine Science, 45*, 101820. https://doi.org/10.1016/j.rsma.2021.101820

UNESCO World Heritage Convention. (2022). *Philippines*. Retrieved March 22, 2022, https://whc.unesco.org/en/statesparties/ph

Urry, J. (1990). *The tourist gaze: Leisure and travel in contemporary societies*. SAGE.

Urry, J. (2002). *The tourist gaze* (2nd ed.). SAGE.

Wendt, R. (1998). Philippine fiesta and colonial culture. *Philippine Studies, 46*(1), 3–23.

Yang, E. C. L., & Ong, F. (2020). Redefining Asian tourism. *Tourism Management Perspectives, 34*, 100667. https://doi.org/10.1016/j.tmp.2020.100667

Zahra, A., & McGehee, N. G. (2013). Volunteer tourism: A host community capital perspective. *Annals of Tourism Research, 42*, 22–45. https://doi.org/10.1016/j.annals.2013.01.008

Richard S. Aquino is a Lecturer of Tourism and Marketing at the UC Business School, University of Canterbury in Christchurch, New Zealand. He holds a Doctor of Philosophy from the Auckland University of Technology in New Zealand, where he also obtained his master's degree in international tourism management, and a Bachelor of Science in Tourism from the University of Santo Tomas in Manila, Philippines. His doctoral research focused on how the adoption of social entrepreneurship through tourism changes host communities in the Philippines. His other research interests include sustainable tourism planning and development, geotourism, tourist behaviour, and recently, the decolonization of tourism knowledge production. Currently, he serves as the research notes editor of *Tourism in Marine Environments* and an editor of the *Advances in Southeast Asian Studies*. Apart from academic work, he has been actively involved in tourism planning consultancy projects in the Philippines and New Zealand.

Brooke A. Porter works in knowledge management as an instructional designer with international aid agencies. Brooke holds a Doctor of Philosophy from the Auckland University of Technology in New Zealand, a master's in education from Chaminade University in Honolulu, Hawai'i, and a bachelor of science in marine biology from the Florida Institute of Technology in Melbourne, Florida. Some of her current work investigates tourism as a development and conservation strategy as well as the role of gender. Her doctoral research explored marine tourism as a supplemental livelihood for fisheries-based communities in the Philippines. Brooke also serves as an Honorary Research Fellow at Auckland University of Technology in New Zealand, and as scientific adviser to The Coral Triangle Conservancy, an NGO in the Philippines.

Part II
The Host Gaze

Exploring Residents' Perceptions of Tourism in a Pilgrimage Destination: The Case of Our Lady of Peñafrancia in Naga City, Philippines

Anne Marie F. Bagadion and Robert Charles G. Capistrano

Abstract This study explores the residents' perceptions of tourism in a pilgrimage destination in the Philippines. Located in Naga City, Camarines Sur in Bicol region, the week-long festivity of Our Lady of Peñafrancia is witnessed by millions of Marian devotees who pay tribute every month of September. Through the lens of social exchange theory, this study addresses the following questions: (1) What are the residents' perceptions on the level of tourism growth brought about by pilgrimage tourism?; (2) What are impacts of pilgrimage tourism in the area?; and (3) How do the residents perceive the management of pilgrimage tourism in the area? Through qualitative inquiry, findings revealed that participants' perceptions and disposition on the level of tourism growth, impacts of pilgrimage tourism and management of tourism in Naga city varies. While the majority still find the level of tourism growth to be satisfactory or reasonable, it cannot be discounted that pilgrimage tourism has greatly impacted residents' lives for the last 10 years. Future studies may examine other religious events in the Philippines where interactions of residents and tourists are occurring, and the implications of these events towards destination management.

Keywords Pilgrimage tourism · Resident perceptions · Social exchange theory · Tourism impacts · Philippines

---

A. M. F. Bagadion (✉)
College of Business and Accountancy, Ateneo de Naga University,
Naga City, Philippines
e-mail: abagadion@gbox.adnu.edu.ph

R. C. G. Capistrano
School of Community Resources and Development, Arizona State University,
Phoenix, AZ, USA

Hainan University – Arizona State University Joint International Tourism College,
Haikou, Hainan, China
e-mail: robert.capistrano@asu.edu

© Springer Nature Singapore Pte Ltd. 2022
R. S. Aquino, B. A. Porter (eds.), *Tourism in the Philippines*, Perspectives on Asian Tourism, https://doi.org/10.1007/978-981-19-4013-2_2

1 Introduction

Tourism is being utilised as a tool in reducing poverty (UNWTO, 2015) and many countries are using it as strategic approach in building their nation and achieve sustainable development (Font & McCabe, 2017; Nunkoo & Gursoy, 2011; Nunkoo & Ramkissoon, 2011). However, many tourism research studies on residents or host communities' perspective give the idea that tourism is an interruption to community life, particularly in rural areas - potentially contributing to the innate discord among either hosts and tourists, or vice versa, at the local community level (Wearing et al., 2010; Woosnam, 2012). In developing countries such as the Philippines, there are substantial efforts to reduce poverty that utilise various forms of tourism, such as culinary tourism (Bender & De Leon, 2018), ecotourism (Brillo, 2016), and farm tourism (Montefrio & Sin, 2019). However, less is known on pilgrimage tourism, specifically from the perspective of residents regarding achieving community development considering that religion plays an important aspect of Filipinos (David & Okazaki, 2006; Lagman et al., 2014).

Tourism engenders both benefits and costs that influence the host or local society. The residents of host communities are the ones who are diametrically influenced by tourism development. Hence, it is crucial to examine resident's views or perceptions of tourism to ascertain the effects of tourism on residents and the locality (Haywood, 2000; Nunkoo & Ramkissoon, 2010a; Simmons, 1994; Snaith & Haley, 1999), regardless of the tourism form being adopted.

Exploring the case of the Peñafrancia festivities, this study explores residents' perceptions of the social and economic impacts of pilgrimage tourism in Naga City, Philippines. Studies related to pilgrimage tourism tend to focus on the tourists rather than host communities (Muresan et al., 2021; Progano, 2018; Woosnam, 2012). Moreover, most of the research studies have highlighted the significance of sustainable development in tourism, but none of them have highlighted the need for such development specifically in pilgrimage tourism (Muresan et al., 2021; Romanelli et al., 2021). Further, it is also vital for tourism destination managers to understand the local community's perceptions towards the impacts of pilgrimage tourism. These are the gaps that this study will explore using the social exchange theory as the conceptual lens. Particularly, this study addresses the following questions: (1) What are the residents' perceptions on the current level of tourism growth brought about by pilgrimage tourism?; (2) What are impacts of pilgrimage tourism in the area?; and (3) How do the residents perceive the management of pilgrimage tourism in the area? This study aims to contribute to the private, public, local government units, and academic sector by providing insights and recommendations on how pilgrimage tourism can be well-managed and become an effective tool as a socio-economic development strategy. Such research may be of benefit not only to Naga City but also to other destinations holding religious events in the Philippines, as well as throughout Southeast Asia.

2 Naga City and the Origin of the Peñafrancia Festivities

2.1 Naga City

Historically, Naga City is called *Ciudad de Nueva Caceres* and was recognized in the order of Spanish Governor-General Francisco de Sande in 1575. The then *Nueva Caceres* received its honoured status as the third Spanish royal city in the Philippine islands, next to Cebu and Manila. Naga City has a land area of 84.48 square kilometres or 32.62 square miles which constitutes 1.54% of Camarines Sur's total area. It is 385 km south of Manila via Pan-Philippine Highway, which takes approximately 8 to 9 hours to travel via land (see Fig. 1). According to the latest census in 2015, the population was 196,003, representing 10.04% of the total population of Camarines Sur province, or 3.38% of the overall population of the Bicol Region. Based on these figures, the population density is computed at 2320 inhabitants per square kilometer or 6009 inhabitants per square mile. According to the Bureau of Local Government Finance, the annual regular revenue of Naga for 2016 was PhP 975,090,393.2 (approximately US$ 19.7 million). The population of Naga grew from 55,506 in 1960 to 196,003 in 2015, an increase of 140,497 people. The 2015 census figures denote a positive growth rate of 2.19%, or an increase of 21,072 people, from the previous population of 174,931 in 2010 (PSA, 2017). Statistics

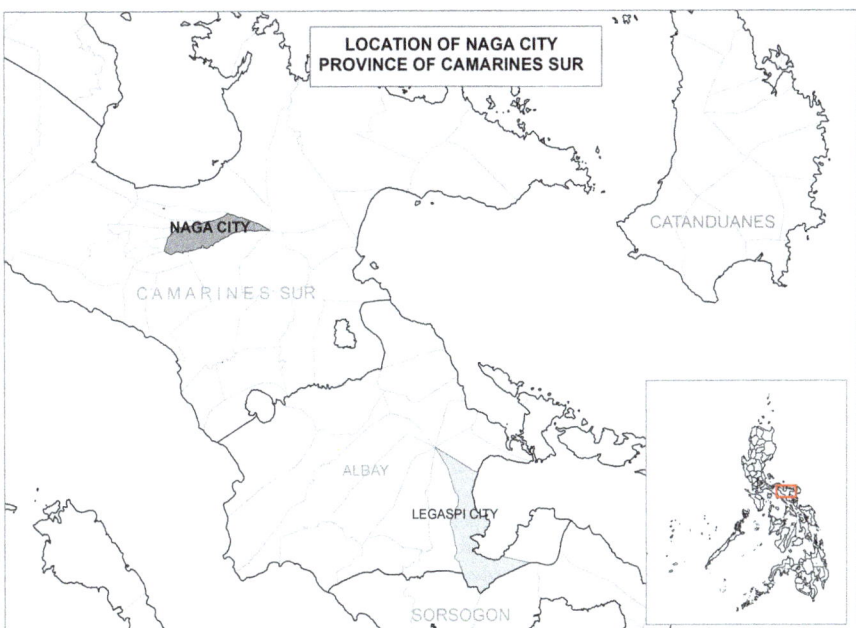

Fig. 1 Area map of Naga city, Camarines Sur and its location in the Philippines (inset). (Map illustration by R. Sontillanosa)

show that Naga had a 6% tourism growth rate from 2018 to 2019 with approximately 1.5 million local and foreign tourists (DOT, 2019).

2.2 Origins of the Peñafrancia Devotion and Festivity

In 2010, the Nagueños (local residents of Naga City) marked their 300 years old devotion to Our Lady of Peñafrancia, which is even older than the famous pilgrim place in the world such as Lourdes (1858) and Fatima (1917; Legazpi, 2008). The region's Feast of Our Lady of Peñafrancia together with Divino Rostro[1] (Holy Face of Jesus) is the only regional feast in the country. For the past three centuries, it has become an epic historical event and part of the Filipino socio-cultural heritage.

The roots of the devotion to the Our Lady of Peñafrancia started in the fifteenth century in France through a devout Catholic named Simon Vela, who came from an affluent French family. With a deep sense of devotion to the Virgin Mary, Mother of Jesus Christ, Simon attested he heard a 'lady's voice' several times instructing him to find an image 'similar to me." With his superior's permission, Simon traversed many roads of France for five years, until he reached Spain where he found the place called *Peñafrancia* which literally means the 'rocky hill of France.' Upon reaching the place, Simon experienced divine instructions from 'Our Lady' on how to find her image. Finally, on May 19, 1434, Simon and his companions found the image of the 'Our Lady with child Jesus in her arms' entrenched among the rocks. Upon discovery of the original image, Our Lady of Peñafrancia showed her miraculous power through inexplicable healings which happened to Simon and his five companions. Immediately, the news on healing spread like wildfire which started the devotion to Our Lady of Peñafrancia from Spain to other parts of the world.

The devotion first came to the Philippines when a young Spanish priest named Fr. Miguel Robles Covarrubias, was ordained, and assigned in Nueva Caceres (now Naga City). Fr. Covarrubias, whose parents originally hailed from Salamanca, Spain, had a strong devoutness to "Our Lady," because he was a sickly boy. His first parish assignment in Nueva Caceres (Naga City) was about 4 km. away from the town proper and nearing the slopes of Mt. Isarog, where many *Agtas* (or Aetas, an indigenous group of people) reside and became his regular parishioners. As promised during his seminary days, Fr. Covarrubias always wanted to build a church in

---

[1] *Divino Nostro* is the image of Jesus that is said to have miraculously appeared on Veronica's veil when she wiped his face en route to the crucifixion. The devotion to the Divino Rostro in Naga City started in 1882 when a cholera epidemic broke out in Manila and reached Naga. Cholera was incurable then, but as locals tell it, on the third day after the image of Divino Rostro was placed at the altar of the Cathedral, the epidemic which had claimed many lives of people in Naga finally ended. Word of mouth spread and fostered devotion to Divino Rostro throughout the region. The Feast of the Divine Face of Jesus is celebrated on the second Friday of September, and the image Our Lady of Peñafrancia is celebrated the following weekend. Both celebrations are important to locals, but the Peñafrancia celebration draws the most vocal and fervent devotion (Fortunado et al., 2019).

honor of Our Lady of Peñafrancia. Upon seeing the growing number of his churchgoers, he expanded his parish church, converting the smaller existing church made from light materials into a bigger church made of "adobe." During the construction, he also ordered for an image of Our Lady of Peñafrancia to be made, similar to the one he prayed to while he was sick in his younger days. Hence, he hired a local craftsman to create the image of Our Lady of Peñafrancia who would be the patroness of the Church, which was finished in 1710. To get the dark finish of the original image of Our Lady from France, a dog was slayed to use its blood to paint and coat the image. After praying for the sacrificed dog with its four legs tied, it was hurled into the river. But after several minutes, many witnessed the dog swim to the riverbanks and run to his master's house. It started the "countless miracles" and "devotion" to "Our Lady of Peñafrancia" which continued throughout the next 300 years (Bagadion, 2018; Carpio, 2002).

Currently, Naga City is known as the home to Our Lady of Peñafrancia festivities, which gather more than a million Marian pilgrims[2] annually. The festivities are commemorated every second week of September, during a two-week celebration where millions of devotees flock into the city to honour the patronnes, the Our Lady of Peñafrancia or *Ina*. The highlight of the celebration is called the *traslacion*,[3] a procession which transfers the image of *Ina* from the original Peñafrancia Shrine to the Metropolitan Cathedral, where the novena is held (see Fig. 2a). After the novena, the image of "Our Lady of Peñafrancia" is brought to the Basilica Minore by a *fluvial procession* through Naga river by the *voyadores*[4] (see Fig. 2b, c).

3 Literature Review

This section discusses the literature encompassing pilgrimage tourism and residents' perceptions of tourism impacts. These phenomena were examined through the lens of social exchange theory.

---

[2] These are pilgrims that have special devotion to Mary, mother of Jesus Christ.

[3] *Traslacion* is the transferring of the miraculous Image of the Virgin, Our Lady of Peñafrancia and image of the Divino Rostro from Our Lady of Peñafrancia Shrine to the Metropolitan Cathedral of Naga City for a (nine day) Novena and Holy Masses via land procession. On the last day which normally falls on a Saturday or the eve of the main festivity, the image is returned to Peñafrancia Basilica Minore following the Naga River route.

[4] *Voyadores* are the men devotee ushering or escort the image of Our Lady of Peñafrancia into her destination. In Fluvial, from Naga Cathedral down to river going to Peñafrancia Basilica Minore. They are those who paddle the boat during the regatta. The City Government of Naga makes it organized due to accidents that happened in the past. They wear headbands and colourful shirts to be identified according to their group affiliation as well as their boat's names.

Fig. 2 (a) Traslacion procession of the Penafrancia image entering Naga Metropolitan Cathedral at the beginning of the 9-day novena; (b) Peñafrancia Image with the *voyadores* during the fluvial procession at the Naga River; (c) Fluvial procession at the Naga river. (Photos by: A. Bagadion, 2018)

3.1 Pilgrimage Tourism

Pilgrimage may be defined in many ways and sometimes the answers converge, compete and to some extent overlap (Nickerson et al., 2018). Amidst different views and definitions, the following are the distinct concepts that support this study: a pilgrimage in its most basic sense is a journey to a special place, in which both the journey and the destination have spiritual significance to the pilgrim (Davidson & Glitz, 2002); and that it is a departure from daily life on a journey in search of spiritual well-being (Bradley, 2009; Collins-Kreiner, 2020).

There is a need to examine the impacts of pilgrimage tourism as this may differ across destinations. For many least developed countries, pilgrimage tourism provides a competitive advantage for which they can efficiently convert domestic cultural resources into foreign exchange (Vijayanand, 2012). Research on pilgrimage tourism remains scant where each geographical regions offer their own unique history and environment (Ebadi, 2014).

Understanding pilgrimage tourism is important for the Philippines because it is Asia's largest Catholic population, and thus, considered a 'religious nation;' more than 86% of the approximately 105 million Filipinos are Catholics (Miller, 2020). In the same vein, scholarly work related to impacts of events and festivals (including pilgrimages) in the Philippines is currently understudied, particularly in terms of the benefits and consequences on local communities (see Aquino, 2019).

A novel approach of this research is that pilgrimage tourism as a socio-cultural phenomenon involving interactions among residents and other stakeholders is explored from a Filipino, Global South, and non-Western perspective. Geographically speaking, this study contributes to knowledge related to Marian pilgrimage where existing studies are focused in a European setting wherein pilgrimage tourism is more established (e.g., Ambrósio et al., 2017; Mylonopoulos et al., 2019). Significantly, pilgrimage tourism is also being understood from a Filipino and Global South perspective, where the Philippines is considered the third largest Catholic nation in the world after Brazil and Mexico and discourse related to pilgrimage tourism is less known considering these countries are formerly shaped by colonisation while recognising its great potential towards tourism and development.

3.2 Resident's Perceptions of Tourism Impacts

In the context of tourism, Smith and Brent (2001) described host-guest relationship as a socially constructed phenomenon that is actively produced by both hosts and guests who create their own meanings within the context of social interaction that varies by time, space, and culture. This influential contribution has also established hospitality and the related concepts of hosts and guests as fundamental to understanding the social interactions between tourists and local residents in both commercial and non-commercial settings (Lynch et al., 2011). While the host-guest interaction represents a human exchange, studies that look at this relationship often focus on tourists and their impact on more traditional social settings, including pilgrimage tourism to which this study contributes.

Current studies on pilgrimage tourism have focused on aspects related to visitors, such as travel motivation, visitor experience or visitor typologies (Progano, 2018). As such, academic discourse tends to the host communities. Nonetheless, it is also vital for tourism destination management to understand the local community's perceptions towards impacts brought by pilgrimage tourism. Previous studies using social exchange theory explored residents-tourists interactions were conducted in the context of island tourism (Moyle et al., 2010), heritage tourism (Deng et al., 2016), and rural tourism (Chuang, 2010). The major idea of social exchange theory is that individuals enter into and or maintain exchange relationships with another individual or parties with the expectation that doing so will be rewarding (Blau, 1964; Homans, 1961) However, the social exchanges occurring in the context of pilgrimage tourism remains underexplored. Therefore, this study significantly contributes in exploring further the social exchanges and interactions occurring while giving voice to residents' spiritual and socio-economic development in pilgrimage tourism.

Social exchange theory started as a marginal utility theory, and later as a sociological and psychological framework. On one hand, Homans (1961) underscores the behaviour of actors' interaction with each other. He defined social exchange as the exchange of activity, tangible or intangible, rewarding or costly, between or among persons. Cost was relevant in the interchange between the actors involved. On the other hand, Blau (1964, 1986) argues that social exchange theory revolves around rewards and cost. However, his view of behaviour is anchored on a more economic and utilitarian perspective as compared with Homans who gave emphasis on reinforcement principles derived from experimental behaviour analysis. Also, Blau saw social exchange as a significant process in the establishment of fundamental relationships between individuals and groups focusing on the reciprocal exchange of material benefits and forms of relations created.

4 Methods

The study utilised a qualitative inquiry approach to explore the phenomenon through the lens of social exchange theory (Belotto, 2018; Yin, 2003, 2011), in order to understand the interactions occurring in pilgrimage tourism in the Philippines which is currently underexplored. Social exchange theory provides a framework for exploring the inter-relationships among the assessment of costs and benefits, positive and negative impacts, and support for tourism (Choi & Murray, 2010; Nunkoo & Ramkissoon, 2010a, b; Perdue et al., 1990). At the individual level, the theory helped explain that that those employed in the tourism sector, who receive more direct benefits from the industry, have more affirmative attitudes or more inclined toward tourists and tourism development (Haley et al., 2005; Haralambopoulos & Pizam, 1996). At the community level, a social exchange entails costs and benefits in economic, environmental, and sociocultural fields that mainly influences attitudes toward tourism development (Ryan & Montgomery, 1994). This study contributes towards understanding the social exchanges occurring in pilgrimage tourism, a non-commercial view where the focus is on the residents. The basic unit of analysis is the relationship between actors and the impacts of these exchanges. Additionally, the exchanges occurring in Naga City, a Marian pilgrimage tourism destination, remains underexplored.

Qualitative case study research approach was adopted as the fundamental method because it is beneficial in exploring possible unknown issues within the locality being studied. Creswell (2003, 2014) proposed that the qualitative research process is iterative, as data collection and analysis methods are continuously re-evaluated to reflect fresh insights gained.

Through an exploratory case study approach, this study established a comprehensive interpretation of a phenomenon, which has developed over time as opposed to examining specific incidents. Moreover, the study enabled the researchers to gain a thorough understanding of the phenomena on how a pilgrimage city develops residents' perceptions towards a growing pilgrimage tourism.

The research locale covers the downtown proper of Naga City where the main route of Our Lady of Peñafrancia's *traslacion* and fluvial procession take place. Purposive cluster sampling was done wherein research participants were identified through one of the lead author's colleagues in a National Catholic membership association which has a chapter in the Bicol region. There were 20 research participants considered in the said study area: six in Peñafrancia Avenue; six in General

Luna Street; five in Elias Angeles Street, and three along Magsaysay Avenue going to the Basilica Minore. The criteria for the selection of participants include those who are at least 18 years old and are currently residing or working in Naga City's downtown proper, that is traversed by the *traslacion* and *fluvial procession* (see routes in Figs. 3 and 4, respectively). Old residents were classified as those who are living/working in the area for more than 5 years, while new residents were categorized as those who are residing/working for less than 5 years. Research participants were briefed in a language comfortable to them: English, Tagalog, or in their native dialect, about the goals of the study, including ethical issues and the risks and benefits of participation.

The inquiry was guided by an interview protocol designed to draw out participants' perceptions on pilgrimage tourism in their community. Face-to-face semi-structured interviews were conducted during the first phase of the data gathering process. Semi-structured interviews were chosen to elicit a deeper explanation of resident's perceptions of tourism. However, the outbreak of COVID-19 in the region affected face-to-face data collection. Therefore, half of the interviews were conducted either through phone calls or Facebook video messenger interviews. A simplified semi-structured questionnaire was patterned after Curto (2006) with eight core questions that covers the research questions stated earlier. The questionnaire was utilised to ensure that same core information can be elicited from each participant, while providing the researchers to probe deeper into the rich data of

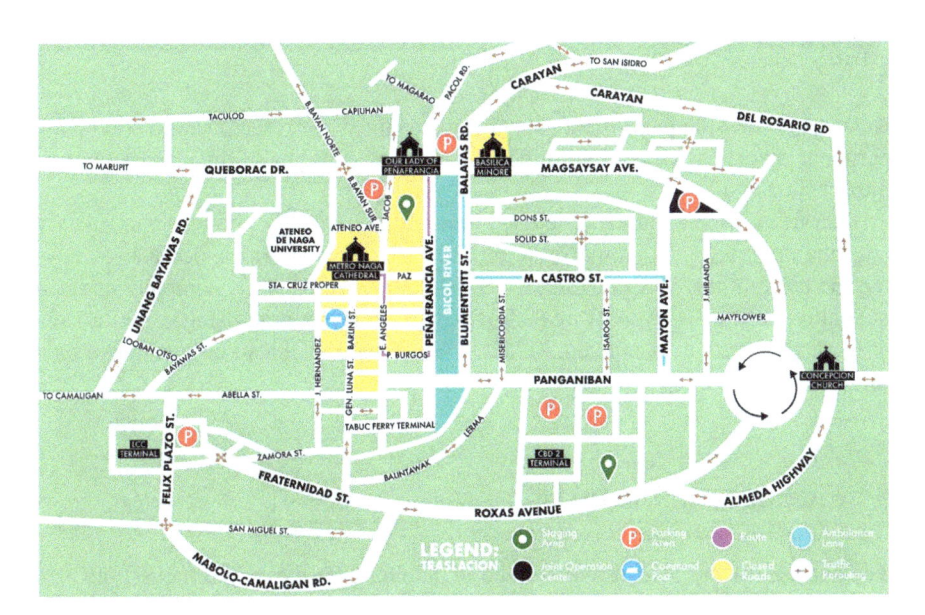

Fig. 3 Map of Downtown Naga showing the route of the *traslacion* (Illustration enhanced by L. Dela Paz; Source: www.naga.gov.ph). Note: *Traslacion* procession route (by land): from Peñafrancia Shrine passes Peñafrancia Ave.; turn right to P. Burgos St.; then turn right to Elias Angeles St.,; enters the Metropolitan Cathedral – and as tradition, the Image will stay there for nine days or what they call *novenario*

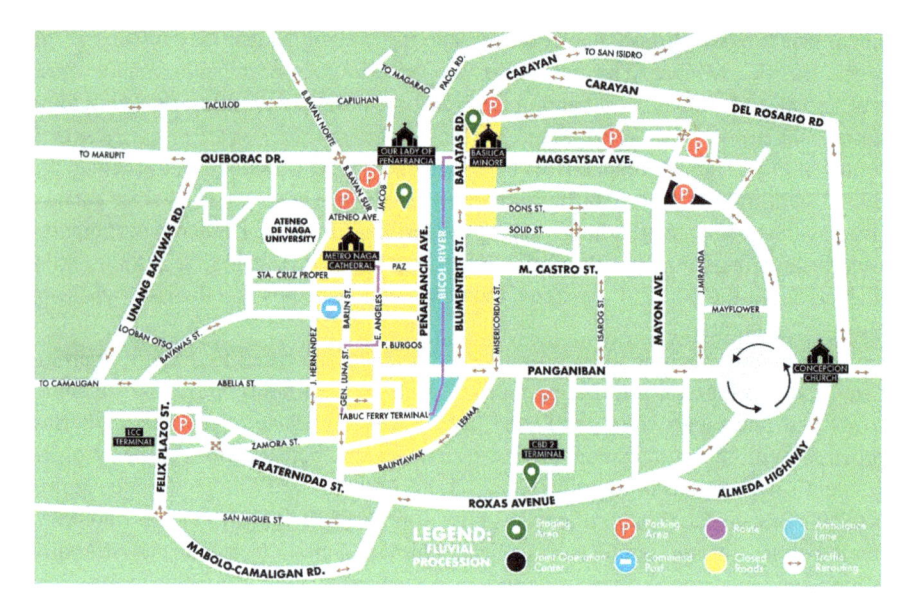

Fig. 4 Map of Downtown Naga showing the route of the *fluvial procession* (Illustration enhanced by L. Dela Paz; Source: www.naga.gov.ph). Note: Fluvial procession route: After nine days in the Metropolitan Cathedral, the procession traverse from Elias Angeles St.; turns right to P. Burgos St.; then left to General Luna St. straight to the Naga City Ferry Terminal wherein the Image is loaded to the pagoda (a small boat that accommodates the *voyadores*[3]) that traverses the Bicol river going to Basilica Minore

experiences that the participant shared. This enabled the researchers to follow the pertinent aspects associated with the residents' perceptions of pilgrimage tourism impacts in Naga City.

Interviews were audio recorded and transcribed manually into text immediately after the interviews. Upon transcription, thematic analysis was undertaken following the conventions of Braun and Clarke (2019). MAXQDA, a computer-assisted qualitative data analysis software (CAQDAS) program for processing large amounts of qualitative data, was utilized. MAXQDA provided insights into qualitative data sets with analyses.

5 Findings and Discussion

The findings of this study are discussed in parallel with the research questions: (1) perceptions on the growth of pilgrimage tourism in Naga City; (2) perceived impacts of pilgrimage tourism in Naga City; and (3) perceptions in the management of Pilgrimage tourism in Naga City.

5.1 Perceptions on the Growth of Pilgrimage Tourism in Naga City

The participants perceived pilgrimage tourism development in locality as satisfactory, as evidenced in the use of expressions such as 'just right'. As tourism is still well-managed in the destination, residents feel that tourists' arrival or growth rate is not exponentially increasing and that the pilgrimage itself is more influenced by a person's faith:

> *Just right, because I noticed that every year, there is a slight increase in the rate of visitors coming, but not necessarily pilgrims. If it is growing too fast, I think it is helpful because it will help boost tourism more.* (P1, Male, 56 years old, dentist, resident of Naga City since birth)

> *The growth of pilgrimage tourism in our place is the effect of a person's spiritual experience rather than as a [tourist] attraction.* (P2, Female, 74 years old, retired educator and government employee, resident for the last 50 years)

> *Just right, though it is not Paris-standard. Growth of pilgrimage tourism in our place is the effect of a person's spiritual experience rather than attraction.* (P4, Female, 48 years old, resident since birth)

The above quotes surmise that residents find the growth of pilgrimage tourism or annual rate of visitors reasonable. It was understood that residents can still cope with the influx of tourists for the last ten years.

5.2 Perceived Impacts of Pilgrimage Tourism in Naga City

Several impacts were perceived by the residents including positive outcomes such as employment and income generation. Meanwhile, the negative impacts that were perceived by residents include public transportation and congestion issues, changing values and culture of the residents, and the potential environmental impacts of overdevelopment.

Economically speaking, residents recognized that pilgrimage tourism has an impact on trade as it opens new business opportunities through increased tourist arrival and employment generation. Small, and medium enterprises benefitted from the festivities as well as boosting a crude economy, thus, when asked – do they perceive that the community as a whole has economically benefited from pilgrimage tourism? – some residents believed that the growth of business only occurs during the month of September.

There are also contrasting views on the contribution of the festivity where pilgrimage tourism is a good economic strategy for Naga city:

> *Naga as a community has benefited because of the promotion and growth of local businesses in the city. Growth in the hotels and other local accommodation services in the city. There is the discovery of local products and business that can be promoted nationwide. And*

> *I think the largest benefits of pilgrimage tourism is the business opportunities and employment to locals.* (P6, Female, 42 years old, food manager and resident for 10 years)

> *Even the less fortunate have the chance to make business like selling candles, foods for the pilgrims.* (P7, Female, 27 years old, banker and resident for 6 years)

> *With the continuing influx of tourists, the watershed of Mt. Isarog is over utilized and the creation of an industrial park at present compromises the ecological resources in the said mountain.* (P17, Female, 52 years old, resident for more than 10 years)

This was also noted by another participant, expressing:

> *Many agricultural lands were given up to pave the way to commercial malls within the last 10 years.* (P2, Female 74 years old, retired educator and government employee, resident for the last 50 years)

Hence, watersheds and many trees are compromised due to the industrial park currently being developed at the slopes of Mt. Isarog in exchange for so-called "economic development" for the city. In addition, such "economic development and opportunities" are contradicting the values of faith and spiritual goodness of the community. To quote the late Archbishop Leonardo Z. Legazpi of Caceres (2010, p. 69):

> We are not against trade and commerce, revelry or merriment. There is nothing wrong with selling bottled mineral water to a thirsty pilgrim […] but everything is wrong with selling a bottle of beer to a minor in the middle of the religious feast. When we say commercialization, we do not want the city and its corporate sponsors to exploit or take advantage of our religious feast.

However, for the residents, pilgrimage tourism also reflects a deep spiritual experience on their Catholic faith. For instance, the annual festivity is a time for deepening and renewal of faith and spirituality. During the festivity, lived experiences related to their physical, mental, and spiritual healing abound. The event is a venue for residents and tourists alike to express gratitude for the blessings sent from above by joining the festive tradition.

> *There were many stories told of healing of physical and mental ailments both from pilgrims and locals. Many have found grace they have longed for through the intercession of Our Lady of Peñafrancia.* (P19, Female 40 years old, housewife, 20 years resident)

> *The Feast of Our Lady of Peñafrancia could be celebrated in many different ways, especially today when religion tries to keep up with the modern world. However, celebrating the festival would only be complete if it served its purpose – prayer, devotion, gratitude and most importantly gratitude.* (P2, Female 74 years old, retired educator and government employee, resident for the last 50 years)

> *On the spiritual side, it deepens the faith of the devotees whether residents or visitors, and also we are freed from all the natural calamities and tragedies that might come along the way because we are being protected by the mantle of Ina. I think all Bicolanos can attest to that.* (P7, Female, 27 years old, banker, resident for 6 years)

5.3 Perceived Management of Pilgrimage Tourism

Residents' perceptions on how the local government manages pilgrimage tourism are contrasting. Challenges are seen by residents during the week-long festivity, such as theft and robbery, traffic congestion, pollution, lesser land space, low accommodation rates of hotel rooms before and after the festivity, unruly and undisciplined devotees and *voyadores,* and other security issues, which should be addressed by local government units particularly the Philippine National Police. However, with the challenges mentioned by some of the research participants, the majority still agreed that Naga city's administrators together with its Arts, Culture and Tourism Office (ACTO) and with other Local government units of nearby municipalities in coordination with Philippine National Police local unit are managing the week-long festivity satisfactorily. Below are some of the quotes from the participants on how they perceive the management of pilgrimage tourism in the city for the last 10 years:

> *I think they manage the pilgrimage tourism or the Peñafrancia festivity satisfactorily.* (P5, Male, 45 years old, Professional/nurse, resident less than 10 years)

> *The annual week-long festivity has always been peaceful. Female, 35 years old, housewife, resident for 5 years*

> *The local government unit (LGU) of Naga together with the other agencies managed the festivity by maintaining peace and order and systematic program of activities. They are doing the planning months before the said festivity. Because of the proper coordination with the different agencies, they have achieved their plans and programs.* (P9, Female, 35 years old, resident for 10 years)

Accordingly, the social exchanges between the residents and tourists can be enhanced through the mediation of the church, the local government units, and other stakeholders' activities, as perceived by another participant:

> *The LGU should coordinate with the Diocese in Naga. Bicol culture and strong faith should be offered and shared to our fellow Filipinos and other tourists. The local tourism department should manage, provide, or offer different pilgrimage activities. We have various churches in the city to be tapped to provide venues and activities for the pilgrims.* (P16, Male, 55 years old, businessperson, resident since birth)

6 Conclusions

This chapter explored residents' perceptions of pilgrimage tourism in Naga City. The findings revealed that residents' perception on the growth, impacts, and management of pilgrimage tourism in Naga City varies. Overall, the residents perceived the level of tourism growth to be satisfactory or reasonable. However, some residents associated the growth rate within the period of 10 years with various impacts to the community. Despite the varied perceptions and dispositions, the majority perceived that the pilgrimage tourism in Naga city has various impacts in their lives such as positive economic impacts (e.g., employment and livelihood opportunities), environmental setback, renewal and deepening of faith both to pilgrims and residents during the weeklong festivity of the Our Lady of Peñafrancia. Moreover, it cannot be discounted that commerce and trade surge during the festivity has benefited thousands of small and medium-scale enterprises that in a way generated income to the residents. However, major setbacks also are perceived by the residents in terms of ecological challenges and compromised moral values, if not managed may create challenges for the next generation.

Pilgrimage tourism has greatly affected the lives of Naga City residents for the past decades in both spiritual and non-spiritual ways. It is imperative that religious and government institutions work together in planning, managing, and implementing measures that would protect and secure factors on: social (moral values, spirituality and faith); political (peace and order); economic (sustainability of business and trade fairs); ecological (environmental protection and preservation); and the use of technology (social media and other applications) that can further promote and sustain pilgrimage tourism in Naga City, which may have an implication to other pilgrimage tourism destinations in the Philippines. Future research may also examine how communities perceive the distribution of costs and benefits among them (Muresan et al., 2021; Progano, 2018). This information could be of valuable use for tourism policy makers, managers, and planners to avoid conflicts between communities and facilitate even development in this time of pandemic. This study also prompts local government units, tourism professionals, planners and strategists to look at how COVID-19 may impact pilgrimage tourism in the future.

Acknowledgement The authors would like to thank the City Government of Naga including the Arts, Culture and Tourism Office (ACTO) with Mr. Alec Santos for allowing us to enhance the city's *translacion* and fluvial procession route maps used in the Naga City website – www.nagacity.gov.ph. Our gratitude also to all our research participants who participated in this study.

References

Ambrósio, V., Krogmann, A., & Fernandes, C. (2017). Marian midsize shrines: Three itineraries between Portugal and Slovakia. *International Journal of Religious Tourism and Pilgrimage, 5*(3), 72–82. https://doi.org/10.21427/D78M5S

Aquino, R. S. (2019). Towards decolonising tourism and hospitality research in the Philippines. *Tourism Management Perspectives, 31*, 72–84. https://doi.org/10.1016/j.tmp.2019.03.014

Bagadion, A. F. (2018). Case study: A look on the economic dimension of pilgrimage tourism. *Journal of Global Business*. CD Journal ISSN No. 2094-7305 Vol 7. 90–98; 11th Association of Training Institutions for Foreign Trade in Asia and the Pacific, Global Business Conference, Manila, March 3, 2018.

Belotto, M. J. (2018). Data analysis methods for qualitative research: Managing the challenges of coding, interrater reliability, and thematic analysis. *The Qualitative Report, 23*(11), 2622–2633. Retrieved from https://nsuworks.nova.edu/tqr/vol23/iss11/2

Bender, D. E., & De Leon, A. (2018). Everybody was boodle fighting: Military histories, culinary tourism, and diasporic dining. *Food, Culture & Society, 21*(1), 25–41. https://doi.org/10.1080/15528014.2017.1398469

Blau, P. M. (1964). *Exchange and power in social life*. Wiley.
Blau, P. (1986). *Exchange and power in social life*. Transaction Publishers.
Bradley, I. (2009). *Pilgrimage: A spiritual and cultural journey*. Lion Hudson.
Braun, V., & Clarke, V. (2019). Reflecting on reflexive thematic analysis. *Qualitative Research in Sport, Exercise and Health, 11*(4), 589–597. https://doi.org/10.1080/2159676X.2019.1628806
Brillo, B. B. C. (2016). Development of a small lake: Ecotourism enterprise for Pandin Lake, San Pablo City, Philippines. *Lakes & Reservoirs: Research & Management, 21*(4), 284–292. https://doi.org/10.1111/lre.12150
Carpio, J. M. Z. (2002). *Ina and the Bikol people: A journey of faith*. Archdiocese of Caceres.
Choi, H. C., & Murray, I. (2010). Resident attitudes toward sustainable community tourism. *Journal of Sustainable Tourism, 18*(4), 575–594. https://doi.org/10.1080/09669580903524852
Chuang, S. (2010). Rural tourism: Perspectives from social exchange theory. *Social Behavior and Personality, 38*(10), 1313–1322. https://doi.org/10.2224/sbp.2010.38.10.1313
Collins-Kreiner, N. (2020). Pilgrimage tourism – Past, present, and future rejuvenation: A perspective article. *Tourism Review, 75*(1), 145–148. https://doi.org/10.1108/TR-04-2019-0130
Creswell, J. W. (2003). *Research design: Qualitative, quantitative, and mixed methods approaches*. Sage Publications.
Creswell, J. W. (2014). *Research design qualitative, quantitative, and mixed methods approaches*. Sage Publications.
Curto, J. (2006). *Resident perceptions of tourism in a rapidly growing mountain tourism destination* [Master's thesis, University of Waterloo, Ontario, Canada]. Retrieved from http://hdl.handle.net/10012/2904
David, E. J. R., & Okazaki, S. (2006). Colonial mentality: A review and recommendation for Filipino American psychology. *Cultural Diversity and Ethnic Minority Psychology, 12*(1),1–16. https://doi.org/10.1037/1099-9809.12.1.1
Davidson, L. K., & Glitz, D. M. (2002). *Pilgrimage from the Ganges to Graceland: An encyclopedia*. ABC-CLIO.
Deng, J., McGill, D., Arbogast, D., & Maumbe, K. (2016). Stakeholders' perceptions of tourism development in Appalachian forest heritage. *Tourism Review International, 20*(4), 235–253. https://doi.org/10.3727/154427216X14791579617579
Department of Tourism Region 5 Office. (2019). Report, Legazpi, Albay, Philippines.
Ebadi, M. (2014). Typologies of the visitors at Khaled Nabi shrine, Iran: Tourists or pilgrims? *International Journal of Culture, Tourism and Hospitality Research, 8*(3), 310–321. https://doi.org/10.1108/IJCTHR-05-2013-0033
Font, X., & McCabe, S. (2017). Sustainability and marketing in tourism: Its context, paradoxes, approaches and challenges. *Journal of Sustainable Tourism, 25*(7), 869–883. https://doi.org/10.1080/09669582.2017.1301721
Fortunado, A. V., Fortunado-Sanches, E., & Landy, T. M. (2019) Peñafrancia Festival & Divino Rostro feature novenas and fluvial procession. Retrieved from www.catholicsandcultures.org/feasts-holy-days/penafrancia-divino-rostro-philippines
Haley, A. J., Snaith, T., & Miller, G. (2005). The social impacts of tourism a case study of Bath, UK. *Annals of Tourism Research, 32*(3), 647–668. https://doi.org/10.1016/j.annals.2004.10.009
Haralambopoulos, N., & Pizam, A. (1996). Perceived impacts of tourism: The case of Samos. *Annals of Tourism Research, 23*(3), 503–526. https://doi.org/10.1016/0160-7383(95)00075-5
Haywood, K. M. (2000). Responsible and responsive tourism planning in the community. In C. Ryan & S. Page (Eds.), *Tourism management: Towards the new millennium* (pp. 167–182). Elsevier Science Ltd.
Homans, G. C. (1961). *Social behavior: Its elementary forms*. Harcourt, Brace & World.
Lagman, R. A., Yoo, G. J., Levine, E. G., Donnell, K. A., & Lim, H. R. (2014). "Leaving it to God" Religion and Spirituality among Filipina Immigrant Breast Cancer Survivors. *Journal of Religion and Health, 53*(2), 449–460. https://doi.org/10.1007/s10943-012-9648-z
Legazpi, L. Z. (2008). Top 30 questions: Caring for our 300 year-old devotion Ateneo de Naga University, Naga City, Philippines.

Lynch, P., Molz, J. G., McIntosh, A., Lugosi, P., & Lashley, C. (2011). Editorial: Theorizing hospitality. *Hospitality and Society Journal*, 1–21. https://doi.org/10.1386/hosp.1.1.3_2

Miller, J. (2020). Religion in the Philippines. Retrieved from https://asiasociety.org/education/religion-philippines

Montefrio, M. J. F., & Sin, H. L. (2019). Elite governance of agritourism in the Philippines. *Journal of Sustainable Tourism, 27*(9), 1338–1354. https://doi.org/10.1080/09669582.2019.1621327

Moyle, B., Croy, G., & Weiler, B. (2010). Tourism interaction on islands: The community and visitor social exchange. *International Journal of Culture, Tourism, and Hospitality Research, 4*(2), 95–107. https://doi.org/10.1108/17506181011045172

Muresan, I. C., Harun, R., Arion, F. H., Fatah, A. O., & Dumitras, D. E. (2021). Exploring residents' perceptions of the socio-cultural benefits of tourism development in the mountain area. *Societies, 11*(3). 1–11. https://EconPapers.repec.org/RePEc:gam:jsoctx:v:11:y:2021:i:3:p:83-:d:597018

Mylonopoulos, D., Moira, P., & Parthenis, S. (2019). Pilgrimages through time and space: The case of Marian pilgrimages in Greece. *International Journal of Religious Tourism and Pilgrimage, 7*(4), 97–105. https://doi.org/10.21427/fwt6-6v41

Nickerson, R. C., Greenia, G. D., McIntosh, I. S., & Quinn, E. M. (2018). What is pilgrimage? A report of the panel at the 2017 symposium on pilgrimage studies, William & Mary October 7, 2017. *International Journal of Religious Tourism and Pilgrimage, 6*(2), 1–6. https://arrow.tudublin.ie/ijrtp/vol6/iss2/2

Nunkoo, R., & Gursoy, D. (2011). Residents' support for tourism: An identity perspective. *Annals of Tourism Research., 39*(1), 243–268. https://doi.org/10.1016/j.annals.2011.05.006

Nunkoo, R., & Ramkissoon, H. (2010a). Small island urban tourism: a residents' perspective. *Current Issues in Tourism, 13*(1), 37–60. https://doi.org/10.1080/13683500802499414

Nunkoo, R., & Ramkissoon, H. (2010b). Community perceptions of tourism in small island states: A conceptual framework. *Journal of Policy Research in Tourism, Leisure & Events, 2*(1), 51–65. https://doi.org/10.1080/19407960903542318

Nunkoo, R., & Ramkissoon, H. (2011). Residents' satisfaction with community attributes and support for tourism. *Journal of Hospitality & Tourism Research, 35*(2), 171–190. https://doi.org/10.1177/1096348010384600

Perdue, R. R., Long, P. T., & Allen, L. (1990). Resident support for tourism development. *Annals of Tourism Research, 17*(4), 586–599. https://doi.org/10.1016/0160-7383(90)90029-Q

Philippine Statistics Authority (PSA) (2017). PSA Report 2017. www.psa.gov.ph

Progano, R. N. (2018). Residents' perceptions of socio-economic impacts on pilgrimage trails: How does the community perceive pilgrimage tourism? *Asian Journal of Tourism Research, 3*(2), 148–178. https://doi.org/10.12982/AJTR.2018.0014

Romanelli, M., Gazzola, P., Grechi, D., & Pollice, F. (2021). Towards a sustainability-oriented religious tourism. *Systems Research and Behavioral Science, 38*, 386–396. https://doi.org/10.1002/sres.2791

Ryan, C., & Montgomery, D. (1994). The attitudes of Bakewell residents to tourism and issues in community responsive tourism. *Tourism Management, 15*(5), 358–369. https://doi.org/10.1016/0261-5177(94)90090-6

Simmons, D. G. (1994). Community participation in tourism planning. *Tourism Management, 15*(2), 98–108. https://doi.org/10.1016/0261-5177(94)90003-5

Smith, V. L., & Brent, M. (Eds.). (2001). *Host and guests revisited: Tourism issues of the 21st century*. Cognizant Communication Corporation.

Snaith, T., & Haley, A. (1999). Residents' opinions of tourism development in the historic city of York, England. *Tourism Management, 20*(5), 595–603. https://doi.org/10.1016/S0261-5177(99)00030-8

UNWTO. (2015). Tourism and poverty alleviation. Retrieved from http://stepunwto.org

Vijayanand, S. (2012). Socio-economic impacts in pilgrimage tourism. *International Journal of Multidisciplinary Research, 2*(1), 329–343. https://doi.org/10.4172/2167-0269.1000387

Wearing, S., Stevenson, D., & Young, T. (2010). *Tourist cultures: Identify, place and the Traveller*. SAGE.

Woosnam, K. M. (2012). Using emotional solidarity to explain residents' attitudes about tourism and tourism development. *Journal of Travel Research, 51*(3), 315–327. https://doi.org/10.1177/0047287511410351

Yin, R. K. (2003). *Case study research: Design and methods* (4th ed.). Sage.

Yin, R. K. (2011). *Qualitative research from start to finish*. Guilford.

Anne Marie F. Bagadion is the current Dean of the College of Business and Accountancy of Ateneo de Naga University in Bicol, Philippines. Her research and teaching interests include tourism, social entrepreneurship, and business research. She has been a convenor of the International Research Conference 2 in 2018 and International Research Conference 3 in 2021, organized by the Ateneo de Naga University

Robert Charles G. Capistrano is an Assistant Professor at Hainan University - Arizona State University Joint International Tourism College (HAITC) based in Hainan China and a Senior Global Futures Scholar, Julie Ann Wrigley Global Futures Laboratory at Arizona State University. His research foci and teaching interests include ecotourism, tourism and conservation, tourism marketing, family tourism, visiting friends and relatives travel, gender and tourism, cross-cultural studies in tourism, and tourism and migration. He has recently facilitated the drafting of the Association of South-East Asian Nations (ASEAN) Gender and Tourism Framework.

Community-Based Tourism: An Analysis of Ugong Rock Adventures Stakeholders' Social Capital in Facilitating Community Participation

Patricia Alace E. Delas Alas, Anne Marie M. Pagador, and Robert Charles G. Capistrano

Abstract This chapter examines community-based tourism (CBT) as a tool for sustainable tourism development. It is argued that social capital is the main catalyst of community participation, a factor which is vital in CBT. Trust, norms, and networks are the main components of social capital considered in this study. The researchers used a qualitative approach to gather data in Ugong Rock Adventures, a successful CBT site in the Philippines. This tourist attraction offers activities such as caving, spelunking, and zip-lining. Key stakeholders of Ugong Rock Adventures, located in *Barangay* Tagabinet in Puerto Princesa City, Palawan, were interviewed. Consequently, this study employed thematic analysis to reveal the emerging themes from the interviews. Results showed that Ugong Rock Adventures' CBT has a strong presence of social capital. This study contributes to existing knowledge that integrates tourism with social capital in the Philippines. This study recognises the need to strengthen the community's social capital for its development.

Keywords Community-based tourism · Social capital · Community participation · Sustainable tourism · Philippines

---

P. A. E. Delas Alas (✉) · A. M. M. Pagador
Asian Institute of Tourism, University of the Philippines – Diliman, Quezon City, Philippines
e-mail: patricia.delasalas@gmail.com; ampagador@up.edu.ph

R. C. G. Capistrano
School of Community Resources and Development, Arizona State University, Phoenix, AZ, USA

Hainan University – Arizona State University Joint International Tourism College, Haikou, Hainan, China
e-mail: robert.capistrano@asu.edu

© Springer Nature Singapore Pte Ltd. 2022
R. S. Aquino, B. A. Porter (eds.), *Tourism in the Philippines*, Perspectives on Asian Tourism, https://doi.org/10.1007/978-981-19-4013-2_3

1 Introduction

Community-based tourism (CBT) is a form of sustainable tourism, commonly applied in rural settings, and focuses on the interaction between the visitors and the host community (Asker et al., 2010). CBT emerged as a form of tourism to counteract the negative impacts of mass tourism (Mtapuri & Giampiccoli, 2017). One of CBT's key features is the involvement of the local communities in tourism development (Hind et al., 2010; Koster, 2007; Schutz, 2017). The participation of local communities at tourism destinations is one of the key factors that generates movement towards long-term development (Ross & Wall, 1999). Sustainable development as a concept deals with meeting the present needs without sacrificing the necessities of future generations (World Commission on Environment and Development [WCED], 1987). The sustainability of tourism development, in social, cultural, economic, and environmental aspects, depends on community sustainability (Richards & Hall, 2000).

Hind et al. (2010) note that CBT usually promotes a bottom-up style of management where locals become self-empowered and eventually lead and manage their respective community sites. Despite the many benefits that may arise from CBT, there are still challenges and problems associated with this approach (Đurkin & Perić, 2017; Giampiccoli & Saayman, 2018), such as the lack of participation of and collaboration within communities (Tosun, 2000). As managers of a CBT site, local communities have a significant role in its development (Asker et al., 2010; Polnyotee & Thadaniti, 2015; Terencia, 2018) and in return, the profits may go directly to the local communities (Giampiccoli & Saayman, 2018; Nataraja & Devidasan, 2014; Polnyotee & Thadaniti, 2015). Generally, government units and private entities are also involved in managing and sustaining the development of a particular CBT site. Thus, stakeholders are essentially interconnected entities in CBT. Their involvement with the CBT project, willingness to cooperate amongst themselves, and their ability to forge partnerships with other stakeholders are key determinants of a successful CBT program (Budeanu, 2005; Park et al., 2017; Simpson, 2001). Cooperation has a vital role in tourism destination communities (Beritelli, 2011). Trust and reciprocity are essential elements for facilitating cooperation (Jones, 2005; Musavengane & Matikiti, 2015). Building trust amongst stakeholders can reduce transaction costs and enable collective action (Pretty & Ward, 2001). Reciprocity, defined as "the social dimension of personal relations" (Torche & Valenzuela, 2011, p. 188), can further develop trust and build stronger stakeholder participation (Musavengane & Matikiti, 2015).

Social capital is defined as the degree of connectedness and the quality and quantity of social relations in each population (Harpham et al., 2002). However, academic discourse addressing social capital in relation to tourism and its development is still developing (Moscardo et al., 2013; Okazaki, 2008). Consequently, there is a need to understand such a relationship because social capital is considered an appropriate tool to harness community participation in tourism development (Thammajinda, 2013). This study contributes to understanding social capital and CBT development in the Philippine setting.

This case study focuses on Ugong Rock Adventures, a CBT site located at *Barangay* Tagabinet in Puerto Princesa City, Palawan, Philippines. A *barangay* is the smallest administrative unit of Philippine society. As an important tourism destination, this area features a 75-foot limestone rock (Ugong Rock) formation that enhances several outdoor activities such as caving, spelunking, and zip-lining. Ugong Rock Adventures is recognised as a successful community-based ecotourism site (Ronquillo, 2012). Specifically, the objectives of this study are to: (a) understand the link between tourism and social capital, and (b) assess the application of social capital at Ugong Rock Adventures. Overall, this study adds to the current limited literature on the incorporation of social capital with tourism in the Philippines (Aquino, 2019). The overarching research questions are: "How is social capital utilised in the Ugong Rock Adventures, a CBT site, and what role did it play towards the site attaining sustainable development?" To answer these main research questions, the following sub-questions further guides the inquiry:

1. How does social capital influence community participation in *Barangay* Tagabinet?; and
2. How is community participation perceived by the stakeholders of Ugong Rock Adventures?

2 Literature Review

2.1 *Community and Its Stakeholders*

This study defines community as a group of socially interdependent people who are involved in policy-making and dialogue (Rovai, 2002). In the context of tourism development, in addition to defining a community by its geographical location, communities can also be created by events that cause people to gather and discuss concerns that are important to them as tourism stakeholders (Thammajinda, 2013). Stakeholders are frequently regarded as individuals or groups of people who are either involved in or affected by the impacts at a particular entity or community. In this study, the stakeholders were considered as entities that have a claim over the community's resources and attention (Bryson, 1995, 2004). Table 1 presents the stakeholders involved in this study, including the local community of Tagabinet, its community organisation leaders, Palawan Council for Sustainable Development (PCSD), the City Tourism Office and ABS-CBN Foundation's *Bantay Kalikasan* (literally translated as 'guarding/protecting nature').

Stakeholder groups are expected to participate in decision-making processes that concern a community. Participation is a concept that is commonly integrated with development (Thammajinda, 2013). Communities can participate in three aspects of tourism development – decision-making phase, sharing of benefits, and establishing development type and measurement (Tosun, 2000). However, conflicts can arise in

Table 1 The stakeholders involved in the study

Stakeholder groups	Definitions/examples
Residents (native and migrant)	They are the people who were born and/or are currently living in the community
Community organisation leaders	They are usually the heads and presidents of organisations in the community, i.e., *Barangay* Tagabinet Captain and Tagabinet Ugong Rock Service Cooperative (TURSCO) General Manager
Local government unit	City government of Puerto Princesa (City Tourism Office)
Government institutions	Palawan Council for Sustainable Development (PCSD)
Non-government organisation	An independent entity which supports the community. It is represented by the ABS-CBN Foundation Inc. *Bantay Kalikasan*

Adopted from Thammajinda (2013)

a community given the diverse interests and concerns within a local community (Richards & Hall, 2000). These conflicts can hinder a community from sustainable development.

2.2 Sustainability and Community Participation

Sustainable development deals with meeting the present generation's needs without sacrificing the necessities of future generations (WCED, 1987). In 2015, the United Nations (UN) General Assembly declared 2017 as the International Year of Sustainable Tourism for Development (United Nations World Tourism Organization, 2015). This declaration highlighted tourism's contribution to the three pillars of sustainability namely, "social, economic, and environmental". Similarly, the UNWTO (2015) also defined sustainable tourism as, "tourism that takes full account of its current and future economic, social and environmental impacts, addressing the needs of visitors, the industry, the environment, and host communities." This asserted that achieving sustainable tourism is an ongoing process; hence, its impacts should be monitored constantly. In sustainable tourism, community participation is promoted, and in return, the local community benefits from the revenues generated by tourism (Polnyotee & Thadaniti, 2015).

CBT strategies are unlikely to provide positive results without community members being aware of tourism assets (Porter et al., 2017). It is, therefore, essential that local community members are informed and involved in the decision-making processes of tourism development activities relevant to their community (Bramwell & Sharman, 2000). However, a higher degree of community participation does not guarantee better outcomes (Breugel, 2013). Research has shown that the community in a tourist destination may attain a higher welfare if it has a higher level of social capital (Jennings & Sanchez-Pages, 2017; Pramanik et al., 2019).

Community participation is also vital in preserving and conserving natural and cultural resources (Albrecht, 2016; Tosun & Timothy, 2003). In this context, tourists, the local communities, and natural resources are the three main entities that are interdependent and fundamental towards achieving sustainable tourism (Ross & Wall, 1999). Yet, there are many complexities underpinning the socio-economic and educational benefits to the community and tourists. For example, Rasoolimanesh and Jaafar (2016) note that community involvement is the community's ability to work in unity for its own benefit. As such, the participation of all stakeholders in all stages of tourism development is a vital factor in achieving sustainable tourism development (Schutz, 2017). Alternatively, Giampiccoli & Saayman (2018) have introduced the concept of "community self-participation" and further argue that mere participation is not enough for a community. However, Thammajinda (2013) suggests that active participation increases awareness, self-confidence and control of the development process. For example, a local community facilitates and takes control over the destination's resources while preventing external agents, such as tour operators, to take over. As such, community participation is about the involvement and representation of diverse social groups and the community's interest in the planning and management of tourism ventures and projects within the community (Thammajinda, 2013).

2.3 Social Capital and Tourism

The concept of social capital has attracted considerable research attention across multiple disciplines over the last few decades (Albrecht, 2016; Okazaki, 2008; Torche & Valenzuela, 2011). Hwang (2012) notes that the social capital theory has been used in several fields of study that deliberate human behaviour in varied social gatherings. The social capital theory demonstrates how resources are organised and distributed to achieve a common goal (Rodriguez-Giron & Vanneste, 2018). However, the body of literature relating to social capital is still fragmented, especially in its application to tourism (Park et al., 2012; Zhao et al., 2011).

Putnam (1995, p. 67) defines social capital as "the features of social organisation such as networks, norms, and social trust that facilitate coordination and cooperation for mutual benefit" (Jones, 2005, p. 304). Social capital is regarded as the capacity to let the members of the community work together (Putnam et al., 1993). Further, Rodriguez-Giron and Vanneste (2018) also consider social capital as the ability of people to act together toward common purposes. Strengthening a community's social capital is a mechanism to foster trust and collective action (Pramanik et al., 2019). Among all definitions that were initially developed, Putnam's (1995) definition has been more widely supported and accepted (Claiborne, 2010; Vermaak, 2009), arguing that Putnam's contribution was "more practical and empirically grounded" (Vermaak, 2009, p. 401). Putnam (1995) also acknowledges that social capital was a resource that developed through social linkages (Vermaak, 2009). Hence, this study utilised Putnam's (1995) conceptualisation.

3 Conceptual Framework

The concepts of social capital, community participation, CBT, and sustainable tourism development are essentially integrated into this study's conceptual framework (Fig. 1). This framework presents the importance of social capital in achieving the end goal of sustainable tourism development in a community.

Figure 1 describes the relationship among the concepts of social capital, community participation, CBT, and sustainable tourism development. This framework (Fig. 1) highlights the significance of social capital in generating and sustaining community involvement. Social capital shapes community participation in tourism (Faizal et al., 2017; Pramanik et al., 2019). CBT, as utilised in this framework, is a form of sustainable tourism development that is very significant in generating positive benefits for a community's economy, culture, environment, and even intellectual wellbeing (Đurkin & Perić, 2017; Nair & Hamzah, 2015). CBT is essentially driven by the level of community participation and involvement at a tourism destination; and is claimed as the most ideal example of sustainable tourism development (Breugel, 2013). Each of these components are discussed in more detail below.

Social capital is acknowledged as a vital feature of CBT development (Choo & Jamal, 2009; Jones, 2005; Nunkoo, 2017; Ooi et al., 2014; Zhang et al., 2020). In this study, social capital pertains to the "features of social organisation such as networks, norms, and social trust that facilitate coordination and cooperation for mutual benefit" (Jones, 2005, p. 304; Putnam, 1995, p. 67). These features can essentially foster and strengthen the level of community participation. Social capital is regarded as a "real" capital that is complemented with other forms of capital (Musavengane & Kloppers, 2020), as it supports a community's ability to work as one. These other forms include financial, natural, built, cultural, human, and political capitals (Moscardo et al., 2013). Among these forms, social capital is the only capital that is built by utilising it (Encarnacion Tadem, 2013). Additionally, social capital is deemed to be the most vital form of capital in sustaining development at a community or organisation, as it refers to the ability of a community to work hand in hand towards the betterment of the community (Encarnacion Tadem, 2013; Putnam et al., 1993). Moreover, social capital can only be completely obtained

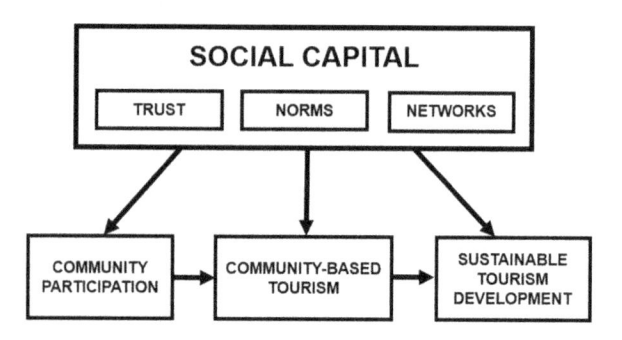

Fig. 1 A Conceptual framework of social capital and community-based tourism

through actual interactions of involved actors toward a common goal (Bourdieu, 1986; Rodriguez-Giron & Vanneste, 2018). Rodriguez-Giron & Vanneste (2018) integrate the destination capitals theory (Sharpley, 2009) with social capital – acknowledging social capital as a special functional resource (Coleman, 1990) which propels other forms of capital into purposive actions. Social capital's essence is most apparent in managing conflicts and reconciling differences in a community. Discussing relevant issues also gives the stakeholders the ability to build up their level of social capital. As such, investing in social capital appears to be the best means of fostering strength and resilience of a community (Musavengane & Kloppers, 2020).

Community participation is influenced by social capital (Faizal, et al., 2017; Pramanik et al., 2019) and is vital in strengthening the ability of a community to sustain its available resources (Albrecht, 2016; Tosun & Timothy, 2003). Tsaur et al. (2006) state that the residents' participation and support of resource conservation could influence the destination's sustainability. However, participation should originate from the community itself, and not be influenced by external entities as true CBT is about people initiating, owning, and controlling the development process from the beginning (Giampiccoli & Saayman, 2018). Hence, the success and development of a CBT is established by having the stakeholders significantly aware about tourism (Porter et al., 2017) and actively involved in the existing social systems at the community (Park et al., 2017). Gutierrez (2019) suggests that local communities will actively participate in tourism development initiatives if they are informed and be made aware of their ability to be involved.

The sustainability of tourism development, in social, cultural, economic, and environmental aspects, depends on community sustainability (Richards & Hall, 2000). This implies a necessity to constantly evaluate the condition of the community to ensure the sustainability of tourism development within the local area. Studies show that sustainable tourism development is a form of tourism that subsequently maintains and enhances all types of capital at a destination, highlighting the significance of human capital (Sinclair-Maragh & Gursoy, 2017; Zhang et al., 2020).

4 Case Study Methods

A case study research method was utilised to address the research questions. This type of method is known to be an effective research strategy (Miles, 1979; Yin, 1989) as it primarily draws data and information from empirical investigation (Robson, 1993). Moreover, Chaiklin (2000) states that a case study concurrently examines multiple factors, making it appropriate for assessing social capital in relation to sustainable tourism development in a community.

The study was conducted in Ugong Rock Adventures (refer to Fig. 2), a tourist destination that features Ugong Rock, a 75-feet limestone formation. It is located at *Barangay* Tagabinet (refer to Figs. 3 and 4) in Puerto Princesa City, Palawan, Philippines. *Barangay* Tagabinet is one of the sixty-six (66) barangays in Puerto

Fig. 2 Entrance signage of Ugong Rock Adventures. (Photo by A. Pagador, 2016a, b)

Princesa City. It has a total land area of 3602.5 hectares, and serves as a buffer zone of the Puerto Princesa City Subterranean River National Park. Hence, it is an area of thinly dispersed population. It lies in the midwest coast of Palawan, approximately 63 km northwest of the Puerto Princesa City proper. Agriculture is the main source of livelihood of the community.

According to the *Barangay* Tagabinet Development Plan, in 2015, there are more than 250 households with around 1400 residents in the community. Ethnic groups such as *Tagbanua, Aklanon, Rombloanon, Antiqueños,* and *Cuyunon* are also present in the area.

Interviews are a basic form of qualitative inquiry and are most consistent with people's ability to make meaning through language (Seidman, 2006). Semi-structured and structured interviews were conducted by the researchers on 19–22 January 2016. Thirteen respondents were interviewed for the purpose of this study; eight of which were residents. Other participants include: Tagabinet's *barangay* captain, ABS-CBN Foundation's *Bantay Kalikasan* (BK), Tagabinet Ugong Rock Service Cooperative (TURSCO), Palawan Council for Sustainable Development (PCSD), and the City Tourism Office of Puerto Princesa. Interviews with the residents lasted for around 16 min each; while interviews with the other respondents averaged at 32 mins each.

The initial analysis of the interview data used a cross-sectional and categorical indexing approach to code the information (Mason, 2002). A thematic analysis approach was then used to identify repeated patterns of meaning (Braun & Clarke, 2008). This approach considered both descriptive categories and analytical themes

Fig. 3 The view on top of Ugong Rock limestone formation after finishing the spelunking course. (Photo by P. Delas Alas, 2016)

(Thomas & Harden, 2008). From the transcribed conversations, themes and patterns were formulated and are discussed in the following section.

5 Results and Discussion

The objectives of this study were to (a) understand the link between tourism and social capital, and (b) assess the application of social capital at Ugong Rock Adventures. Guiding this study, the overarching research questions were: "How is social capital utilised in the Ugong Rock Adventures, a CBT site, and what role did it play towards the site attaining sustainable development?"

Three key themes emerged that addressed the influence of social capital in catalysing community participation and how community participation was perceived by the stakeholders. The first emergent theme presented the role of social capital in facilitating community participation in tourism development. This theme encompassed the application of the concepts of trust, norms, and networks in *Barangay* Tagabinet, Puerto Princesa City, Palawan. The second theme described the facilitation of community participation at CBT sites. This theme was further divided into

Fig. 4 The view of Barangay Tagabinet on top of Ugong Rock limestone formation. (Photo by A. Pagador, 2016a, b)

two forms: the facilitation of community participation in tourism planning and decision-making; and the facilitation of community participation in tourism operation and management. The last theme explored the benefits of participation in CBT.

5.1 The Role of Social Capital in Facilitating Community Participation in Tourism Development

Social capital catalyses community participation in *Barangay* Tagabinet. Its three main components – trust, norms, and networks – facilitate the level of participation in the community. All residents that were interviewed for this study declared that they do trust the local people as well as the officials in their *barangay*. However, trusting non-residents was challenging for the residents. On the other hand, there was minimal indication of trust towards public officials, as some of the respondents pointed out that politics hinders them from fully trusting officials. One resident said that she only trusts about 80% of the officials in position. After stating this, she refused to talk about her trust in the officials of Puerto Princesa.

Norms, known as informal rules that guide social interactions (Dandaneau, 2007), also help in facilitating participation in the *barangay*. Most of the interviewed residents indicated their willingness to provide time and money to those who are in need of such resources. A resident specifically mentioned that he was very willing to give donations if a death of a family member occurs. Another expressed that she is willing to reach out to those in need saying,

> Of course [I will help]. We need to think of ways on how to help and reach out to other people. Even though we consider ourselves poor, we must not always think of ourselves all the time. There are those who need more help.

Further, the researchers inferred that the concept of *bayanihan* is also fundamentally seen in the community as the residents continue to help others. *Bayanihan*, from the root word *bayan* which means "nation" (Ealdama, 2012), is a concept rooted in agricultural communities' collective efforts (Beza et al., 2018; Eadie & Su, 2018). It has been integrated into Filipino culture and has developed into a representation of "cooperative action" (Ealdama, 2012). In essence, *bayanihan* is the "Filipino principle of mutual effort" (Eadie & Su, 2018). It essentially portrays the service and solidarity of the Filipino society (Ealdama, 2012). It also proves how communities achieve their goals by coordinating well and achieving genuine team spirit (Beza et al., 2018). *Bayanihan*, as a cultural norm, is associated together with social capital (Eadie & Su, 2018). The residents of *Barangay* Tagabinet live out *bayanihan* in continuing to heighten the community's level of social capital; thus, highly associating the concepts of trust, norms, and networks. A resident especially mentioned, "*Yes, people here are used to [living out]* bayanihan. *We know that it is important to live harmoniously. If not, who else will we rely on?*"

The last component of social capital in this study covered networks which are linked with relationships established between people (Bourdieu, 1986). Networks foster internal and external relations in the community. For internal matters, meetings and assemblies with TURSCO and their barangay officials served as the primary means to discuss the residents' concerns about their community. In terms of external relations, *Barangay* Tagabinet's Ugong Rock Adventures had established coordination and partnerships with private individuals and other entities such as the ABS-CBN Foundation Inc. *Bantay Kalikasan*, the Department of Science and Technology, City Tourism Office, Palawan Cooperative Union, and academic institutions namely, Palawan State University and Western Philippine University. Thammajinda (2013) regards the establishment of networks with external stakeholders, such as marketing and educational networks, as a vital factor in obtaining knowledge and skills to facilitate higher income for the community.

Trust, norms, and networks ultimately drive the community residents to participate in developing tourism at *Barangay* Tagabinet. This was most apparent in their *bayanihan* efforts which include implementing the barangay beautification project and using Ugong Rock Adventures' community development fund to provide financial support to selected community members. In the same context, Pramanik et al. (2019) report that the Indonesian community (Kampung Tajur) members participated in activities such as religious meetings, tourism initiatives, and community works – highlighting the significance of trust and collective action which are also apparent in the present case study.

5.2 The Facilitation of Community Participation in Community-Based Tourism (CBT) Site

Community participation was perceived by the stakeholders of Ugong Rock Adventures in two forms: (1) tourism planning and decision-making; and (2) tourism operation and management.

5.2.1 The Facilitation of Community Participation in Tourism Planning and Decision-Making

Through meetings and assemblies, the residents did the planning as TURSCO members. When asked about how they formulate their plans, the TURSCO General Manager stated,

> We study about it. Higher authority does research. Bantay Kalikasan or BK's community organiser helps us out. They are with us and their ideas and experiences are of great help, especially in bringing in tourists, motivating the members, and dealing with challenges.

Meetings and assemblies are the main indication of the community's participation in tourism planning and decision-making. These meetings come in many forms such as general assemblies, *Barangay* Council meetings, and special meetings. These assemblies enabled the stakeholders to voice out their ideas and opinions. One resident revealed that she regularly attends the meetings because she believes it is necessary to do so, expressing, *"If I don't attend any of these assemblies, I won't be aware of the current condition of my barangay – what to follow and what projects will be implemented."* This finding resonates with Gutierrez's (2019) study of Kawit's community-based heritage tourism in the Philippines which showed that the community has the ability to "negotiate with those in power"; and thus, partakes in decision-making and planning.

5.2.2 The Facilitation of Community Participation in Tourism Operation and Management

Tourism operation and management comprises the community's tourism projects, policies, and necessities. According to *BK's* community organiser, the residents primarily identified the tourism products and services to be offered in the site. These activities included caving, spelunking, and zip-lining. Aside from selecting activities to be offered, the community initiated projects, such as the maintenance of Ugong Rock Adventures, *Barangay* Tagabinet beautification efforts, and the construction of a footbridge for a coastal community. *BK's* community organiser revealed that,

> As far as I can remember, they identified a project to help a community build a bridge. The children are having a hard time [to go to school] because it is a coastal community. The

Community-Based Tourism: An Analysis of Ugong Rock Adventures Stakeholders... 47

resources used for that [project] came from tourism. They also have the beautification project, not just only in Ugong Rock but in the entire barangay. Everyone is encouraged to join. It is a project not only intended to beautify Ugong Rock but also the other parts where tourists will pass by. [Others include] Street gardening type, street beautification. ABS-CBN Foundation's main role is to support that project.

Policies, on the other hand, also facilitate tourism development in the community. Most of these policies are adhered to at a local level. Although local policies were being implemented, there are still lapses in enforcing these. The TURSCO General Manager added that the lack of education hinders them from successfully implementing policies as a result of limited knowledge. Generally, enforcement is the main problem seen by the authorities, testified by the BK community organiser. Ugong Rock, as a CBT, involves the local people in its operation and management, which is in accordance with the local ordinance. Furthermore, policies and regulations relevant to carrying capacity were also mentioned by the BK's community organiser. He shared,

For example, Ugong Rock's environmental carrying capacity should not exceed 300 visitors per day. You can develop the area, however, you must consider the social carrying capacity – ask if the community can handle the developments, as these might affect the day-to-day [operations] of Ugong Rock or cause cultural problems. Eventually, Ugong Rock might be too commercialised, as well. I think that policies that deal with limits or regulations should be strictly followed.

Lastly, in terms of necessities, Ugong Rock Adventures, which is still at its developmental stage according to Palawan Council for Sustainable Development (PCSD), has its apparent needs such as marketing support.

5.3 The Benefits of Community Participation in Community-Based Tourism (CBT)

The benefits of community participation in CBT are categorised into three classifications: economic, socio-cultural, and environmental benefits.

5.3.1 Economic Benefits

Economic benefits were evident in the *barangay*; residents were able to increase their income by thinking of ways on how to utilise the impacts of tourism. For instance, more *sari-sari* stores (local convenience stores) emerged as tourism developed in the area. One resident shared that,

For me, the tourists that go here are sure to spend. In return, the community renders service to them. [With the generated income,] the cost of beautification and maintenance of the surroundings generates higher return to the community.

Another resident mentioned that because of tourism, they could send their children to school. Tourism, according to her, empowered the residents to share their own resources whenever there were occasions in the community. She was hopeful for the next generations to adapt to this. In addition, she shared that the community development fund from Ugong Rock Adventures was being utilised to provide some needs of the barangay, most especially the school. TURSCO generates a community development fund to sustain their community projects every year. TURSCO General Manager said that these projects include the provision of a set of drum and lyre and an electric generator for the school, the contribution to teacher's salary, and the construction of a footbridge for a coastal community within *Barangay* Tagabinet. These projects are a way of giving back to the community.

The beautification project in *Barangay* Tagabinet was also a benefit generated by tourism in the community. This project aimed to enhance the visual aspect of *Barangay* Tagabinet's *sitios* [smaller settlements], and not only Ugong Rock Adventures. The Barangay Council and TURSCO worked hand in hand to make this project a successful venture. Both organizations relied on community participation to make it work. The economic benefits that were generated from tourism generally helped in improving not just the welfare of the employees of Ugong Rock Adventures, but also the well-being of the residents in *Barangay* Tagabinet. This enabled the community residents to maximise their participation in developing tourism at *Barangay* Tagabinet.

5.3.2 Socio-cultural Benefits

Ugong Rock was once the fortress of indigenous people such as the *Batacs* and the *Tagbanuas*. Despite the tourism and development, *Barangay* Tagabinet simultaneously promotes and conserves its culture, as the residents give high value to its cultural resources. One resident asserted that the community members promote the maintenance of their indigenous people's culture. She revealed that, *"We don't stop them from being civilised, but we still want to maintain and preserve their culture."* In addition, according to one resident, she thinks their culture is still preserved – *"it's still Filipino style, not American style or whatever."*

The rock is approximately 23 million years old; the community manages to protect it for its cultural value, as well as for its environmental value. According to the BK community organiser, initially, their motivation was to just protect their environment, but the residents knew they needed to generate income, as well, to send their children to school in the community. They wanted to capitalise on the strategic location of the *barangay* that is found along the road that leads to the world-famous Puerto Princesa Underground River. Thus, they considered developing their area for tourism.

The residents were also happy and proud that visitors came to their place. Porter and Orams (2014) and Porter (2015) also reported the same feeling of "general happiness" from the residents of coastal communities in the Philippines when asked about how they felt towards the arrival of tourists. According to the residents of

Barangay Tagabinet, the interaction did not only entail more income for them, as it also enabled them to learn to speak in English. A participant shared that he was only able to learn to speak English when he became a community guide. He revealed that he gradually learned it through interacting with tourists and not through formal education, saying, "*I used to be shy about it, but now, I am confident in using English to communicate with the tourists. Many of us did not finish our education here, so we learned how to speak English through interacting with the tourists.*" One participant even conveyed that grammar is not a big deal, saying, "*Interacting with tourists, of course, will somehow make you learn English. Even though it [grammar] is wrong or if it is [done] with gestures/actions, I think it is enough.*" Hence, residents got to know more about the culture of their visitors and gained additional knowledge from them while sharing their own experiences and culture to the tourists.

5.3.3 Environmental Benefits

The TURSCO General Manager advocated the significance of environmental awareness. She said that lectures are conducted for the TURSCO members to understand the need to protect their environment. The TURSCO General Manager asserted that, "*Sometimes, the environment gets destroyed because of the attitude of people. If they are not aware [of its significance], they continue to exploit it.*" In a study of a community in Laos, Park et al. (2017) highlighted the importance of providing training programmes that will enable the community members to understand tourism and its development, and eventually take a higher form of participation. In this way, knowledge gaps are addressed.

Regarding perceived environmental benefits, Ugong Rock Adventures and its stakeholders believed that the development of the site has not only contributed to the wellness of the community, but also to the conservation and protection of the environment. For example, *kaingin* (slash-and-burn farming) has decreased in frequency. Other problems regarding the destruction of their environment were also addressed.

Residents also reported an increased awareness of the relevance of their natural resources to the development and growth of the community. One resident noted that their natural resources are not exploited, and that "*they are even protected, so that the tourists will come and visit us.*" Another resident, a community guide, said that his father used to practice *kaingin*, but because of the new opportunities brought about by tourism, his family stopped the practice. Further, he said that, "*If it were not because of tourism, I might have ended up cutting trees and doing* kaingin, *as well.*"

TURSCO General Manager said that residents began an initiative to plant more trees in the area. According to her, "*The residents are more aware now [of environmental impacts of tourism]. They are then motivated to get rid of activities that are hazardous to the environment.*" The City Tourism Office stated that as a CBT site, the residents recognised that the protection of the natural environment is essential in attaining sustainability because they can set their own limits in terms of the number of visitors per day. BK community organiser emphasised that Ugong Rock Adventures must limit its visitors with respect to its environmental carrying capacity, as it affects the natural state of the rocks and formations inside the cave. The residents also practised proper waste disposal and management in the area, and participated in *"OPLAN Linis"*, the cleanliness program, of the site. A resident asserted, *"Our decision-making procedures as a barangay cover the cleanliness program. We recognise being responsible in keeping our barangay clean and pleasant, so that we can attract tourists."*

Based on the findings, it can be deduced that *Barangay* Tagabinet has a strong presence of social capital because of the well-established trust, norms, and networks in the community. This social capital influences the residents' community participation, as significantly evidenced in their CBT programs. More importantly, the stakeholders of Ugong Rock Adventures are aware that community participation is significant to attain sustainable development (Okazaki, 2008). They mentioned that there is a need for *Barangay* Tagabinet residents to support and participate in activities that aim to develop CBT.

6 Conclusion

This study was guided by the role of social capital in the Ugong Rock Adventures, a CBT site, and its contribution towards attaining sustainable development at the community level. The study focused on analysing the link between tourism and social capital, and assessing the application of social capital in Ugong Rock Adventures. Essentially, this study addressed the limited literature that incorporates social capital with tourism development in the Philippines.

Through a case study method, the stakeholders' social capital in Ugong Rock Adventures, one of the country's most successful CBT sites (Ronquillo, 2012), was analyzed using Putnam's (1995) definition of social capital (e.g., trust, norms, and networks). Based on the interviews conducted, the stakeholders of Ugong Rock Adventures emphasized the importance of community participation in enhancing CBT development. The community was truly aware of the benefits that Ugong Rock Adventures generates as they continue to preserve and conserve their natural and cultural resources. Participant responses indicated that the three factors explored – economic, socio-cultural, and environmental benefits – are equally given of great importance in participating in tourism activities towards sustainable development. Therefore, suggesting the strong presence of social capital is an indicator of organisational capability to yield desired social change.

This study recognises the need to conduct future studies in exploring social capital in other CBT sites in the Philippines. This study was limited to Ugong Rock Adventures which has a small population. Future studies may explore social capital in other CBT sites in the Philippines. The relatedness of social capital in the cultural context of *bayanihan* in other CBT sites may also be explored. Lastly, the study did not seek to elaborate on the integration of other forms of capital (i.e., financial, natural, built, cultural, human, and political) into the community; therefore, these capitals should be incorporated in future research.

The findings support the idea that social capital is a main driving catalyst of community participation in Ugong Rock Adventures in Palawan, Philippines. From this, we assume the success of Ugong Rock Adventures to be influenced by social capital. While previous research shows that community participation to be highly essential in CBT (Budeanu, 2005; Giampiccoli & Saayman, 2018; Park et al., 2017; Simpson, 2001), a novel approach of this study shows the cultural context of the significance of *bayanihan* spirit within a Filipino CBT site. With the established trust, norms, and networks, the residents were able to implement projects altogether and even help one another in times of need.

Acknowledgments We would like to express our deepest gratitude to our Ugong Rock Adventures tour guides, *Barangay* Tagabinet residents, TURSCO, *Bantay Kalikasan* community organiser, PCSD, and Puerto Princesa City Tourism Office. We would like to especially thank Dr. Lisette Muaror-Wilson (Dalhousie University) who reviewed and provided comments in the latter stage of revising the manuscript.

References

Albrecht, S. (2016). *How social capital shapes community participation: A case study on a community-based-ecotourism intervention in Amboseli, Kenya* [Unpublished masteral thesis]. Wageningen University.

Aquino, R. S. (2019). Towards decolonising tourism and hospitality research in the Philippines. *Tourism Management Perspectives, 31*, 72–84. https://doi.org/10.1016/j.tmp.2019.03.014

Asker, S., Boronyak, L., Carrad, N., & Paddon, M. (2010, June). *Effective community based tourism: A best practice manual* (Publication). Retrieved January 03, 2019, from Sustainable Tourism Cooperative Research Centre 2010 website: http://publications.apec.org/-/media/APEC/Publications/2010/6/Effective-Community-Based-Tourism-A-Best-Practice-Manual-June-2010/210_twg_CommunityBasedTourismWEB.pdf

Beritelli, P. (2011). Cooperation among prominent actors in a tourist destination. *Annals of Tourism Research, 38*(2), 607–629. https://doi.org/10.1016/j.annals.2010.11.015

Beza, B., Johnson, M., & Fuentes, A. (2018). Women and their roles in peace building in conflict vulnerable areas of Mindanao, Philippines. In G. Marsh et al. (Eds.), *Community engagement in post-disaster recovery* (pp. 131–144). Routledge.

Bourdieu, P. (1986). The forms of capital. In J. G. Richardson (Ed.), *Handbook of theory and research for the sociology of education* (pp. 241–258). Greenwood Press. 973842196 755530221.

Bramwell, G., & Sharman, A. (2000). The community: A sustainable concept in tourism development. In G. Richards & D. Hall (Eds.), *Tourism and sustainable community development*. Routledge.

Braun, V., & Clarke, V. (2008). Using thematic analysis in psychology. *Qualitative Research in Psychology, 3*(2), 77–101. https://doi.org/10.1191/1478088706qp063oa

Breugel, L. V. (2013). *Community-based tourism: Local Participation and perceived impact. A Comparative study between two communities in Thailand* [Unpublished masteral thesis]. Radboud University.

Bryson, J. M. (1995). *Strategic planning for public and non-profit organizations* (Revised ed.). Jossey-Bass.

Bryson, J. M. (2004). What to do when stakeholders matter: Stakeholder identification and analysis techniques. *Public Management Review, 6*(1), 21–53. https://doi.org/10.1080/14719030410001675722

Budeanu, A. (2005). Impacts and responsibilities for sustainable tourism: A tour operator's perspective. *Journal of Cleaner Production, 13*(2), 89–97.

Chaiklin, H. (2000). Doing case study research. *American Journal of Dance Therapy, 22*(1), 47–59.

Choo, H., & Jamal, T. (2009). Tourism on organic farms in South Korea: A new form of ecotourism. *Journal of Sustainable Tourism, 17*(4), 431–454. https://doi.org/10.1080/09669580802713440

Claiborne, P. (2010). *Community participation in tourism development and the value of social capital* [Unpublished masteral thesis]. University of Gothenburg.

Coleman, J. S. (1990). *Foundations of social theory*. Belknap Press of Harvard University Press.

Dandaneau, S. P. (2007). Norms. In G. Ritzer (Ed.), *The Blackwell encyclopedia of sociology* (pp. 1–4). Wiley. https://doi.org/10.1002/9781405165518.wbeosn029

Delas Alas, P. (2016). *The view on top of Ugong Rock limestone formation after finishing the spelunking course* [Photograph].

Đurkin, J., & Perić, M. (2017). Organising for community-based tourism: Comparing attitudes of local residents and local tourism entrepreneurs in Ravna Gora, Croatia. *Local Economy: The Journal of the Local Economy Policy Unit, 32*(7), 678–691. https://doi.org/10.1177/0269094217734811

Eadie, P., & Su, Y. (2018). Post-disaster social capital: Trust, equity, bayanihan and Typhoon Yolanda. *Disaster Prevention and Management: An International Journal, 27*(3), 334–345. https://doi.org/10.1108/dpm-02-2018-0060

Ealdama, Y. (2012, November). *BAYANIHAN: The indigenous Filipino strengths perspective* [Paper presentation]. International Conference on Strengths Based Practice in Social Work and Human Services, Kathmandu, Nepal.

Encarnacion Tadem, T. S. (2013). Social capital and the martial law technocracy: The making and unmaking of a power elite. *Kritika Kultura, 20*, 69–94. https://doi.org/10.13185/kk2013.02004

Faizal, M. I., Hakim, L., & Harahap, N. (2017). Factors affecting level of participation in the management of mangroves as ecotourism attraction: Lesson learned from Cengkrong Watulimo, Trenggalek. *Journal of Indonesian Tourism and Development Studies, 5*(1), 19–24. https://doi.org/10.21776/ub.jitode.2017.005.01.03

Giampiccoli, A., & Saayman, M. (2018). Community-based tourism development model and community participation. *African Journal of Hospitality, Tourism and Leisure, 7*(4), 1–27. Retrieved 2020, from https://www.ajhtl.com/uploads/7/1/6/3/7163688/article_16_vol_7_4__2018.pdf

Gutierrez, E. M. (2019). Participation in tourism: Cases on community-based tourism (CBT) in the Philippines. *Ritsumeikan Journal of Asia Pacific Studies, 37*, 23–36.

Harpham, T., Grant, E., & Thomas, E. (2002). Measuring social capital within health surveys: Key issues. *Health Policy and Planning, 17*, 106–111.

Hind, E. J., Hiponia, M. C., & Gray, T. S. (2010). From community-based to centralised national management--A wrong turning for the governance of the marine protected area in Apo Island, Philippines? *Marine Policy, 34*(1), 54–62.

Hwang, D. (2012). *Influence of social capital on community-based action in tourism development: A study of social network analysis* [Unpublished doctorate dissertation]. University of Illinois at Urbana-Champaign.

Jennings, C., & Sanchez-Pages, S. (2017). Social capital, conflict and welfare. *Journal of Development Economics, 124*, 157–167. https://doi.org/10.1016/j.jdeveco.2016.09.005

Jones, S. (2005). Community-based ecotourism: The significance of social capital. *Annals of Tourism Research*, 303–324. https://doi.org/10.1016/j.annals.2004.06.007

Koster, R. (2007). An evaluation of community-based tourism development: How theory intersects with practice. *Prairie Perspectives, 67*–88. Retrieved from http://pcag.uwinnipeg.ca/Prairie-Perspectives/PP-Vol10/Koster.pdf

Mason, J. (2002). *Qualitative researching* (2nd ed.). SAGE Publications.

Miles, M. B. (1979). Qualitative data as an attractive nuisance: The problem of analysis. *Administrative Science Quarterly, 24*(4), 590–601.

Moscardo, G., Schurmann, A., Konovalov, E., & McGehee, N. G. (2013). *Best Education Network Think Tank XIII Theme: Engaging Communities in Sustainable Tourism Development* (pp. 219–236). Taylor's University, Kuala Lumpur, Malaysia.

Mtapuri, O., & Giampiccoli, A. (2017). A conceptual coalescence: Towards luxury community-based tourism. *African Journal of Hospitality, Tourism and Leisure, 6*(3), 1–14.

Musavengane, R., & Kloppers, R. (2020). Social capital: An investment towards community resilience in the collaborative natural resources management of community-based tourism schemes. *Tourism Management Perspectives, 34*, 100654. https://doi.org/10.1016/j.tmp.2020.100654

Musavengane, R., & Matikiti, R. (2015). Does social capital really enhance community-based ecotourism? A review of the literature. *African Journal of Hospitality, Tourism and Leisure, 4*(1), 1–18.

Nair, V., & Hamzah, A. (2015). Successful community-based tourism approaches for rural destinations. *Worldwide Hospitality and Tourism Themes, 7*(5), 429–439. https://doi.org/10.1108/whatt-06-2015-0023

Nataraja, T. C., & Devidasan, S. D. (2014). Community based tourism: Case study on potential of Shivanahalli village. *Compass, 1*(2), 67–75.

Nunkoo, R. (2017). Governance and sustainable tourism: What is the role of trust, power and social capital? *Journal of Destination Marketing & Management, 6*(4), 277–285. https://doi.org/10.1016/j.jdmm.2017.10.003

Okazaki, E. (2008). A community-based tourism model: Its conception and use. *Journal of Sustainable Tourism, 16*(5), 511–529.

Ooi, N., Laing, J., & Mair, J. (2014). Social capital as a heuristic device to explore sociocultural sustainability: A case study of mountain resort tourism in the community of Steamboat Springs, Colorado, USA. *Journal of Sustainable Tourism, 23*(3), 417–436. https://doi.org/10.1080/09669582.2014.957211

Pagador, A. (2016a). *Entrance signage of Ugong Rock Adventures* [Photograph].

Pagador, A. (2016b). *The view of Barangay Tagabinet on top of Ugong Rock limestone formation* [Photograph].

Park, D., Lee, K., Choi, H., & Yoon, Y. (2012). Factors influencing social capital in rural tourism communities in South Korea. *Tourism Management, 33*(6), 1511–1520. https://doi.org/10.1016/j.tourman.2012.02.005

Park, E., Phandanouvong, T., & Kim, S. (2017). Evaluating participation in community-based tourism: A local perspective in Laos. *Current Issues in Tourism, 21*(2), 128–132. https://doi.org/10.1080/13683500.2017.1323851

Polnyotee, M., & Thadaniti, S. (2015). Community-based tourism: A strategy for sustainable tourism development of Patong Beach, Phuket Island, Thailand. *Asian Social Science, 11*(27), 90–98. https://doi.org/10.5539/ass.v11n27p90

Porter, B. A. (2015). Starstruck fisherfolk: Perceptions of social importance of tourism development among artisanal fisherfolk in the Philippines. In M. Lück, J. Velvin, & B. Eisenstein (Eds.), *The social side of tourism: The interface between tourism, society, and the environment: Answers to global questions from the International Competence Network of Tourism Research and Education (ICNT)* (Vol. 9, pp. 71–85). Peter Lang.

Porter, B. A., & Orams, M. B. (2014). Exploring tourism as a potential development strategy for an artisanal fishing community in the Philippines: The case of Barangay Victory in Bolinao. *Tourism in Marine Environments, 10*(1–2), 49–70. https://doi.org/10.3727/154427314X14056884441743

Porter, B. A., Orams, M. B., & Lück, M. (2017). Sustainable entrepreneurship tourism: An alternative development approach for remote coastal communities where awareness of tourism is low. *Tourism Planning & Development, 15*(2), 149–165. https://doi.org/10.1080/21568316.2017.1312507

Pramanik, P., Ingkadijaya, R., & Achmadi, M. (2019). The role of social capital in community based tourism. *Journal of Indonesian Tourism and Development Studies, 7*, 62–73. https://doi.org/10.21776/ub.jitode.2019.007.02.02

Pretty, J., & Ward, H. (2001). Social capital and the environment. *World Development, 29*(2), 209–227. https://doi.org/10.1016/s0305-750x(00)00098-x

Putnam, R. D. (1995). Bowling alone: America's declining social capital. *Journal of Democracy, 1*, 65–78.

Putnam, R., Leonardi, R., & Nanetti, R. (1993). *Making democracy work: Civic traditions in modern Italy*. Princeton University Press.

Rasoolimanesh, S. M., & Jaafar, M. (2016). Community participation toward tourism development and conservation program in rural World Heritage Sites. In M. Jaafar (Ed.), *Tourism – From empirical research towards practical application* (pp. 1–14). In Tech. 1143813120 860814005. https://doi.org/10.5772/62293

Richards, G., & Hall, D. (2000). The community: A sustainable concept in tourism development. In G. Richards & D. Hall (Eds.), *Tourism and sustainable community development*. Routledge.

Robson, C. (1993). *Real world research: A resource for social scientists and practitioner researchers*. Blackwell.

Rodriguez-Giron, S., & Vanneste, D. (2018). Social capital at the tourist destination level: Determining the dimensions to assess and improve collective action in tourism. *Tourist Studies, 19*(1), 23–42. https://doi.org/10.1177/1468797618790109

Ronquillo, L. B. (2012, April 27). *Palawan's Ugong Rock balances economy and the ecosystem*. Retrieved from http://puertoprincesa.ph/?q=articles/feature-palawan's-ugong-rock-balances-economy-and-ecosystem

Ross, S., & Wall, G. (1999). Ecotourism towards congruence between theory and practice. *Tourism Management, 20*, 123–132.

Rovai, A. P. (2002). Building sense of community at a distance. *The International Review of Research in Open and Distributed Learning, 3*(1), 1–16. https://doi.org/10.19173/irrodl.v3i1.79

Schutz, M. (2017). *A community based assessment: An analysis of community based tourism cooperatives in Kalache and Hulgol India* [Unpublished masteral thesis]. University of North Texas, Denton, United States of America.

Seidman, I. (2006). *Interviewing as qualitative research: A guide for researchers in education and the social sciences* (3rd ed.). Teachers College Press.

Sharpley, R. (2009). *Tourism development and the environment: Beyond sustainability?* Earthscan.

Simpson, K. (2001). Strategic planning and community involvement as contributors to sustainable tourism development. *Current Issues in Tourism, 4*(1), 3–41.

Sinclair-Maragh, G., & Gursoy, D. (2017). Residents' identity and tourism development: The Jamaican perspective. *International Journal of Tourism Sciences, 17*(2), 107–125. https://doi.org/10.1080/15980634.2017.1313472

Terencia, N. M. (2018). Community based tourism and development in third world countries: The case of the Bamileke region of Cameroon. *International Journal of Social and Tourism Sciences, 12*(1), 26–30.

Thammajinda, R. (2013). *Community participation and social capital in tourism planning and management in a Thai context* [Unpublished doctorate thesis]. Lincoln University, New Zealand. Retrieved from https://researcharchive.lincoln.ac.nz/bitstream/handle/10182/5423/thammajinda_phd.pdf

Thomas, J., & Harden, A. (2008). Methods for the thematic synthesis of qualitative research in systematic reviews. *BMC Medical Research Methodology, 8*(45). Retrieved from http://www.biomedcentral.com/1471-2288/8/45

Torche, F., & Valenzuela, E. (2011). Trust and reciprocity: A theoretical distinction of the sources of social capital. *European Journal of Social Theory, 14*(2), 181–198. https://doi.org/10.1177/1368431011403461

Tosun, C. (2000). Limits to community participation in tourism development process in developing countries. *Tourism Management, 21*, 613–633. https://doi.org/10.1016/S0261-5177(00)00009-1

Tosun, C., & Timothy, D. J. (2003). Arguments for community participation in the tourism development process. *Journal of Tourism Studies, 14*(2), 2–15.

Tsaur, S.-H., Yu-Chiang, L., & Lin, J.-H. (2006). Evaluating ecotourism sustainability from the integrated perspective of resource, community and tourism. *Tourism Management, 27,* 64–653.

United Nations World Tourism Organization. (2015, December 07). *United Nations declares 2017 as the international year of sustainable tourism for development* [Press release]. Retrieved from https://www.unwto.org/archive/global/press-release/2015-12-07/united-nations-declares-2017-international-year-sustainable-tourism-develop

Vermaak, J. (2009). Reassessing the concept of social capital: Considering resources for satisfying the needs of rural communities. *Development Southern Africa, 26*(3), 399–409.

World Commission on Environment and Development. (1987). *Our common future; chapter 2: Towards sustainable development* (pp. 41–59, Rep.). Oxford University Press. Retrieved from http://www.un-documents.net/ocf-02.htm

Yin, R. K. (1989). *Case study research: Design and methods.* SAGE Publications.

Zhang, Y., Xiong, Y., Lee, T. J., Ye, M., & Nunkoo, R. (2020). Sociocultural sustainability and the formation of social capital from community-based tourism. *Journal of Travel Research,* 1–14. https://doi.org/10.1177/0047287520933673

Zhao, W., Ritchie, J. B., & Echtner, C. M. (2011). Social capital and tourism entrepreneurship. *Annals of Tourism Research, 38*(4), 1570–1593. https://doi.org/10.1016/j.annals.2011.02.006

Patricia Alace E. Delas Alas graduated *magna cum laude* from the University of the Philippines (UP) Asian Institute of Tourism (AIT) in 2016. She was awarded as the "Natatanging Mag-aaral ng Turismo" (Most Outstanding Student of Tourism) of the same year. Although currently working as an integrated media planner, she served as a Market Analyst II of the Tourism Promotions Board, Philippines for more than three years. She has always been interested in studying about community-based tourism and destination marketing management and is eager to conduct relevant studies in the Philippines.

Anne Marie M. Pagador is a University Research Associate at the University of the Philippines Diliman, where she also obtained her undergraduate degree in tourism (*cum laude*). Her work focuses on the historical research of degree programs and course offerings of the university relevant to the review of curricular proposals. She also conducted research for the formulation of policy guidelines on academic field activities and created the Academic Field Activity Handbook in 2019. Eventually, she plans to pursue a postgraduate degree in public policy and management.

Robert Charles G. Capistrano is Assistant Professor at Hainan University - Arizona State University Joint International Tourism College (HAITC) based in Hainan China and a Senior Global Futures Scholar, Julie Ann Wrigley Global Futures Laboratory at Arizona State University. His research foci and teaching interests include ecotourism, tourism and conservation, tourism marketing, family tourism, visiting friends and relatives travel, gender and tourism, cross-cultural studies in tourism, and tourism and migration. He has recently facilitated the drafting of the Association of South-East Asian Nations (ASEAN) Gender and Tourism Framework.

Part III
The Tourist Gaze

Strolling Between Shanties: Tourists' Perceptions and Experiences of Manila's Slums

Jonna C. Baquillas and Brian C. Gozun

Abstract In tourism, destination image is a key factor in destination selection among potential tourists. While there is abundant literature in understanding the image of typical tourist destinations, there is scant literature in understanding the image of slums as a tourist destination. This study investigates the perceptions and experiences of tourists visiting Manila slums (BASECO, Happyland, Smokey Mountain) based on 359 English user-generated reviews of Smokey Tours' slum tour in the online platform, TripAdvisor. NVivo for Mac was used to code and analyze the reviews based on themes of destination image (affective, cognitive, conative) and memorable tourism experience (ambiance, socialization, emotion and reflection). The reviews demonstrated a positive image of slum tourism in Manila, Philippines, carved from the tourists' "real" and "authentic" experience of Manila slums. Contributing to the memorable experience of the tourists are the novelty of the destination providing a backdrop in the multi-sensory experience, meaningful interactions with the tour guide and slum residents, and appreciation of the whole experience. This study is relevant in designing tourism activities that rely on providing a novel or non-typical experience, as well as contribute to the still developing literature on understanding slum's destination image and memorable tourism experience.

Keywords Content analysis · TripAdvisor · Slum tourism · Destination image · Memorable tourism experience · Pro-poor tourism · Urban poverty · Philippines

---

J. C. Baquillas (✉)
Management and Organization Department, De La Salle University, Manila, Philippines
e-mail: jonalyn_baquillas@dlsu.edu.ph

B. C. Gozun (Deceased)
Decision Sciences and Innovation, De La Salle University, Manila, Philippines

1 Introduction

Urban poverty, fueled by population explosion in urban areas, exists in different cities across Asia and the globe. Rapid increases in urbanization overwhelm infrastructures and basic services in less developed countries, as these nations are unable to cope effectively with the demands of population growth (Mahabir et al., 2016). The United Nation's (UN) Habitat (n.d.) projects that by 2030, people living in slums will be at three billion, from one billion in 2016.

Poverty alleviation is a primary global concern; the UN's first Sustainable Development Goal (SDG) for 2030 focuses on ending poverty, in all its forms, everywhere. While different sectors and agencies are creating programs and policies for inclusive economic growth, tourism continues to be suggested for promoting local economic development (UNWTO, 2002; Zhao & Ritchie, 2007). Previously, the traditional approach of tourism development relied on regional economic growth, with hopes that the economic benefits of widespread tourism activities would trickle down to the poorer members of the community, ultimately resulting in poverty reduction (Zhao & Ritchie, 2007; Truong et al., 2014). To further maximize the potential of tourism in poverty alleviation, pro-poor tourism (PPT) became an alternative strategy to effectively open opportunities for the poor rather than only focusing on overall expansion of the tourism sector in general tourism development (UNWTO, 2002).

1.1 Pro-poor Tourism (PPT) and Slum Tours

Tourism's unique characteristics offer opportunities for wide participation of people from different groups, including those in the informal sector. Being dependent on resources, tourism may draw from those already owned by people in impoverished communities. As a labor-intensive sector, tourism activities generate employment for various members of the communities (Truong et al., 2014). PPT aims to enable tourism strategies that directly benefit the poor through activities that focus on creating primary opportunities and strategies for the poverty-stricken members of the community (Chok et al., 2007; Harrison, 2008; UNWTO, 2002; Zhao & Ritchie, 2007). To clarify, PPT is not a stand-alone strategy; it harnesses the potentials of different stakeholders within the tourism realm in order to afford collective benefits for the community, as well as provides access to previously inaccessible markets (Harrison, 2008). PPT strategies can be incorporated into existing tourism systems, and applied to any kind of tourism, ranging from large scale to small-sized tourism activities (Harrison, 2008).

Visiting slums is a distinct niche form of tourism that emerged in the last three decades (Frenzel & Koens, 2012). Slum tourism has widely looked into the application of PPT into its strategies, and has been getting a lot of attention for its poverty alleviation potential (Mekawy, 2012). It involves going to impoverished areas, and has also been called poverty tourism, urban poverty tourism, township tourism, or slumming (Mekawy, 2012). Whereas, "slumming" often consists of upper and upper-middle classes visitors to poorer quarters of urban areas, (e.g., Meschkank, 2011), the modern roots of slum tourism are traced back to the cities of the global south where guided tours bring tourists to the impoverished slums of Brazil (favelas) and South Africa (Booyens & Rogerson, 2019; Meschkank, 2011).

The inclusion of poverty in the tourism activities is no longer seen as just an avenue to alleviate poor conditions, but touristic valorization has turned it into an attraction (Booyens & Rogerson, 2019; Frenzel et al., 2015). Slum tours can range from community-based strategy where the residents are heavily involved in the design and delivery of activities, to an entirely entrepreneurial endeavor with limited involvement of community members (Dürr & Jaffe, 2012). Slum tourism is marked by a widespread desire to connect with how others live. It is presented as a "reality tour" or "places of authenticity", showing the true day-to-day life of the cities being visited (Meschkank, 2011). This type of tourism has attracted various tourist profiles from budget travelers, gap-year students, to development workers, journalists, high profile politicians and luxury tourists (Dürr et al., 2019; Dürr & Jaffe, 2012). To date, a focus of the literature has been the motivations of tourists participating in slum tours, with findings indicating interest in foreign cultures and living conditions visited. Other research has shown curiosity in poverty and squalor, to be another motivation to engage in slum tourism (Meschkank, 2011; Rolfes, 2010).

1.2 Perceptions of Slum Tourism

Discourses about slum tourism frequently point to the ethical implications of the practice; some see it as using poverty as a tourist commodity and has been described as voyeurism and exploitation (Meschkank, 2011). However, the potential economic benefits of slum tourism may also empower the community, especially through the active participation of the public sector and the support of the government (Frenzel & Koens, 2012; Frenzel et al., 2015). Aside from the economic opportunities presented by slum tourism, some tour operators emphasize the reality aspect of the tours – giving authentic peek into the culture and history, and showing their way of life as a way to present an unadulterated truth about their activities (Rolfes, 2010).

In Rocinha, Brazil, research has shown that the perspectives of the slum residents in the largest favela are largely positive with residents reporting a sense of pride in showcasing their place, and a reduction in social isolation (Meschkank, 2011; Steinbrink, 2012; Frenzel et al., 2015). Meanwhile, slum tours in Cape Town noted an optimistic viewpoint from the tourists. TripAdvisor reviews focus on the slums as places of hope instead of despair, noting that the residents are wealthy in nonmaterial things and have goals for constant self-improvement. On a personal level, tourists viewed the tours as ethical, moral, and a cultural experience (Huysamen et al., 2020), rather than the "poverty porn" perspective where the tour is viewed as voyeurism and commoditization of the experience (Iqani, 2016). Similar positive perceptions have been reported from slum tourists in India (Nisbett, 2017; Meschkank, 2011). Slum residents were viewed by tourists as owning the values of industry and community, emphasizing their independence and self-sufficiency. The experience was viewed as transformative and eye-opening (Nisbett, 2017). In addition to the quest for real and authentic experiences, the popularization of the media of slums, such as the movie "Slumdog Millionaire" has driven visitors to Dharavi, India's slum tour (Meschkank, 2011).

For tourists, a slum tour may be a highlight of their trip, emphasizing that while it is a tourism commodity because of the exchange of monetary value for service, the activity is regarded as morally and culturally educational due to the benefits accorded to both the slum residents (economic) and tourists (experiential; Iqani, 2016, Meschkank, 2011, Burgold & Rolfes, 2013). Such visits may also transform prior negative perceptions of slums into positive perspectives associated with hope and dream creation (Burgold & Rolfes; 2013, Iqani, 2016).

1.3 Theoretical Lens

This study employs the concepts of destination image and memorable tourism experience (MTE) as the theoretical lenses in analyzing participants' perception and experiences of slum tours. The image of a tourist destination is an important element in tourism because it influences the perceptions and behavior towards the destination (Gallarza et al., 2001). It also depends on how the destination image being portrayed reflects the real experience (Marques et al., 2021; Papadimitriou et al., 2015). It is a significant decision-making consideration, and it differentiates one destination from another in the minds of the tourists (Marques et al., 2021). Destination image is also a key attribute of tourist satisfaction and influences the intention to revisit and/or recommend a destination (Marques et al., 2021; Papadimitriou et al., 2015).

The multidimensional nature of destination image acknowledges the different aspects considered by tourists when they visit a destination. Gartner (1994) described the image formation process as it relates to destination image using three interrelated components: cognitive, affective, and conative. Related to destination image, the cognitive image component refers to information that is known or what people may think they know, in an intellectual way, about a destination (Gartner, 1994; Kladou & Mavragani, 2015). The cognitive image contains analysis of attributes pertaining to natural/cultural resources, tourist infrastructures, and social environment (Meng et al., 2021); attributes formed based on factual knowledge, and the amount of external stimuli coming from various sources lead to forming an internally accepted cognitive image of a destination (Gartner, 1994; Boulding, 1956; Papadimitriou et al., 2015).

The affective component of image refers to the feelings and emotions that a certain destination may evoke or that a person may hold towards a place; this can be classified into favorable (positive), unfavorable (negative), or neutral (Kladou & Mavragani, 2015; Meng et al., 2021; Marques et al., 2021). As the affective component involves emotions attached to the experience, it is found to be more volatile than the cognitive component (Marques et al., 2021). It is also based on what a person hopes to obtain from visiting a destination – the motives – and can affect the way the destination is being perceived (Gartner, 1994; Boulding, 1956). Lastly, the conative image component describes the behavior that the person chooses to act on to make a decision. Tourists decide on whether the experience of a destination will make them revisit or recommend the destination (Kladou & Mavragani, 2015; Gartner, 1994).

Destination image helps shape the experience of tourists, and a pleasant experience makes the visit memorable (Zhang et al., 2018; Kim, 2014). Turning an ordinary experience into a memorable one relies on various tourism components embedded in the offerings of the destination, as well as assessment of these attributes that are anchored on how the individual tourist processes the experience (Coelho et al., 2018; Kim, 2014).

Memorable tourism experiences (MTE) are highly personal and subjective, and several studies point to its connection to the novelty of the tourism offering and emotions generated during the experience (Servidio & Ruffolo, 2016; Skavronskaya et al., 2020). Kim et al. (2010) noted that "affective feelings, cognitive evaluations, and novel events" (p. 13) augment the memorability of a tourism experience. While MTE is still a complex concept due to its highly subjective nature, there have been some attempts to identify its dimensions (Hosseini et al., 2021). To measure MTE, Kim et al. (2010) developed a scale focusing on the following seven dimensions: hedonism, refreshment, novelty, social interaction and local culture, involvement, knowledge, and meaningfulness. Hedonism pertains to the thrill and pleasure of the new experience; refreshment is feeling a sense of freedom and being revitalized; novelty is new or unique experience; local culture is the impressions on the interaction with the local people; involvement is the extent to which the tourist is involved in or attached to the tourist activity; knowledge involves acquired information or facts; and lastly, meaningfulness is the sense of doing something of great value or significance (Kim, 2014; Kim et al., 2010; Zhang et al., 2018).

Meanwhile, Coelho et al. (2018) posited environmental/cultural influences, relational influences, and personal influences as dimensions of MTE, corresponding to the core processes that make an experience memorable to the tourist: ambiance, socialization, and emotion and reflection. Ambiance points to the cultural exchange during the tourist's immersion where the tourism activity happened, which includes the personal experience of attractions, infrastructures, and other destination elements (Kim, 2014; Coelho et al., 2018). It also covers activities prior to arrival that involve finding information relevant to planning the trip (Coelho et al., 2018). Socialization is acquired in interpersonal interactions, which may remain even beyond the travel experience. This can happen between the tourist and the travel companion, among tourists, and contact with tourism intermediaries (Trauer & Ryan, 2005). Emotion and reflection are attributed to the tourist's experience of heightened emotions and evoked thoughts, which may be positive or negative. It is also connected to fulfilling one's dreams and desires, and the diversity of tourism activities are central to the tourist's lived emotions (Servidio & Ruffolo, 2016; Skavronskaya et al., 2020). Coelho et al. (2018) emphasized that these processes are not exclusive to each other and may be experienced in one tourism activity (for example, river rafting all involve the processes of ambiance pertaining to the environment where the activity is happening, socialization with companions and tour guide, and emotion and reflection brought on by the thrill or novelty of the experience).

1.4 Study Aim and Objectives

This research aims to understand the perceptions and experiences of Smokey Tours' slum tour participants based on user-generated TripAdvisor reviews. Specifically, it seeks to investigate tourists' perceptions of Manila slums in BASECO, Happyland, and Smokey Mountain based on cognitive, affective, and conative components of destination image. It also aims to understand tourists' experiences of Smokey Tours' slum tour by determining how the dimensions of a memorable tourism experience have manifested in their reviews.

2 Manila's Slum Tourism: Smokey Tours

In the Philippines, Smokey Tours started offering slum visits in 2011 as a "photo tour" of Smokey Mountain, a city landfill located in Tondo, Manila. The goal of Smokey Tours is to be able to shed light on societal issues concerning slum dwellers, and embody inspiration among visitors to bring about social change (About Smokey Tours, n.d.). It was founded by Juliet Kwee, a Dutch national who started recruiting and training tour leaders from the slums. The group was coached by Chris Way, founder of Reality Tours & Travel, who pioneered slum tours in India. Since Smokey Mountain has closed, Smokey Tours now offers a similar tour at Bataan Shipping and Engineering Company, known locally as BASECO (About Smokey Tours, n.d.; Berdnarz, 2018). Formerly known as the National Shipyard and Steel Corporation, BASECO compound spans an area of more or less 520,000 m^2 located in Port Area, Manila (Cepeda, 2020). In 2002, it was proclaimed open for disposition to its actual occupants, granting the residents a certificate of award (Proclamation No. 145, 2002). As of the 2015 population census, 59,847 people were inhabiting the area (Cepeda, 2020).

With steady jobs difficult to secure, most of the slum residents of BASECO are garbage pickers earning about US$2 to 3 per day if working alone; earnings can be doubled if they join a scavenging group that requires travel to visit another area. Aside from scavenging, other common livelihoods include charcoal-making (a sack can be sold for US$10), peeling garlic (earnings equate to US$1.20 per sack), and fishing in nearby polluted waters. Some enterprising community members gather discarded and left-over food from fast-food establishments, where pieces of meat are carefully cleaned, re-cooked, and then re-sold to their neighbors. This meal is called *pagpag*, literally meaning "to shake off dust or dirt" (Roxas & Santiago, 2018; Berdnarz, 2018). In the earlier years, BASECO became known as "Isla Walang Bato" (Alburo, 2007), loosely translated as an island (of people) without kidneys– a moniker that came about when, stricken with extreme poverty, men were recruited to donate their kidney for a fee, usually between US$3900 to 5800 (Promchertoo, 2019) – a hefty amount for someone living in impoverished conditions (Promchertoo, 2019; Ventura, 2014; Aravilla, 2001; Yea, 2010).

Improving living conditions in the host community is one of the key projects of Smokey Tours. One hundred percent of the profit of the slum tour is given back to the community. As a result of the organization's efforts, a health center was opened in 2017 in BASECO. The health center provides medical consultation, treatments, and even medicines when necessary (About Smokey Tours, n.d.; Roxas & Santiago, 2018). In addition to providing direct community benefits, Smokey Tours aims to inspire people from all walks of life to become agents of positive change through exposure in urban realities (Cepeda, 2020; Roxas & Santiago, 2018).

To support the fair distribution of wealth, tour leaders are only allowed to stay in the post for two years. In the first year, they are trained to speak English and handle finances. A talent development program is provided in the second year, where they are taught transferable skills such as how to build their resume and apply for a job. After two years, some tour leaders would put up their own small store business, or work abroad as an Overseas Filipino Worker (OFW). Smokey Tours' BASECO slum tour catered to around 1,500 tourists in 2018, mostly coming from Japan, Australia, Netherlands, Germany, and China (Cepeda, 2020).

3 Methodology

This paper used a qualitative research approach in analyzing secondary web-based data from TripAdvisor. As an online platform where users can share their reviews of tourist products (e.g., a country, a specific destination, or restaurant), TripAdvisor has been an important tool for informing tourists about potential destinations. Likewise, the platform has become important for destination stakeholders in understanding what the tourists are saying about and how they are perceiving destinations through user-generated reviews (O'Connor, 2010). Anyone of legal age with online access can create an account in TripAdvisor, and the user has the option to share or leave out their personal details such as age and household income (Kladou & Mavragani, 2015). Platforms like TripAdvisor are important for both the tourists and tourism entities in accessing detailed information based on personal experiences (Kim et al., 2020). The advent of online platforms, where user-generated content is shared, has influenced and shaped the decision-making processes, and contributed to the formations of destination images based on shared experiences (Kladou & Mavragani, 2015; O'Connor, 2010).

3.1 Data Collection: TripAdvisor Reviews

This research is focused on understanding the perceptions and experiences of visitors to Manila slums located in BASECO, and formerly in Smokey Mountain, based on TripAdvisor reviews. Tourists' memorable tourism experiences based on the slum tours offered by Smokey Tours, particularly focusing on the dimension of meaningfulness are also analyzed in this research.

The data used for this research were reviews posted between February 2014 and March 2020. As of March 2020, Smokey Tours had a total of 562 reviews on TripAdvisor. Non-English reviews (Chinese, Dutch, Japanese, German, French, Italian, and Serbian), totaling to 109 reviews were eliminated, leaving 453 English reviews. To collect the data, user-generated reviews of Smokey Tours' slum tour on the platform TripAdvisor were copied and pasted into a Microsoft Word document. Username, user's country of origin, and the star rating were likewise collected. Data was cleaned by removing reviews (n = 94) that pertain to the other offerings of Smokey Tours – market tour, cemetery tour, and bike tour – as these are not covered by the scope of this study. A total of 359 reviews qualified for this research.

3.2 Data Analysis

A deductive approach in analyzing data was employed in this research, using destination image components as the basis of classifying and coding user-generated reviews from TripAdvisor. Reviews were classified and coded based on destination image components – cognitive, conative, affective, to help elucidate tourists' perceptions of Manila slums (Kladou & Mavragani, 2015; Meng et al., 2021).

Using the software NVivo for Mac, word frequency was generated to reveal the words that were frequently used in the reviews. The words "slum", "tours", and "tours", and "Manila" were eliminated from the list. Reviews were coded based on destination image components: cognitive (tour experience, social environment, infrastructure, place), affective (positive, negative, neutral), and conative (recommend, revisit, desire to help, purchase). Likewise, in order to determine Memorable Tourism Experience (MTE), reviews were looked into for insights on ambiance (observable destination elements such as infrastructure, sights, and sounds), socialization (interpersonal interactions between the tourist and travel companion, among tourists, and with tour guides and residents), and emotion and reflection (experience of heightened emotions and fulfilling of one's desire). To ensure accuracy and consistency of thematic coding, the coded data were revisited twice.

4 Findings

A total of 359 reviews of Smokey Tours' slum tour were used for this study with 353 (98.3%) rating the tours as either very good or excellent. Only six reviews (1.7%) rated Smokey Tours slum tour as average, poor, or terrible. The breakdown of the ratings is shown in Table 1.

A word cloud was generated from the 100 most frequently mentioned words in the analyzed reviews (see Fig. 1). The word size reflects the number of times a certain word was mentioned in the reviews. The words "people", "guide", "living", "see", and "experience" were in the top five. "People" reflected how the tourists described the residents of the slum, talking about their living conditions, their activities, their sources of living, and descriptions of how they felt about them. "Guide" was mentioned frequently as a lot of reviews gave praises to their tour guide, describing their personality, how they interacted with the group, and how impactful their presence was in the tour. "Living" pertained to how people in the slums lived their lives, carefully narrating their observations of their insights on their situation. "See" reflected in sentences that provided the opportunity to get a glimpse of the "reality of life" in the slums; it was also often mentioned in the recommendations as a "must-see" activity in Manila. "Experience" was often referred to when summarizing their total impression of the whole activity, often going along with adjectives such as "great", "eye opening", and "unforgettable".

The reviews were first coded based on the three tourist destination image components: cognitive, affective, and conative (Gartner, 1994). A total of 752 coding references for the 359 reviews was generated, suggesting that reviews contain at least two destination image components (mean: 2.10). As seen in Table 2, most reviews analyzed focused on the cognitive image (44%) aspects of their experience. This was followed by the affective image (35%) component, and the conative image (21%) component.

The reviews were then revisited to identify sub-themes (see Table 3). The emergent sub-themes included four for cognitive (place, tour experience, social environment, infrastructure), three for affective (positive, negative, neutral, reflective), and four for conative (recommend, revisit, help, and purchase).

Table 1 Breakdown of Smokey Tours' slum tourism TripAdvisor reviews

Rating	Number of reviews	Percentage
5 – Excellent	312	86.90
4 –Very good	41	11.42
3 – Average	2	0.56
2 – Poor	3	0.84
1 – Terrible	1	0.28
Total	**359**	**100%**

Fig. 1 Word cloud generated from Smokey Tours' TripAdvisor reviews

Table 2 Summary of number of references per destination image component

Destination image component	Frequency	Percentage
Cognitive	331	44%
Affective	263	35%
Conative	158	21%
Total	**752**	**100%**

4.1 Cognitive Image Component

The cognitive image component included guest reactions towards the slums, infrastructure (availability or lack of facilities in the area particularly water, electricity, toilet, and school), tour experience, and the social environment (activities, behavior, and general information about the residents). For example, reviews detailed the notable imagery of the slums:

Table 3 Themes and sub-themes of Smokey Tours' slum tourism TripAdvisor reviews

Key themes	Sub-themes	Description
Cognitive information that are known or what people may think they know, in an intellectual way, about a destination (Gartner, 1994; Kladou & Mavragani, 2015)	Place	Factual description of how the area appeals to the senses (look, feel, sound, smell)
	Tour experience	Narration of tour specifics
	Social environment	Information about the people, their activities, and their behavior
	Infrastructure	Description of available facilities for the residents in the area
Affective feelings and emotions that a certain destination may evoke or that a person may hold towards a place (Kladou & Mavragani, 2015; Meng et al., 2021; Marques et al., 2021)	Positive	Favorable sentiments about the tour
	Negative	Unfavorable sentiments about the tour
	Neutral	Sentiments that do not appear as favorable or unfavorable
Conative behavior that the person chooses to act on to make a decision (Kladou & Mavragani, 2015; Gartner, 1994)	Recommend	Encourage other people to take the tour
	Revisit	Wanting to visit again, or have visited again
	Help	Desire to help, or act of donating (e.g. books for the library)
	Purchase	Buying products sold by Smokey Tours

> Baseco is right on the harbor and its elevation probably varies from under 1 to, maybe, 3 or 4 meters above sea level. Just an extreme high tide is enough to flood many homes and storms wreck a good portion of Baseco over and over. The website for the tour mentions a 'grey' beach. 'Grey' is a four-letter word like another four-letter word that starts with 's' and ends with 't'. It is the equivalent English word for the name that the locals use for their beach. This beach is the children's toilet. The adults use buckets that they empty on the beach. (Minnesota, USA, 5 stars)

Other reviews described the smells of the place:

> The smells and sights have to be experienced in order to get an understanding of how these people live. If you have a weak stomach, think twice about doing this tour. Several of us four struggled with the odours in the slums. (grumpee-58, Australia, 5 stars)

The only review that rated the slum tours as terrible took issue with both the sights and smells:

> I've been here last year and it's really not a good experience to be here.. Foul odor.. really bad.. We need to think of other ways to make this place become more pleasing to the eyes. (1 star)

Other reviews suggest components relating to cognitive image components, such as what was learned, and the abilities of the tour guides:

> Found the slum tour very informative and has given us a unique perspective on life in Baseco. The tour was conducted sensitively and covered the realities and opportunities for the residents. Not always comfortable to see the realities of life in a slum. (New Zealand, 5 stars)

Safety was mentioned several times in reviews as a key attribute of their experience:

> This is one of the highlights of my trip in Manila. If you are concerned about the safety, don't worry it is safe there in Baseco with our tour guide Tessie (who is also from this area.). You will know what I mean when you get there. (Thailand, 5 stars)

> It was just a wonderful experience. The tour leader was from the slum, it means totally guaranteed safety (Non Iwamoto, Philippines, 5 stars).

In general, the social environment was widely mentioned in the reviews. For example, the spirit of the slum residents was frequently commended. In addition, visitors' interactions with residents with described as genuine:

> Children would smile and wave, some even running up to hold our hands. Every person we met was genuine and positive, in spite of their plight. They lived with strength beyond words. (Taiwan, 5 stars)

> The locals of the slum are very hard-working people and poor, but also warm and welcoming, full of smiles, and going about their daily lives despite the struggles they face. I felt safe the entire time and it was interesting and humbling to learn about and see how others make their living. (United Kingdom, 5 stars)

The reviews under the cognitive image component provided highly detailed expression of what they saw, smelled, heard, and felt during their participation of the slum tours in BASECO and Smokey Mountain, depicting a multisensory experience for the tourists. For most, it was an extraordinary immersion into the "other side" of the city, giving them a glimpse of the life in the slums – the depiction of their dwelling places showing cramped spaces, the noise generated by children laughing, people chatting, and going through their whereabouts, the feel of the heat and humidity, and the smell of garbage and Manila Bay waters. The visual, olfactory, auditory, and tactile senses provided a multi-sensory experience for the tourists.

The tourists also shared the tour specifics in much detail, emphasizing the importance of the tour guides who ushered them in navigating through the slums. Most of them noted how important that the guides are from the slums, and are well-trained and knowledgeable in imparting information among the tourists.

4.2 Affective Image Component

The affective image component was coded as positive, negative, and neutral. Positive sentiments consisted of emotions and feelings attached to the activity and how it compared to previous tour experiences:

> I have traveled around the world and done tons of tours, however this was by far the one that I have liked the most. (Colombia, 5 stars)
>
> This was such an interesting, insightful and eye-opening experience that I will struggle to match again in my life I think. (Ireland, 5 stars)

Negative sentiments related to the company's photo-taking policy were highlighted in the comments. Smokey Tours does not allow taking photographs during the tour, to maintain decency and respect for the residents (so as not to make them feel that they are being gawked at). A few mentioned that they agree and are okay with this policy, but there were some who felt the need to document the experience with photos.

> The only regret is that no photos may be taken. (Belgium, 5 stars)
>
> It bothered me a bit when we were clearly instructed not to film any of people's livelihood, but there was another guest who insisted filming everything with her GoPro. I advise you to walk away from this tour if you wish to acquire an Instagram shot. (5 stars)

There were also some who were unhappy with the surroundings, and noted how their first experience was "better", done in the previous location.

> I've been here last year and it's really not a good experience to be here.. Foul odor.. really bad.. We need to think of other ways to make this place become more pleasing to the eyes. (1 star)
>
> The true slum tour through Smokey tours was at "happyland tondo Manila". It was here where you really got a raw gut wrenching appreciation and a deep sense of sorrow for the atrocious life of the people of happyland tondo. It was here where you got to see the people working, living, breathing and also eating trash.
>
> The new slum tour at BASECO doesn't come anywhere near close to the slum tour at happyland. (Australia, 2 stars)

The affective component covered how the tourists felt about the whole experience of walking between shanties and witnessing a day in the lives of the residents. The largely positive sentiments credited their slum tour experience as unique and an eye-opener, giving them an insightful glimpse into what is not commonly visited. There was some commendation for arranging tours in small groups making the experience intimate and authentic, and although some wanted to take photos, there was general acceptance of the policy to respect the privacy of the residents. A lot of people noted that this is the highlight of their trip, with some even comparing this with tours they have taken in other parts of the world claiming that this is more memorable, heartwarming, and inspiring. While some people noted that it was heartbreaking to see the living conditions of the people in their slums, they were glad to be able to help alleviate the situation by availing of the tour, noting that the profits are poured back to the community by helping fund some of the facilities for the residents.

Although quite few, the negative sentiments mentioned of the area having foul smell, suggested to the tour organizer to do something to make the place more "pleasing". There were also some mentions of minor inconveniences such as the tour being hot and humid, or that the meeting place is difficult to find, and the inability to document the experience by taking photos. There was an expressed concern for the possibility of picking up airborne diseases, with the tourist sharing an advice not to come unless needed, and if so, to wear a mask and proper clothing for protection. For those that have visited Smokey Mountain or Happyland previously and then have recently gone to BASECO, they noted the previous locations being better in terms of the total sensory experience.

4.3 Conative Component

The conative component was populated with messages of recommendations, urging those who are reading the reviews to take the tour:

> Do it! At least for one time do something different. Leave the pub crawl for another day, do the bike tour in another city, and for at least one time try to put yourself in someone else's shoes that lives completely different from you. (Colombia, 5 stars)

> Go meet the wonderful people of Baseco slums. You won't ever see the world in the same way again. (5 stars)

There were a few references for revisiting:

> It was very touching, and inspired me to find a way to look for a way to help those less fortunate than me. I hope to return soon. Janet, the Smokey Tours guide, was very helpful and informative. I recommend the tour wholeheartedly. (Ben B, South Korea, 5 stars)

> This tour was well worth it and I will be back to do another tour next time I am in Manila. (Dubrovnik, 4 stars)

There were also a few mentions of wanting to help:

> If I had planned better I would have brought books for the community library and supplies for maternity care services. Check out their Facebook page for their current projects serving the community. (5 stars)

> I really hope that this tour and review will ENTICE MORE LOCALS to create AWARENESS that our fellow Filipinos living in extreme poverty are just "ON THE OTHER SIDE" of the city. (5 stars)

Reviews highly recommending the tours dominated the conative component. Among the reasons why tourists are recommending the tour include the chance for a novel and different tourism experience, the emotions evoked in seeing the plight of the slum residents, the visit being an authentic cultural and educational encounter, and the opportunity to indirectly help people (through the tour charges) while benefiting from the experience at the same time.

4.4 Memorable Tourism Experience

As a multi-sensory experience, tourists who have taken Smokey Tours' slum tour expressed how memorable and meaningful the activity was.

While the slum is not a typical tourist destination, the ambiance was highlighted in most of the tourists' reviews. In their recollection of the environment, they emphasized the stark difference between the slums and the rest of Manila, where tall buildings and highly urbanized sights can be observed. Their memory allowed them to vividly recount in detail how the houses looked like and what condition they are in, the surroundings where the shanties are located, and the day-to-day activities of the residents. Learning about the living conditions of the residents, their source of livelihood, and how residents make do with the limited facilities and infrastructures available in their community was an educational and cultural experience for most of them.

> Baseco is right on the harbor and its elevation probably varies from under one to, maybe, three or four meters above sea level. Just an extreme high tide is enough to flood many homes and storms wreck a good portion of Baseco over and over. The website for the tour mentions a 'grey' beach. 'Grey' is a four-letter word like another four-letter word that starts with 's' and ends with 't'. It is the equivalent English word for the name that the locals use for their beach. This beach is the children's toilet. The adults use buckets that they empty on the beach. (Minnesota, USA, 5 stars)

> The walking tour itself is very confronting, you 'visit' the poorest part of Manila. Where water and electricity cannot be taken for granted. Where thousands of people live together on a few square kilometers without (or few) conflicts. (Belgium, 5 stars)

This interspersed often with the socialization process, articulating their interactions with the tour guide and the residents. Many highlighted the valuable role that the tour guides provided in making their experience remarkable. The fact that the tour guide grew up in the slum communities gave them a sense of safety and security, but also provided them with extraordinary "insider" information about life in the slums. Another thing that most tourists highlighted in their reviews is the warm and hospitable mood of the residents, who, despite their difficulties in life, always offer a smile to the visitors. They saw hope in them, instead of despair. The tourists also noted that most children are happily playing as they go along.

> Me and my brother went for the Slum Tour with Melanie (guide). She has lived there for 20 years so she was able to tell us the reality. All the people we met were happy to see us. We played basketball with the kids and peeled garlic. We went there by jeepney and tricycle, it was our first time and it was really fun. This was an awesome visit and I would highly recommend it to anybody. (Canada, 5 stars)

> We visited women who peeled garlic to earn 80 pesos (roughly 1.6 dollars) a day, learnt about men who risked being shot to collect mussels from a ship, saw children who swam in the muddy waters of "Miami beach" near a dumpsite, and visited projects run by Smokey Tours such as a local library. Children would smile and wave, some even running up to hold our hands. Every person we met was genuine and positive, in spite of their plight. They lived with strength beyond words. (Taiwan, 5 stars)

Many studies have recounted the importance of emotion in evoking a memorable tourism experience (Skavronskaya et al., 2020), and in the slum tour, this is particularly evident. Emotion and reflection attributed to the slum tourists' distinct recollections, pertaining to how they felt during the activity and the thoughts that they reflected on after. The experience evoked heightened emotions of compassion for the residents, as well as admiration for their hard work and cheerful disposition despite the situation. This also revealed their realization of how privileged their lives are, being able to live comfortably with everything they need.

> It was indeed a humbling experience for me and I have to say that my perspective and outlook on life has changed. Smokey Tour showed me how fortunate I am compared to all the slum tour residents. Not only I realized that any problems or struggles that I am going through in my life are nowhere near theirs. I recommend this tour to those who wish to see the other side of life and reality of life itself. (Philippines, 5 stars)

> The slum tour of the Baseco area was a very eye opening and humbling experience. Initially it's shocking to see people living in such conditions, but then you begin to see that although they are needy, and living below the poverty line, they are still beautiful, friendly, and happy people there. The children are playing, and many people are working. It was very touching, and inspired me to find a way to look for a way to help those less fortunate than me. (South Korea, 5 stars)

Memorable tourism experiences that were generated by participating in Smokey Tours' slum tour highlighted the core processes as suggested by Coelho et al. (2018). The user-generated reviews demonstrated that these core processes are interrelated and that some or all processes may be present in the experience. To illustrate, the ambiance process provided an important backdrop in the multi-sensory experience, providing context in the activity. The sights, sounds, and smell were key elements in the lived experiences of the tourist. Socialization process allowed meaningful interactions with the tour guide, as well as the locals, and provided a more holistic and deeper insight into the tourism experience. Lastly, emotion and reflection process lent itself important during the tourism activity as well as the post-activity realizations of the tourists. As the slum tour emphasizes interaction with the "reality" of life in the slums, it evoked certain emotions and thoughts among those who participated in the tour.

5 Discussion and Conclusion

This study investigated the perceptions and experiences of visitors to Manila slums (BASECO, Happyland, and Smokey Mountain), by analyzing the cognitive, affective, and conative components of destination image, as well as their memorable tourism experiences. Results showed an overwhelming positive response to the slum tours of Smokey Tours. The cognitive component revolved around the authenticity of the tour, from describing the place visited, to recounting their tour experience. It painted a multi-sensory picture of what to expect; as a slum tour is not a usual tourist product, a clear understanding of what it entails is key to managing one's expectations – the visual, auditory, and olfactory depiction of their experience help clarify these. Oftentimes, Smokey Tours' slum tour was described as "real" and "authentic", and this achieves the goal of the organization to present the reality of the slums. Because tourism services cannot be "pre-tested" prior to availing them (Gartner, 1994), perceptions based on reviews, and particularly, the cognitive aspect of the reviews, can aid the potential tourist in the decision-making process. These important insights also help shape potential visitors' perceptions of and expectations from the tourism experience.

The affective component was, likewise, populated with positive sentiments, showing that the slum tour elicits positive emotions and feelings despite the nature of the activity. It demonstrated a reflective action, which can potentially spark social change, which was one of the objectives of the organization. Marques et al. (2021) noted that while cognitive components were a more dominant factor in creating images among non-visitors, the affective component becomes stronger upon visiting the place. For example, the emotions evoked by their encounters with the environment and with the people are vividly recalled in their reviews, and while they may already have had some pre-conceived images of a slum prior to the activity, the emotions associated with the lived experience created a stronger impression. The novelty of the experience also contributed to the heightened feelings associated with the tour.

Finally, the conative component illustrated how positively the tourists perceived the slum tour, by recommending it to the readers – which dominated the references in this component. Gartner (1994) posits that the conative aspect is directly related to the previously discussed components – the behavior or action would be determined by how well the image was demonstrated in the cognitive and affective aspects. In the case of Smokey Tours' slum tour visitors, the basis for their recommendation is anchored on how well the tour was organized, how they were able to gain insights from the whole experience, and how relevant the activity is to their lives.

Memorable tourism experiences of the slum tour were punctuated by the interrelatedness of the core processes of ambiance, socialization, and emotion and reflection (e.g., Coelho et al., 2018). The tangible elements of ambiance provided context for where socialization took place. The activity allowed the visitors to interact with the environment as well as with the people in the slums. They learned about the daily activities of the slum residents, and witnessed how they work in their livelihood sources. These meaningful interactions evoked remarkable emotions and initiated a reflection process, making them contemplate on the relevance of the experience in appreciating what they have in life, as well as in sparking the spirit of compassion and helping in some.

Social media sources and user-generated content are easily becoming an important resource for academic investigations, given its capacity to influence people and aid in the construction of brand images (Kladou & Mavragani, 2015; Garay, 2019). For Smokey Tours, TripAdvisor seems to be an essential tool in image formation of its services, particularly the slum tour. Participants in their tours are mostly foreigners looking to experience the "real" Manila. Findings suggest that Smokey Tours' slum tourism reviews shaped a positive destination image, punctuated by a unique experience that tugs on the emotional side of a tourist. For the most part, the people who decided to visit have had favorable and memorable experiences, with positive sentiments rooted in the deep reflections formed through their connection with reality.

While a slum is not a typical tourist destination, Manila slums (BASECO, Happyland, Smokey Mountain) as offered in Smokey Tours' slum tour, provided a novel experience to tourists who were looking for cultural or educational interactions. A glimpse into the life of the slum dwellers offered lessons on hope, hard work, and resilience, and the cheerful disposition of the locals provided a warm and kindhearted environment for the visitors. The image that the slum tours offer is an authentic and real experience that has been highlighted through tourists' perceptions.

As this inquiry is exploratory in nature, future research may involve a comparative look into the image formed through the reviews, and the image that the company wants to portray. From a marketing perspective, this is relevant to ensure alignment of brand activities. It may also benefit from a comparative analysis of reviews done for slum tourism activities in other areas, to investigate whether slum tourism generates the same responses despite differences in location.

References

About Smokey Tours. (n.d.). *Smokey Tours.* Retrieved April 03, 2021, http://www.smokeytours.com/home-2

Alburo, K. (2007, September). Kidneys for sale: Regulating bodies through medical tourism in the Philippines. *Philippine Quarterly of Culture and Society, 35*, 196–212. https://www.jstor.org/stable/29792618

Aravilla, J. (2001, September 19). Barangay Baseco: The lost city of stilts and half. *Philippine Star.* https://www.philstar.com/metro/2001/09/19/134167/barangay-baseco-lost-city-stilts-and-half

Berdnarz, C. (2018, April 25). Inside the controversial world of slum tourism. *National Geographic.* https://www.nationalgeographic.com/travel/article/history-controversy-debate-slum-tourism

Booyens, I., & Rogerson, C. (2019). Re-creating slum tourism: Perspectives from South Africa. *Urbani izziv, 30*(supplement 2019), 52–63. https://doi.org/10.5379/urbani-izziv-en-2019-30-supplement-004

Boulding, K. (1956). *The image – Knowledge in life and society.* University of Michigan Press.

Burgold, J., & Rolfes, M. (2013). Of voyeuristic safari tours and responsible tourism with educational value: Observing moral communication in slum and township tourism in Cape Town and Mumbai. *DIE ERDE – Journal of the Geographical Society of Berlin, 144*(2), 161–174. https://doi.org/10.12854/erde-144-12

Cepeda, C. (2020, March 2). Baseco and the 'kick' from slum tourism. *Philippine Daily Inquirer.* https://newsinfo.inquirer.net/1235528/baseco-and-the-kick-from-slum-tourism

Chok, S., Macbeth, J., & Warren, C. (2007). Tourism as a tool for poverty alleviation: A critical analysis of "pro-poor tourism" and implications for sustainability. *Current Issues in Tourism, 10*(2–3), 144–165. https://doi.org/10.2167/cit303

Coelho, M., Gosling, M., & Almeida, A. (2018). Tourism experiences: Core processes of memorable trips. *Journal of Hospitality and Tourism Management, 37*, 11–22. https://doi.org/10.1016/j.jhtm.2018.08.004

Dürr, E., & Jaffe, R. (2012, October). Theorizing slum tourism: Performing, negotiating and transforming inequality. *European Review of Latin American and Caribbean Studies, 93*, 113–123. http://www.jstor.org/stable/23294474

Dürr, E., Jaffe, R., & Jones, G. (2019). Brokers and tours: Selling urban poverty and violence in Latin America and the Caribbean. *Space and Culture*, 1–11. https://doi.org/10.1177/1206331219865684

Frenzel, F., & Koens, K. (2012). Slum tourism: Developments in a young field of interdisciplinary tourism research. *Tourism Geographies, 14*(2), 195–212. https://doi.org/10.1080/14616688.2012.633222

Frenzel, F., Koens, K., Steinbrink, M., & Rogerson, C. (2015). Slum tourism: State of art. *Tourism Review International, 18*, 237–252. https://doi.org/10.3727/154427215X14230549904017

Gallarza, M., Saura, I., & Garcia, H. (2001). Destination image: Towards a conceptual framework. *Annals of Tourism Research, 29*(1), 56–78.

Garay, L. (2019). #Visitspain. Breaking down affective and cognitive attributes in the social media construction of the tourist destination image. *Tourism Management Perspectives, 32*, 1–11. https://doi.org/10.1016/j.tmp.2019.100560

Gartner, W. (1994). Image formation process. *Journal of Travel & Tourism Marketing, 2*(2–3), 191–216. https://doi.org/10.1300/J073v02n02_12

Harrison, D. (2008). Pro-poor tourism: A critique. *Third World Quarterly, 29*(5), 851–868. https://doi.org/10.1080/01436590802105983

Hosseini, S., Macias, R., & Garcia, F. (2021). Memorable tourism experience research: A systematic review of the literature. *Tourism Recreation Research*. https://doi.org/10.1080/0250828 1.2021.1922206

Huysamen, M., Barnett, J., & Fraser, D. (2020). Slums of hope: Sanitising silences within township tour reviews. *Geoforum, 110*, 87–96. https://doi.org/10.1016/j.geoforum.2020.01.006

Iqani, M. (2016). Slum tourism and the consumption of poverty in TripAdvisor reviews: The cases of Langa, Dharavi and Santa Marta. In *Consumption, media and the global south: Aspiration contested* (pp. 51–86). Palgrave Macmillan.

Kim, J.-H. (2014). The antecedents of memorable tourism experiences: The development of a scale to measure the destination attributes associated with memorable experiences. *Tourism Management, 44*, 34–45. https://doi.org/10.1016/j.tourman.2014.02.007

Kim, J.-H., Ritchie, J. R. B., & McCormick, B. (2010). Development of a scale to measure memorable tourism experiences. *Journal of Travel Research, 51*(1), 12–25. https://doi.org/10.1177/0047287510385467

Kim, Y., Rahman, I., & Bernard, S. (2020). Comparing online reviews of hyper-local restaurants using deductive T content analysis. *International Journal of Hospitality and Management, 86*. https://doi.org/10.1016/j.ijhm.2019.102445

Kladou, S., & Mavragani, E. (2015). Assessing destination image: An online marketing approach and the case of TripAdvisor. *Journal of Destination Marketing, 4*, 187–193. https://doi.org/10.1016/j.jdmm.2015.04.003

Mahabir, R., Crooks, A., Croitoru, A., & Agouris, P. (2016). The study of slums as social and physical constructs: Challenges and emerging research opportunities. *Regional Studies, Regional Science, 3*(1), 399–419. https://doi.org/10.1080/21681376.2016.1229130

Marques, C., da Silva, R., & Antova, S. (2021). Image, satisfaction, destination, and product post-visit behaviors: How do they relate in emerging destinations? *Tourism Management, 85*, 1–12. https://doi.org/10.1016/j.tourman.2021.104293

Mekawy, M. (2012). Responsible slum tourism: Egyptian experience. *Annals of Tourism Research, 39*(4), 2092–2113. https://doi.org/10.1016/j.annals.2012.07.006

Meng, L., Liu, Y., Wang, Y., & Li, X. (2021). A big-data approach for investigating destination image gap in Sanya City: When will the online and the offline goes parted? *Regional Sustainability, 2*, 98–108. https://doi.org/10.1016/j.regsus.2021.02.001

Meschkank, J. (2011). Investigations into slum tourism in Mumbai: Poverty tourism and the tensions between different constructions of reality. *GeoJournal, 76*(1), 47–62. http://www.jstor.org/stable/41148435

Nisbett, M. (2017). Empowering the empowered? Slum tourism and the depoliticization of poverty. *Geoforum, 85*, 37–45. https://doi.org/10.1016/j.geoforum.2017.07.007

O'Connor, P. (2010). Managing a hotel's image on TripAdvisor. *Journal of Hospitality Marketing & Management, 19*(7), 754–772. https://doi.org/10.1080/19368623.2010.508007

Papadimitriou, D., Kaplanidou, K., & Apostolopoulou, A. (2015). Destination image components and word-of-mouth intentions in urban tourism: A multigroup approach. *Journal of Hospitality & Tourism Research, 42*(4), 503–527. https://doi.org/10.1177/1096348015584443

Proclamation No. 145 s. 2002. (PHL).

Promchertoo, P. (2019, October 19). Kidney for sale: Inside Philippines' illegal organ trade. *Channel News Asia.* https://www.channelnewsasia.com/news/asia/kidney-for-sale-philippines-illegal-organ-trade-12007722

Rolfes, M. (2010). Poverty tourism: Theoretical reflections and empirical findings regarding an extraordinary form of tourism. *GeoJournal, 75,* 421–442. https://doi.org/10.1007/s10708-009-9311-8

Roxas, F., & Santiago, A. (2018). Smokey Tours: The other side of Manila. *Emerald Emerging Markets Case Studies, 8*(1), 1–22. https://doi.org/10.1108/EEMCS-06-2017-0116

Servidio, R., & Ruffolo, I. (2016). Exploring the relationship between emotions and memorable tourism experiences through narratives. *Tourism Management Perspectives, 20,* 151–160. https://doi.org/10.1016/j.tmp.2016.07.010

Skavronskaya, L., Moyle, B., Scott, N., & Kralj, A. (2020). The psychology of novelty in memorable tourism experiences. *Current Issues in Tourism, 23*(21), 2683–2698. https://doi.org/10.1080/13683500.2019.1664422

Steinbrink, M. (2012). 'We did the slum!' – Urban poverty tourism in historical perspective. *Tourism Geographies, 14*(2), 213–234. https://doi.org/10.1080/14616688.2012.633216

Trauer, B., & Ryan, C. (2005). Destination image, romance and place experience – An application of intimacy theory in tourism. *Tourism Management, 26*(4), 481–491.

Truong, V. D., Hall, M., & Garry, T. (2014). Tourism and poverty alleviation: Perceptions and experiences of poor people in Sapa, Vietnam. *Journal of Sustainable Tourism, 22*(7), 1071–1089. https://doi.org/10.1080/09669582.2013.871019

UN Habitat. (n.d.). *The Participatory Slum Upgrading Programme (PSUP) | UN-Habitat.* Retrieved January 29, 2022, from https://unhabitat.org/programme/the-participatory-slum-upgrading-programme-psup

United Nations World Tourism Organization. (2002). *Tourism and poverty alleviation.* https://www.e-unwto.org/doi/pdf/10.18111/9789284405497

Ventura, R. (2014). A suitable donor: Harvesting kidneys in the Philippines. *The Asia-Pacific Journal, 12*(50). https://apjjf.org/2014/12/50/Rey-Ventura/4235.html

Yea, S. (2010). Trafficking in part(s): The commercial kidney market in a Manila slum, Philippines. *Global Social Policy: An Interdisciplinary Journal of Public Policy and Social Development, 10*(3), 358–376. https://doi.org/10.1177/1468018110379989

Zhang, H., Wu, Y., & Buhalis, D. (2018). A model of perceived image, memorable tourism experiences and revisit intention. *Journal of Destination Marketing and Management, 8,* 326–336. https://doi.org/10.1016/j.jdmm.2017.06.004

Zhao, W., & Ritchie, J. R. (2007). Tourism and poverty alleviation: An integrative research framework. *Current Issues in Tourism, 10*(2–3), 119–143. https://doi.org/10.2167/cit296.0

Jonna C. Baquillas is a communications strategist, marketing specialist, seasoned educator, and an experienced researcher. She is a member of the Board of Trustees of the Asia Pacific Roundtable for Sustainable Consumption and Production, and has been involved in various projects under the UN Environment Programme, UN Development Programme, EU SWITCH-Asia, USAID, and NZAID. Her research interests are in the following areas: sustainable consumption and production, circular economy, sustainable tourism, climate action, consumer behavior, and disaster space. She completed her Doctor of Business Administration degree from De La Salle University (DLSU).

Brian C. Gozun was the Dean of the Ramon V. del Rosario College of Business at De La Salle University Manila from 2010 to 2019. He completed his Ph.D. in Social Systems Analysis at the National Graduate Institute for Policy Studies in Tokyo, Japan, and undertook his post-doctoral fellowship at the Universitat Ramon Llull in Barcelona, Spain. His research works focused on entrepreneurship, systems analysis, structural equation modeling, sustainable transport, and content analysis. He was a full professor at the Decision Sciences and Innovation Department of DLSU.

Home Away from Home: Foreign Vloggers' Gaze of the Philippines during the COVID-19 Pandemic

Maria Criselda G. Badilla, Adrian Lawrence Carvajal, Carl Francis Castro, and Maria Paz Castro

Abstract Vlogs (video blogs) are shaping tourism experiences and destination brands while COVID-19 continues to change the ways we view and experience the contemporary world. The romantic and collective gaze of travel vloggers (video bloggers) on a destination is immediately mediatized through the internet and mobile technology, which makes the vloggers' narratives a rich resource of insights for creating better tourist experiences. Anchored in Urry's (*The tourist gaze*. Sage Publications Ltd., 2002) tourist gaze, this study examines popular foreign travel vloggers' perceptions of the Philippines during the first 4 months of quarantine in the country. It explores their experiences, how they coped with their situation, and their images of Filipinos and the Philippines, that they have presented in their vlogs. The analysis revealed five dominant themes, namely: Quarantine Experience and Protocols, Incomparable Sites, Filipino Qualities, Food Experience, and Philippines as (Second) Home. The themes suggested that stranded foreign vloggers held a positive view of the Philippines and Filipinos despite being stranded.

Keywords Travel vlogs · COVID-19 · Destination branding · Tourist gaze · Destination image · Stranded tourists · Filipino culture

---

M. C. G. Badilla (✉)
University of the Philippines – Diliman, Quezon City, Philippines

A. L. Carvajal
Chantology Limited, Camberley, United Kingdom

C. F. Castro
La Consolacion College Manila, Manila, Philippines

M. P. Castro
Our Lady of Fatima University, Quezon City, Philippines

1 Introduction

Technology-enabled tools have revolutionized marketing methods by increasing performance, reach, and efficiency of marketing messages (Graesh et al., 2021). Websites, mobile applications, and social media channels such as Youtube, Facebook, and Instagram, as sources of information for tourists, have grown in recent years. Alongside this growth is an increasing popularity of travel vlogs (video blogs) as sources of travel information. Technological advancements have empowered ordinary people to create content and videos more efficiently, giving rise to the popularity of many professional and amateur vloggers (Cheng et al., 2020). What was once limited to static content, the travel blog has now morphed into vlogs which articulate the many aspects of tourism such as travel activities, accommodations, food, and adventures (Peralta, 2019). Vlogs are among the most popular types of travel videos watched on YouTube and have great marketing potential because of their important role in customers' decision-making (Lodha & Philip, 2019).

Recent studies on travel vlogs have revealed their impacts on tourism. For example, Peralta (2019) found that travel vloggers and the content they share on Facebook play a key role in creating an online destination image. Hill et al. (2020) showed that vlogging has more effect on the customer regarding experience products rather than search products; their research also showed that the perceived expertise and trustworthiness of a vlogger was influenced by the number of viewers and subscribers (Hill et al., 2020). Such research suggests the increasing value of vlogs for the tourism sector. Cheng et al. (2020) showed the effect of watching vlogs on behavioral intention. Schouten et al. (2020) recognized the commercial value of vlogs as a marketing tool. In specific relevance to the tourism sector, Lodha and Philip (2019) demonstrated the impact of images of beauty and travel vloggers on decision-making and purchase intention of consumers. Garner (2021) explored how posting to Instagram can visually narrate travel experiences and, thus, showing its important role in shaping narratives associated with places. Both academia and the hospitality and tourism industry stand to benefit from a more in-depth understanding of travel vlogs (Lodha & Philip, 2019). Given the enormous marketing possibilities and the potential influence of travel vlogs on travel intention, analyzing travel vlog content can help marketers understand its role in influencing travel behavior.

As countries imposed COVID-19-related border lockdowns and other quarantine measures, leisure travel came to a complete halt. On March 12, 2020, the Philippines imposed a travel ban on all countries (CNN Philippines, 2020). The national lockdown and border closure also resulted in many foreign tourists being stranded in tourist destinations in the Philippines. Among those stranded were popular foreign vloggers who documented and shared their experiences during the lockdown.

This study examines the foreign vloggers' perception of the Philippines while stranded in the country during the COVID-19 pandemic. This chapter explores positive and negative experiences of the vloggers related to the travel ban in the Philippines. In doing so, it explores the images of the Philippines from the gaze of these stranded tourists as presented in their vlogs. It contributes to the literature on vlogging and tourism and more specifically, on how foreign vloggers viewed a destination during a global crisis.

Our inquiry was guided by Urry's (2002) 'Tourist Gaze'. The tourist gaze is a sociological and technologically patterned way of seeing touristic objects (Urry, 2002). Videos have become a primary medium for sharing travel experiences in recent years resulting in a restructuring of the tourist gaze. Garner (2021) called for studies to redefine the touristic experience and the tourist gaze. Two concepts of the tourist gaze (Urry, 2002) aided our analysis of stranded travel vloggers' perceptions of the Philippines during the COVID-19 pandemic. First, was the idea of seeing, and in turn, being seen. Second, was the simulated character of the contemporary cultural experience (referred to as hyper-reality) and the construction of themed environments waiting to be viewed by the omnivorous visual consumer (Urry, 2002).

2 Methodology

There is a rising trend in the popularity of many professional and amateur vloggers, including those who focus on travel content creation (Cheng et al. 2020). Such travel vlogs are a convenient data source, especially during the pandemic when movements were restricted. To understand perceptions that are present in the travel vlogs, we used a qualitative research approach that included gathering and evaluating non-numerical data. Qualitative data allows researchers to gain insights into people's attitudes, behaviors, motivations, and aspirations, as well as, their contexts and lifestyles (Portus et al. 2018).

We purposefully identified seven top foreign vloggers who were stranded in the Philippines during the COVID-19 pandemic (Table 1), and had vlogged about their experiences being in the country during the lockdown. The selected videos for analysis were limited to those posted on YouTube between March 15, 2020 and to-July 15, 2020, because these captured the vloggers' quarantine experiences in the Philippines during the first wave of COVID-19 pandemic. Aa total of 45 videos and 744.02 min (12 h and 40 min) of content were collected and analyzed for this study.

The data gathered for this study were analyzed using a combination of content analysis and thematic analysis. In a recent study of travel vlogs, thematic analysis was used to look into the perspective of involvement in reaching audiences through travel vlogs (Xu et al., 2021). Studies that need to interrogate media such as videos and film use qualitative content analysis which helps interpret or assess text to perceive its particular significance (Portus et al., 2018). Analyzing text involves describing, interpreting and evaluating the text then finding themes and patterns to it (Portus et al. 2018). In this study, the vlogs were viewed and verbatim quotes were captured and assigned into codes. Thereafter, these codes were categorized into prevalent themes. Five major recurring themes were found during the analysis process: (1) Quarantine Experience and Protocols; (2) Incomparable Sites; (3) Filipino Qualities; (4) Food Experience; and (5) the Philippines as (Second) Home.

Table 1 Profile of the selected travel vloggers

Vlogger's name	Nationality/ies	Descriptions and locations of quarantine	Name of vlog/s	Approximate number of YouTube subscribers (as of January 4, 2021)
1. Carson and Zowie	American Filipino Australian	Carson Moody is Caucasian but speaks fluent Bisaya (a Philippine dialect). Together with girlfriend Zoe, they were stranded in Dumaguete City when the lockdown was imposed.	*Bisayang Hilaw*	883,000
2. George and Lucy	British	George and Lucy are British vloggers who got stranded in El Nido, Palawan.	*Juicy Vlog*	470,000
3. Mike and Nelly	Austrian and British	Mike and Nelly are an Austrian couple based in Makati, Metro Manila. They were stranded in Siargao during the quarantine.	*Making it Happen; and What's up Philippines*	467,000 and 128,000
4. Jmayel and Sacha	British	Jmayel and Sacha make family-friendly vlogs with their daughter, Story. They were stranded in Siargao during the global pandemic and have fallen in love with island life and considered making that permanent.	*Eight Miles from Home*	186,000
5. Chris and Carol	British and Brazilian	Forced to ride out the quarantine in El Nido, Palawan thinking it was better and safer for them to stay on the island for better amenities.	*Jumping Places*	127,000
6. Martin Solhaugen	Norwegian	Martin met his Filipina girlfriend and fellow vlogger, Ave, on one of his trips. He has been locked down while in Siargao and he plans to stay in the Philippines indefinitely.	*Martin Solhaugen*	115,000
7. Anna and Trevor	Canadian	A web-designer Canadian couple who got locked down while in El Nido and have since gotten back to Canada.	*Delightful Travellers*	74,500

3 Findings and Discussion

3.1 Quarantine Experiences and Protocols

Crises have been said to reveal the character of people and places. The people and tourist places in the Philippines were notably impacted by the COVID-19 pandemic. Kock et al. (2020) suggested that the current pandemic constitutes a paradigm shift in tourists' behavior and decision-making. Similarly, we found the quarantine experiences in the Philippines impacting the behaviors and perceptions presented in the foreigners' vlogs. For example, Eight Miles from Home earnestly revealed in their vlogs:

> *Ever since we touched down on this island, our lives have completely changed. This pandemic has stranded us here and we think that there is a huge signal from something or somewhere that we are meant to be thinking about this as a possible home in the future. Never have we felt the way we do right now about a place.*

Most of the foreign vloggers felt safe in the Philippines compared to being in their home countries. Mike and Nelly disclosed, *"I feel like I'm safer here because Austria has so many cases that, for the size of the country, it's kind of too much. It's like being in the top 12 countries worldwide."* This feeling of safety stemmed from the perception that, *"the government handled everything. They did a very, very good job locking down the place…really, really well done"* (Delightful Travellers). What's Up Philippines expressed similar sentiments: *"super impressed with how everyone here is behaving; everyone here is social distancing."*

When borders were partially opened, the vloggers had evaluated their situation and had chosen to stay in the Philippines. A local news outlet explained that a Canadian couple Anna and Trevor, who were in El Nido on March 14, 2020, chose to remain in the country rather than take a flight out due to health and safety concerns, including the cost of repatriation (see Laririt, 2020).

While the foreign travel vloggers acknowledged that they needed to obey national and local quarantine protocols, some reported poor and uncoordinated information from sources such as local authorities. As Jumpin' Places noted:

> *There are a lot of tourists that are gonna be stranded. If we're stranded, we have to just abide by the rules that the locals do. However, it's confusing so check out this sign here… all tourists need to leave (the) Philippines on or before March 19th. I say guests still need to fly out before the 19th. What's the date today alright I guess we got to leave today then yeah… where to? It's weird though… it's not like it sounds official but it's just the tourists coming yet so I'm putting in the government papers that we read it doesn't really say that.*

Other media coverage reported residents as an important factor in alleviating the impact of the crisis, noting that the "Filipinos' positive outlook helps (foreign vloggers) power through the COVID-19 pandemic" (Robillos 2020, p. 89). Likewise, Jumpin' Places observed that Filipinos had a positive sensitivity to situations in the time of the pandemic:

> *We actually checked into this new place, kind of like a little apartment I guess, it's called fisheye and we're paying about $20 a night. I think this is usually over a hundred dollars but yeah everywhere is kind of lowering the prices and stuff. There are also a lot of places that are closing down, a lot of hotels but this place stayed open.*

3.2 Incomparable Sites

One of the major reasons why people travel is to see new places and experience new things (Crompton, 1979). Pull motivators include cognitive factors such as landscape, climate and facilities (Correia et al., 2013) The travel vloggers demonstrated a fascination and wonder with the places they had stayed in during the quarantine period which highlighted the natural beauty of sites in Coron, El Nido, Siargao, Manila, Dumaguete, and Romblon. For instance, several of the vloggers singled out how remarkable the sunsets were, with 8 Miles from Home saying he did not get tired of the sunset:

> *So we always come down here every day to watch the sunset, whatever has happened throughout the day, coming out here just to watch this little sunset is just our little moment to be thankful for where we are and just take that moment even (if) it's just a fleeting glance at the sunset.*

The Delightful Travellers seconded this by saying *"The things we're gonna remember the most are this beautiful view that we look at every single day – that sunset"*. The Philippines is as close to a tropical idyll as you'll find in Southeast Asia, with gentle coastlines and made-for-Instagram sunsets (Canoy et al. 2020). The Philippine sunset has been famous as one of the best sunsets in the world, the common reference of the vloggers to the beauty of the sights reiterates the beauty of the destination.

The content of some vlogs mentioned more than just the popular tourist places. For example, Jumping Places described places 'off the beaten path' in Romblon:

> *Yeah, so the Philippines just gets more and more mind-blowing every day especially on this trip since we do in like the more off the beaten path to finding all these gems that not really that that popular obviously a lot of these places require you to go in a bit of adventure to arrive here but definitely a rewarding adventure.*

Discovering 'hidden gems' of the Philippines illustrated above is indicative of a tourist gaze associated with anticipation, and different scenes from customarily encountered (Urry, 2002).

3.3 Filipino Qualities

Although colonized my various countries, many of their core value systems of Filipinos remained intact and are still practiced to this day. One of the unique qualities of the Filipinos that is known in the whole world is the way the Filipinos welcome and receive their guests, more popularly known as the Filipino hospitality. Filipinos have been described as warmly welcoming visitors to their home, especially strangers and foreigners (Carson-Arenas, 2004). Such hospitality may include offering one's home to visitors as a place to stay for the night, sharing food and drinks, greeting visitors with a warm smile, and making arrangements that suit the visitors' convenience (Saito et al., 2010). Similar hospitality was experienced by Making It Happen, as narrated in their vlog:

> The best memories were the people that we met during the quarantine in Siargao and the kindness...people inviting us to their homes to eat and just seeing a community come together ...Anywhere, people are eager to share experiences, food, and knowledge. It's a nice mentality and I feel like we've adopted that ourselves.

Similarly, What's Up Philippines' described their surprise at their hospitality experience:

> Everybody was smiling and having fun and singing; and you know just greeting us. It was just so heartwarming for us that we even said, like something must be wrong. Why are these people so friendly with the food, like inviting us to join in the meal?

Filipinos' tendency to get along with each other shows how friendly and amicable they are, a trait that permeates in their private lives, workplaces, and relationships with their neighbors (Saito et al., 2010). Filipinos' sense of camaraderie, friendship, neighborliness or empathy towards others leads to helping each other in difficult situations (Saito et al., 2010). Many vlogs supported these previous findings:

> They treat tourists more like a friend than a customer. It leads to a very different type of travel and adventure. Your guides will really take care of you. (Martin Solhaugen)

> It always comes down to a few key things - the people, super friendly people, really welcoming locals...the openness, the friendliness. How welcome we felt here by the people that we meet when we travel around. (Juicy Vlog)

> Everyone is just kind of in this together and helping one another. In this unexpected situation, (it was a) very strange, very scary time, people were so kind to us, so welcoming, and so helpful. The Filipino people where we stayed at the hotel, all the staff and people who work there now basically feel like family to us now... Everyone's been very welcoming to us all the expats here; been very kind. We definitely made some friends for life... In quarantine, one of the hotels we stayed at when we first got here, we're still in touch with them and they've been helping us get local news, getting us food. (Delightful Travellers)

> I really like the fact that we're starting to form friendships with the people here not just like with other Westerners but the locals too. (Eight Miles from Home)

Similar to the findings of Cabanlit (2011) who described the Filipino brand of hospitality, the vloggers reported extensive acts of hospitality from securing food, to finding shelter, and sharing information with genuine care.

Beyond Filipino hospitality, another quality that was repeatedly recognized in the blogs were the language abilities of many Filipinos, specifically fluency in the English. Multiple vloggers described the ease in communicating with Filipinos. The Filipinos ability to converse well in English as stated by Martin Solhaugen added to the destination's appeal to the tourists. Also, the Filipinos ability to empathize and give special emergency discounts to the tourists was noticeable. As discussed by Eight Miles from Home, kindness was shown by the Filipinos at the time of emergency, it would have been an opportunity to earn more but the locals did not take advantage of the situation but instead gave a special rate.

Making It Happen expressed their admiration for the openness, kindness, togetherness and resilience of the Filipinos:

> *I'm grateful that I'm surrounded by people who actually put a smile on my face... I feel more relaxed because people here are very positive; it keeps me motivated to stay positive and share a smile and always look on the bright side...Anywhere, the people are eager to share experiences, food and knowledge. It's a nice mentality and we feel like we've adopted that ourselves. Filipino's kindness and dedication to help each other out; we learn resilience from Filipinos; the way the Philippines handles all these situations is one-of-a-kind because no matter how difficult the situation seems at that moment, everybody tries to make the best out of it.*

The Delightful Travellers were also amazed by the friendliness of the Filipinos as they share in their vlogs:

> *First impression, wow, straight up is a beautiful city...People are super friendly. We know Filipino people are extremely nice and they're exceeding it already. What are the most positive things in our lives at the moment and it occurred to us that it's possibly the best thing, the most positive thing and happiest thing is the Filipino people themselves.*

Friendliness goes beyond being nice. This quality of the Filipinos stands out as the best thing that ever happened to some vloggers. The Filipinos were even able to go over and beyond the first impression the Delightful Travellers have set. During this pandemic, the vloggers have realized the positive contribution of the Filipinos in their being stranded in the Philippines. Bisayang Hilaw described how he fell in love with the Filipinos:

> *What I love about the Philippines is just the greatest people. The culture's awesome...such a kickback relaxed atmosphere here that makes us stay. It's always good vibes here in the Philippines, such a good atmosphere.*

The laidback attitude of Filipinos has endeared them to the vloggers. Being surrounded by positive and fun-loving people provides good vibes and the perfect ambiance for a holiday. Eight Miles from Home was very thankful for the kindness of the Filipinos during the lockdown experience:

> *We have to extend our rental for the tuktuk for another 20 to 30 days. It's actually been a good little vehicle for us the whole time we've been here, (we were given a) kind of special emergency discount from the owner who is very kind.*

Based on the experiences of these vloggers, what really makes the nation so endearing are the very people that made them feel at home. Experiencing these notable Filipino qualities, through their socializations with their hosts, could have contributed to the development of the vloggers' place attachment, which is further explored in the theme, The Philippines as Home (see Sect. 3.5). As Brown and Raymond (2007) suggest, place attachment is formed through positive emotional bonds that develop between individuals and their environment. Because of the multiple visits and countless human interactions with the Filipinos, the statements of the vloggers expressed an emotional connection to the people which resulted in making them stay longer or for good.

3.4 Food Experience

Urry and Larsen (2011) acknowledge that gaze is entangled with olfactory, sonic, and tactile oral experiences. The travel vloggers' experiences were multi-sensory, providing a deeper experience of the destination. More than the visuals, these social and cultural traits made their gaze on the destination more extraordinary. For most vloggers, Filipino cuisine is not the main reason for coming to the Philippines. The vloggers highlighted the cuisine selection which proved to be better than what they expected. Delightful Travellers were surprised while Making It Happen were delighted upon experiencing Filipino food:

> *Aside from chicken adobo, I had no idea what Filipino food was about; we were in for a surprise. Oh wow! It lived up to the hype and better than expectations. (The) cuisine has surprised us. We didn't know a whole lot about it coming in. We knew there were some dishes that were popular...Not enough credit is given to (the) food...We both agree that the food is phenomenal...with great flavor.*

As with other countries in Asia, rice is a constant commodity in Filipino society, being valued as a symbol of cultural unity and sustenance across the country (Gonzales, 2020). It is a primary consumer product that is consumed by Filipinos regardless of their social status (Aguilar Jr., 2008). As a staple that is prepared and served at every meal, Martin Solhaugen and Delightful Travellers observed the Filipino preference for rice as a peculiarity.

> *As a normal Filipino, (my girlfriend) eats rice for breakfast, lunch, and dinner.* (Martin Solhaugen)

> *It's really strange for us to have rice for breakfast.* (Delightful Travellers)

However, the love for rice has been adapted by the vloggers. Juicy Vlog has developed a liking for rice and has adopted the practice of having rice with their meals: *"Using a rice cooker has changed my life. Because it's so handy"*. They appreciated the easy process of cooking rice using a rice cooker, while Delightful Travellers expressed preference to the garlic rice variety: *"I have to say, I'm loving garlic rice."* Local meals made vegetarian-friendly were also discovered by the vloggers. Jumping Places, being vegan and wanting to keep costs down due to the lockdown, found a way to make their own vegetarian version of the local fare:

> *We really enjoy cooking the local meals. We've been cooking vegetarian versions, using something we've never used before, (a) sizzling plate for sizzling tofu - very, very tasty.*

The lockdown imposed restrictions in gathering food supply from stores and commercial establishments which is the usual practice even in the islands and provinces. Residents were forced to go back to basics and produce or forage ingredients to make their meals. Likewise, the foreign vloggers were not only concerned about sourcing food but also on the quality of the food that was available at that time. Maintaining a healthy lifestyle even under the circumstances was considered important. Martin Solhaugen and Making It Happen witnessed the back-to-basics production of food, with the latter experiencing organic farming first-hand.

> *My concern (for) staying here is the produce, vegetables since I'm European. What I'm so impressed about when it comes to Siargao, I don't know if the whole Philippines is like this.* (Martin Solhaugen)

> *Everyone started farming, foraging, fishing; self-providing which is really cool.* (Making It Happen)

Food is also considered as a major element of a social event and a celebration. As Filipinos believe in the term *pakikisama* or smooth interpersonal relationships, food is used to express this desire for harmony; as sharing for the sake of solidarity and integration (Florendo, 2019). Making It Happen and The Juicy Vlog came to love the Filipino brand of community or family-style dining.

> *Spending time together enjoying food; celebrate food, celebrate eating events; these fiestas where there are tons and tons of delicious food.* (Making It Happen)

> *I love and I'm gonna do forever now family-style ordering in restaurants; family dining…family size meals for two to three people. In the UK, you order your own meal; seldom shared with family or friends.* (Juicy Vlog)

Good Filipino food came as a surprise to many of the vloggers. The vlog entries suggested a positive view of Filipino food and how under-rated it was until they were able to try it themselves. The vlogs revealed that the Filipinos should promote its cuisine more and give it the level of importance for the tourist's list of expectations. The collective gaze of the tourist vloggers showed the quality of Filipino cuisine and suggests that Filipino food may be comparable to its Asian counterparts and could probably be a potential differentiating factor for tourist decision-making.

3.5 The Philippines as (Second) Home

The binary structure of "home" and "away" has a long history in tourism research (Franklin, 2004). Tourists tend to go to other places due to different types of travel motivators which could be physical, interpersonal, cultural, or for status and prestige. They visit destinations and attractions and as time goes by, place attachment develops in them. Thus, tourists may embrace their destination as a second home along in the pursuit of exotic and extraordinary experiences (Wildish et al., 2016).

While place attachment is a phenomenon common to tourism (Tao et al., 2022), the circumstances surrounding the pandemic created a novel situation. From the vlogs examined during the period of this study, Eight Miles from Home, Making it Happen, Jumping Places, Bisayang Hilaw and Martin Solhaugen have chosen to relocate indefinitely to the Philippines, as a result of the experiences associated with the unplanned and extended stay. The content shared on their blogs demonstrate an attachment to the country and culture. Personal attachment was also observable. At the time of the study, Bisayang Hilaw decided to stay in the country permanently together with his Australia-based half-Filipina girlfriend Zoe. He narrated, *"Definitely, (it's) the people that attract us to the Philippines. It makes us want to stay here even more."* George and Lucy of the Juicy Vlog happily told their story about why they chose the Philippines as their new home:

> We love the nature, the diversity, the beautiful mountains, the clear ocean, and amazing cities. There's so many things that we really love here that it feels like home. Having lived in Manila for over a year now, been in the Philippines for two years on and off, we noticed that Filipinos do which is different to the UK.

The Delightful Travellers returned to their home in Canada after travel restrictions have been lifted. However, they mentioned how grateful they were to be stuck in the Philippines than elsewhere: *"just being in this country, we're gonna have a special connection to it, I think forever. No matter what, we'll definitely be back after all this is over"*.

Zhang and Lei (2010) suggested that place attachment is a variable that expresses the meanings people assign to a specific setting through their experience with it. It is likely that the vloggers' experiences in the Philippines influenced their decisions on remaining in the Philippines. As George and George (2004) point out, if people become attached to places, they tend to have higher levels of satisfaction and a higher likelihood to revisit the destination, or potentially stay as demonstrated by the statements and experiences of the stranded vloggers.

4 Conclusions

Our study explored stranded foreign vloggers' perception of the Philippines during the COVID-19 pandemic. Through a qualitative content and thematic analysis of travel vlogs, we explored the images of the Philippines and Filipinos from the gaze of these tourists as presented in their vlogs. The vlogger's gaze of their quarantine experiences, revealed unique characteristics of the Philippines as encompassed in the five emergent themes discussed above.

Except for Delightful Travellers, all other vloggers chose to stay in the Philippines indefinitely. All vlogs showed reverence for the natural beauty; however, the most important were the qualities of the people, more specifically, the Filipino hospitality. The vloggers' descriptions of Filipinos as warm, friendly, helpful, hospitable, laidback, and easy-going, added to the literature on the Filipino brand of hospitality. This study has shown that travel vlogs can be used in market research as a good way of gaining tourist insights. However, the vlogs analyzed in this study have only captured the perceptions and experiences of foreign travel vloggers during the first 4 months of the pandemic. We suggest future research to examine the experiences of foreign vloggers in the latter periods of the pandemic. Research on local Filipino vloggers' travel content around the country during the pandemic should be conducted as well, and compare these with the content of their foreign counterparts. Finally, studies should also be conducted on the use of travel vlogging as a marketing tool for local destinations in country.

References

Aguilar, F. V., Jr. (2008). Rice in the filipino diet and culture. Research Paper Series (RPS) 2008–03. *Philippine Institute for Development Studies*.

Brown and Raymond (2007). The Relationship between Place Attachment and Landscape Values: Towards Mapping Place Attachment. *Applied Geography 27*(2), 89–111.

Cabanlit, E. A. (2011). Set operations for determining similarities and differences in traits, practices and beliefs of Filipinos in Mindanao. In *Mathematics of peace, war and terrorism* (pp. 1–17). Cabanlit Research, Development and Publication Center.

Canoy, N. A., Roxas, G. K., Robles, A. M., Alingasa, A. P., & Ceperiano, A. M. (2020). From cesspool to fortified paradise: Analyzing news media territorial assemblages of rehabilitating Boracay Island, Western Philippines. *Journal of Sustainable Tourism, 28*(8), 1138–1157. https://doi.org/10.1080/09669582.2020.1726934

Carson-Arenas, A. (2004). *Introduction to psychology*. Rex Book Store, Inc.

Cheng, Y., Wei, W., & Zhang, L. (2020). Seeing destinations through vlogs: Implications for leveraging customer engagement behavior to increase travel intention. *International Journal of Contemporary Hospitality Management, 30*(10), 3227–3248.

CNN Philippines. (2020, March 12). *Philippines expands travel ban to all countries with local COVID-19 transmission*. Retrieved from https://cnnphilippines.com/news/2020/3/12/Philippines-expands-travel-ban-to-all-countries-with-local-COVID-19-transmission.html

Correia, A., Kozak, M., & Ferradeira, J. (2013). From tourist motivations to tourist satisfaction. *International Journal of Culture, Tourism and Hospitality Research, 7*(4), 411–424. https://doi.org/10.1108/IJCTHR-05-2012-0022

Crompton, J. L. (1979 October/December). Motivations for Pleasure Vacations. *Annals of Tourism Research, VI*(4), 408–424.

Florendo, J. (2019) *Colonizing the Filipino palate*. 12th DLSU Arts Congress De La Salle University, Manila, Philippines February 20, 21 and 22, 2019.

Franklin, A. (2004). Tourism as an ordering: Towards a new ontology of tourism. *Tourism Studies, 4*, 277–301.

Garner, A. (2021). I came, I saw, I selfied: Travelling in the age of Instagram. In M. Mansson, A. Buchmann, C. Cassinger, & L. Eskilsson (Eds.), *The Routledge companion to media and tourism* (pp. 316–325). Routledge.

George, B., & George, B. (2004). Past visits and the intention to revisit a destination: Place attachment as the mediator and novelty seeking as the moderator. *Journal of Tourism Studies, 15*(2), 37–50. Retrieved from https://papers.ssrn.com/sol3/papers.cfm?abstract_id=2111025

Gonzales, M. (2020). *A Historical and Analytical Perspective on Rice and its Significance within Filipino Culture*. Re: Locations, University of Toronto Online Journal accessed on June 30, 2022. https://relocationsutoronto.wordpress.com/2020/07/02/rice-and-its-significance-within-filipino-culture/

Graesh, J. P., Hensel-Borner, S., & Henseler, J. (2021). Information technology and marketing: An important partnership for decades. *Industrial Management and Data Systems, 121*(1), 123–157.

Hill, S., Troshani, I., & Chandrasekar, D. (2020). Signalling effects of vlogger popularity on online consumers. *Journal of Computer Information Systems, 60*(1), 76–84. https://doi.org/10.1080/08874417.2017.1400929

Kock, F., Norfelt, A., Josiassen, A., Assaf, A., & Tsionas, M. (2020, November). Understanding the Covid-19 tourist psyche: The evolutionary tourism paradigm. *Annals of Tourism Research, 85*. https://doi.org/10.1016/j.annals.2020.103053

Laririt, P. (2020, April 21). Foreign vloggers share quarantine experiences from El Nido. *Palawan News Online*. Retrieved from https://palawan-news.com/foreign-vloggers-share-quarantine-experiences-from-el-nido/

Lodha, R., & Philip, L. (2019). Impact of travel blogs and vlogs on decision-making among students of Bangalore. *International Journal of Scientific Research and Review, 7*(3), 2279–2543.

Peralta, R. (2019). How vlogging promotes a destination image: A narrative analysis of popular travel vlogs about the Philippines. *Place Branding and Public Diplomacy, 15*, 244–256. https://doi.org/10.1057/s41254-019-00134-6

Portus, L., Barrios, E., Conaco, M., & Go, S. (2018). *Doing social science research: A guidebook*. Philippine Social Science Council.

Robillos, A. (2020, May 30). Quarantine in the Philippines: Is it more fun? These foreigners tell all. Retrieved December 2020, from TripZilla.com: https://www.tripzilla.com/foreigners-quarantine-in-the-philippines/110953

Saito, I., Imamura, T., & Miyagi, M. (2010). Filipino personality traits and values for social support: FOW as human resources for work life balance in Japan. Retrieved from https://core.ac.uk/download/pdf/268585064.pdf

Schouten, A. P., Janssen, L., & Verspaget, M. (2020). Celebrity vs influencer endorsements in advertising: The role of identification, credibility, and product-endorser fit. *International Journal of Advertising, 39*(2), 258–281.

Tao, H., Zhou, Q., Tian, D., & Zhu, I. (2022). The effect of leisure involvement on place attachment: Flow experience as mediating role. *Land, 11*, 151.

Urry, J. (2002). *The tourist gaze* (2nd ed.). Sage Publications Ltd.

Urry, J., & Larsen, J. (2011). *The tourist gaze 3.0: Theory, culture, and society* (3rd ed.). Sage Publications.

Wildish, B., Kearns, R., & Collins, D. (2016). At home away from home: Visitor accommodation and place attachment. *Annals of Leisure Research, 19*, 117–133.

Xu, D., Chen, T., Pearce, J., Mohammadi, Z., & Pearce, P. (2021). Reaching audiences through travel vlogs: The perspective of involvement. *Tourism Management, 86*, 1–15.

Zhang, H., & Lei, S. L. (2010). Effects of place attachment on participation intentions for local tourism development. *WIT Transactions on Ecology and the Environment, 139*, 501–509.

Maria Criselda G. Badilla is an Associate Professor of the University of the Philippines Asian Institute of Tourism teaching graduate and undergraduate students after 15 years of hospitality industry experience. She has worked on various training programs and tourism and infrastructure master plans with local government units and national agencies. Her research interests include destination marketing, consumer behavior, new media and education tourism.

Adrian Lawrence Carvajal is Lead Researcher and Senior Project Manager, Chanthology Limited, United Kingdom. He was former Dean and Professor for Business, Management, Research and Education. He is also a consultant for national and international organizations for training, publications, leadership and research. His research interests include marketing, management, leadership, quality assurance and education.

Carl Francis Castro is currently the Chairperson of the School of International Tourism and Hospitality Management at La Consolacion College Manila. He is also a co-author of a reference book for Senior High School students in the Philippines. He is a registered environmental planner and being an advocate of sustainable development, he is a consultant to various LGUs in making local climate change action plans. His research interests include sustainable development, environmental planning and climate change mitigation.

Maria Paz Castro is Assistant Professor, College of Hospitality and Institutional Management, Our Lady of Fatima University, Quezon City. She is a business management professor and lecturer for business, tourism and hospitality colleges of several universities in Metro Manila. She also served in government as Project Planner, Fishing Ports Project Management Office, Department of Transportation and Communications and Department of Public Works and Highways. Her research interests include food innovation & sensory studies, consumer behavior, hospitality and toursim education and industry studies, culture and heritage.

The Traveling Filipina in Periodicals (1898–1938)

Katherine G. Lacson and Brian C. Gozun

Abstract Tourism has become a significant player in income and job creation for many countries all over the world. With its impact on a country's economy, many studies on the subject tackle current issues and developments, with tourism history left as a footnote. This chapter addresses two topics that have been left by the wayside – tourism history and women's history, which adds to the richness of knowledge creation under the umbrella of Philippine tourism. This chapter explores the details in the life of the Filipina traveler during the American Period. This was done by utilizing periodicals available in the Philippines from 1898–1938, providing a better perspective on the details of the Filipina's life as she expanded her world view through travel. There has been a dearth of information to encapsulate the Filipino woman's story as she discovered the different parts of her country and the places outside it. This chapter hopes to add another layer to the rich tapestry of the Filipino women's story in history.

Keywords Filipina traveler · Women history · Philippine history · American period · Tourism · Images and representation

The reconstruction of women's history has its set of challenges due to the poverty of sources that documented her activities. This is due to the relegation of her experiences in the private sphere. With the help of existing primary sources such as the periodical, one can piece together bits and pieces of the Filipina's historical narrative. During the American period, the Filipina was given opportunities to actively engage in the public sphere. She fought for her right to suffrage, matriculated in schools, became part of the economic force, and took part in the social and cultural transformation of the country. These opportunities gave her a chance to explore the

K. G. Lacson (✉)
Department of History, Ateneo de Manila University, Quezon City, Philippines
e-mail: klacson@ateneo.edu

B. C. Gozun (Deceased)
Decision Sciences and Innovation, De La Salle University, Manila, Philippines
e-mail: brian.gozun@dlsu.edu.ph

world and step out of the domestic sphere. The periodicals captured her meaningful sojourns at home and abroad as she participated in various tourism experiences that changed and empowered her. Using a historical-feminist perspective to study the narratives and adopting Alan McKee's (2005) interrogation of Jurgen Habermas' ideas on the public sphere in the face of feminist historiography, this chapter offers a glimpse of the experiences of the everyday and the extraordinary through the eyes of the Filipina traveler as she explored the world, inadvertently becoming a representative and an ambassador of the Filipino. She defined and redefined perceived representations of what a Filipino was during this period in time, in the process, expanding her view of herself and her place in the world.

1 Itinerary: A Planned Route or Journey

Periodicals like the *Philippines Free Press, Graphic,* and *The Tribune* provided a rich tapestry of valuable historical tidbits on the Filipina traveler's story. Feature articles, travelogues, narratives, photos, and advertisements captured her peregrinations. These articles, illustrations, and photographs provided the different types of female travelers, her itinerary, the various reasons for her perambulation, the activities she joined, whom she traveled with, and her experiences and impressions of the world outside her own home.

During the first decade of the American period, it was challenging to find the story of the Filipina traveler. Most pieces were bent on selling Manila as a tourist town. As the world opened up and the infrastructure of travel was created, so did the increase of articles on women travelers. By the second decade of American occupation, the Filipina and her journeys became visible as periodicals published more articles on her various sojourns.

A variety of female travel experiences, both domestic and international, were captured by the articles published in this period's extant periodicals. With the availability of various modes of transportation, the Filipina traveler had a choice of visiting nearby destinations through automobiles, buses, or Manila Railway Company trains that reached different parts of Luzon ("Manila Railroad Company," 1914, 1932; San Martin, 1928b). Modern steamships made traveling to the other islands possible, while bigger ones crisscrossing the globe opened up the world to the globetrotting Filipina ("Smith, Bell & Co's.," 1915; "Pacific Mail S.S. Co.," 1915; "United States Lines," 1925) The favorite haunts featured in periodicals were Manila, Baguio, Antipolo, Cavite, Laguna, Iloilo, Cebu, Davao, and Zamboanga. The yearly pilgrimage to Antipolo and the summer exodus to Baguio were the most popularly featured domestic destinations ("To Baguio Kid, to Baguio! Leave the Oven," 1919; "On With the Dust," 1928; Montalban, 1928; "All Aboard for Baguio," 1929). Those from the provinces looked forward to visiting the capitol, especially during the carnival season celebrated every February ("Mindanao, Luzon and Visayas United," 1923, p. 14). Favorite international destinations were Hongkong, China, Japan, the United States, and European countries such as Britain, Italy, and France.

2 Jaunt: A Short Trip or Excursion, Usually for Pleasure

There were Filipinas who traveled for pleasure. During the American period, domestic trips were in the form of excursions, field trips, outings, picnics, and vacations. Families, companies, students, and social clubs took the time to visit nearby destinations to fulfil their desire to explore. Photo sections of periodicals such as *Graphic* and *Philippines Free Press* were full of happy pictures of employees on excursions, students making field trips, and friends and families gallivanting to nearby sites. Various photos and articles contained stories of picnics, which were considered as grand events that started early in the morning and finished at the end of the day ("A Page for the Young Reader," 1913; "Ilongos in Manila Celebrate Annual Reunion," 1926). The destinations were usually idyllic venues near nature such as mountains, forests, and lakes. Games, speeches, and dances filled the program for the day. Picnics were well-attended shindigs such as the intercollegiate girl's picnic in Los Baños, where well-known co-eds and bachelors started the event with parlor games like the blind man's bluff as soon as they rode the train from Manila. They continued the fun as they reached the venue where they partook in activities such as swimming, cycling, and dancing ("Foto News Editor Joins Kalaw Picnic," 1938).

The writers and picnic participants usually waxed poetic about the lady attendees of these events, not just for their beauty but also for their skills in the kitchen. In most of the picnics, women were always the ones who took care of the meal. The food prepared was always lavish. Filipino dishes like *adobo, sinigang*, and *lechon* were part of the usual spread ("A Page for the Young Reader," 1913). A social club from Manila called Barangay had themed picnics. One was called "Let's Go Native," where over a hundred picnickers wearing colorful *barong tagalogs* (an embroidered long-sleeved formal shirt for men) and the traditional *Balintawak* (a native costume of Filipino women consisting of a bodice, a skirt, a *tapiz* worn over the skirt and a *panuelo* worn either as a wimple or merely draped over the shoulders) motored to Kawit, Cavite for a Sunday pleasure-bent affair of dancing and fishing. In line with the theme, food was served on fresh banana leaves and was eaten using one's bare hand ("Barangay Goes Picnicking," 1938). The penchant for picnics was so that Filipinas continued this favorite pastime abroad. For example, a picnic was held to celebrate the visit of Hon. Ignacio Villamor, president of the University of the Philippines (UP) in the picturesque town of Tsurumi ("Filipino Picnic in Japan," 1916). Mrs. Natividad, Mrs. del Rosario, and Miss Carmen Lacson attended this event. Another example was the annual picnic that the Filipino Youth Association of Vallejo held in various parts of America ("Big Filipino Picnic" 1920).

3 Summertime: The Season or Period of Summer

Summer was an important time for the Filipina traveler, whether it be domestic or international. A flurry of activity happened in preparation for the mass migration. Students finalized their goodbyes as they went back to their homes, while society made "a frantic effort to finish off their social obligations" before they hid in their summer houses or left for travels abroad ("Capital Society Moves Center to Cooler Place," 1931, p. 23).

Various periodicals were full of advice columns to prepare the traveler for a chic and safe summer. Articles extensively discussed shopping recommendations on wardrobes such as sleeveless dresses, bathing suits, sports, and traveling clothes that were in vogue ("Before You Go Shopping," 1933; "Fashion: Summertime Means Swimming, New Bathing Suits," 1938). Essential must-haves such as deodorants, creams, and other toilet preparations were written. Even quick removal of excess hair and depilatories were included ("Some Suggestions for Making You Fresh and Dainty," 1933). Lists were created to ensure that the Filipina had a complete beauty kit ready for any occasion or summer activity. According to Juan Cristobal of the Aguinaldo Hair Science and Beauty Culture Institute, the first aids to beauty were "a jar of cleansing cream, a bottle of astringent lotion, favorite powder, rouge (paste or powder), lipstick, skin oil, vanishing cream, and a generous supply of facial tissues. And of course, a stiff hairbrush and a good bath soap" ("Vacation Make-up," 1937, p. 34, 38).

Those who decided to stay in the country to try to escape the summer heat and the dusty season in Manila ("On With the Dust," 1928) joined the annual exodus to Baguio known as the mountain resort or "the health and sports center of the Orient" ("Why Go to Baguio," 1935, p. 134). Aside from the train services of Manila Railway Company, Baguio became more accessible due to the availability of air taxis managed by the Philippine Aerial Taxi Co. ("Philippine Aerial Taxicab Co.," 1931). Many women coming from the upper echelons of society like the Araneta's and their peers were featured doing various activities in the summer capital during society's migration to cooler climes ("Capital Society Moves Center to Cooler Place," 1931). Bowling, tennis, hiking, small house parties, *tete-a tetes*, get-together parties, and dances ("Enjoy Baguio's Balmy Breezes," 1931) were regular pastimes and features of Baguio vacations for the society women ("Members of Smart Set are Already in Baguio," 1928).

Not everybody moved to Baguio during the summer. There were those who craved a glimpse of foreign lands. Hongkong and Shanghai were the preferred destinations of those who wanted to do temporary migrations during the summer season, while those who had more time began their whirlwind trip to the United States and Europe ("Capital Society Moves Center to Cooler Place," 1931).

To those who were upwardly mobile, vacation connoted a complete change of scenery. However, for a good majority, vacation meant short weekend getaways to Pasay and Parañaque beaches and public swimming pools that served as a respite from the summer heat ("Manila Browses on Sunday," 1938). For students, "vacation simply means going back to their home provinces" ("What to Do During Your Vacation," 1933, p. 37). It was a time to bond with their families and help out their mothers with housework ("What to Do During Your Vacation," 1933; "Vacation days!" 1922). Dr. Felisa Nicolas, a medical staff of the UP infirmary, suggested that girls focus on their health and physical education by improving sanitary conditions in the home during this time ("What to Do During Your Vacation," 1933). In line with this, some girls participated in summer camps like the Red Cross summer camp in Nagcarlan ("Red Cross Summer Camp in Nagcarlan," 1923) and the Girl Reserve Camp at YWCA at Canlubang Laguna ("What to Do During Your Vacation," 1933). To those who did not have the opportunity to join these summer camps, Ms. Filomena Alonso suggested that the camping idea "can be carried out in our own homes, without going out of town and sleeping in tents" ("What to Do During Your Vacation," 1933, p. 37).

Other students engaged in civic activities in their communities, like the youth leaders of Alabat, Tayabas province, who jump started thrift and health campaigns. These campaigns were in line with the movement inaugurated by Jorge Bocobo of the University of the Philippines to arouse the youth's interest in public affairs and social work. An example of one of the activities that were done by the youth leaders of Alabat, Tayabas province was to give a series of lectures on topics such as the "Necessity of Cooperation with Town Officials" and "Importance of Beautiful and Neat Surroundings," to name a few ("Making the Most of Vacation," 1928, p. 14). Centro Escolar directress Miss Librada Avelino pushed the tenets of learning through experience by chartering the steamship *Islas Filipinas* where 130 students from the famous girl's school did a summer cruise to various Philippine islands and provinces for recreation and study ("The Floating Centro Escolarina," 1928). The Floating Centro Escolarina project was partly inspired by the world's first floating university housed in the S.S. Ryndam, where 450 students went on a world cruise for eight months ("Floating University Visit Manila," 1926). Miss Avelino stated "that our girls know more of other countries from what they have learned from books, than of their own land," a problem that she wished to correct with this endeavor ("Floating University Visit Manila," 1926, p. 2).

4 Gadabout: A Person Who Travels Often or to Many Different Places for Pleasure

Leisurely pursuits such as outings, excursions, pilgrimages, field trips, and picnics were accessible to most Filipinas in all social classes, for they were usually domestic and entailed short term travel. However, in the featured narratives, there was a limitation for those in the lower social classes when it came to travel. Class privilege was visible in the travel narratives of the Filipina. Since traveling entailed certain costs, those who were able to travel most of the time came from the middle and upper classes. To those who have time and money, the world became their playground.

Many of the ladies featured who traveled for leisure came from society's upper echelon and had money to burn. They were wives, mothers, sisters, and daughters of prominent politicians, businessmen, and the landed gentry from Manila and provinces such as Negros ("These Farm Trained Girls from Negros Can make City Society Girls Sit Up," 1925; "Traveling Through Europe and America with Three Society Girls," 1931). Some were even known to have money of their own. Their grand tours lasted for a minimum of a year to five years. Due to this, *despedidas*[1] and welcome back parties became *de rigueur*, as these events became the opportunity for them to say farewell to their friends before they disappeared for a year or so. For example, Mrs. Pura Villanueva Kalaw, the first Carnival Queen and one of the mavens of Manila society, hosted a *despedida* tea party at their residence to honor the departure of Eduardo del Rosario Tan Kiang. It consisted of an evening musical program ("Director and Mrs. Kalaw Entertain at Despedida Tea Yesterday," 1931). Miss Ofelia Pamintuan, who was to stay in Europe for a year with a group of Manila society girls, was given numerous *despedidas* hosted by her friends in Manila and Angeles, Pampanga ("Miss Pamintuan to Go to Europe," 1931). While Dr. Maria Paz Mendoza-Guazon and Miss Milagros Hernandez gave a farewell party at their residence in Chicago to Miss Encarnacion Alzona, who was leaving for Radcliffe, Massachusetts. The farewell party was full of visitors who gave short talks and toasts, which seemed to be an essential feature of any self-respecting *despedida* (Hernandez, 1919). Upon their return after a long trip overseas, they would attend several welcome back parties hosted by good friends. This became a chance to embrace them back to the fold as they adjusted to Philippine life once again. Each welcome back party had its unique twist, such as a "lumpia" party to celebrate the arrival of Mrs. Primo Arambulo, who went with the Philippine trade mission to various important Japanese cities ("Mrs. Arambulo Welcomed Back," 1933).

Many of those who traveled far and wide were part of the smart set of the Philippines. They traveled with their parents, their relatives, or with friends. Many of these society girls toured the world, like Remedios Sunico, who joined the Bayot family in their sojourn ("Society Girl to Tour the World," 1931). While the triumvirate of Dolores Paterno, Maria Osmeña, and Natividad Quiogue, daughters of prominent Filipinos, related their magnificent trip through Paris, London, the Riviera, Rome, Hollywood, Washington DC, and New York ("Traveling Through Europe and America with Three Society Girls," 1931). They met Hollywood actors in Los Angeles, tried their luck in the gambling tables of Monte Carlo, enjoyed the charm of the Englishmen, and were even granted a special audience with His Holiness, Pope Pius XI in Rome. When asked about their favorite destination, the three ladies were most enchanted with Paris ("Traveling Through Europe and America with Three Society Girls," 1931).

---

[1] A social event to mark a person's departure; a farewell party or leaving party. *Despedida | Definition of Despedida by Oxford Dictionary on Lexico.com also meaning of Despedida.* (n.d.). Retrieved October 26, 2020, from https://www.lexico.com/definition/despedida

Paris was the favorite city of the *crème de la crème* of Philippine society. Various travel narratives pertained to the Filipino woman as she visited the city of lights. According to Dr. Francisco Villanueva Jr. (1929a), "Many Filipino women have become great patronizers of the different *galleries*, which sell all sorts of merchandise from the most insignificant needle to the most expensive gown" (p. 2). Besides visiting sites and buying things, they also enjoyed the social life, attended opera performances in Paris, and watched Parisian movie films. Some were there to take advantage of their stay. They studied dressmaking, cooked French food, attended lectures, or perfected their mastery of the French language (Villanueva Jr., 1929a). Others entered the leading finishing schools like Misses Macaria and Pacita Madrigal y Paterno, daughters of Vicente Madrigal, and Mrs. Susana Paterno de Madrigal ("Daughters of Vicente Madrigal Leaving for French Finishing School," 1931). Some took part in special events like the de la Rama Family, and other society ladies such as Mrs. Manuel Eloriaga and Mrs. Arsenio Luz, who attended the Paris Exposition (Villanueva Jr., 1929b; "Filipino Women Grace Exposition," 1931). Misses Natividad Marquez and Salud Marquez of Lucena, Tayabas arrived in Paris to make a reality of their dream to fly over Paris (Villanueva Jr., 1929c).

Suffragist, educator, physician, and one of the most respected women of her time, Dr. Maria Paz Mendoza-Guazon, usually traveled with her sister Guillermina Mendoza and was even featured as the most traveled Filipino women "touring not only the beaten paths of the average round-the-world globe trotter but also visiting other nations not frequented by Filipinos," ("Most Travelled Filipino Women," 1927, p. 4). This might be an overstatement, especially when one heard about the travels of the two daughters of Don Esteban de la Rama, Amparing and Leonor de la Rama, 23 and 19 years old, respectively. They were given a blank check by their father to go to any part of the world they deemed interesting. They could stay in any country as long as they pleased, were given no time limit, and could decide to come back to the Philippines when they were tired of traveling and ready to manage their millionaire father's estate and business. The most extraordinary part was that the two sisters traveled without any chaperones, which was frowned upon during that time. However, Don Esteban de la Rama was the one who conceived of the bold idea and stated that "I am sending my daughters on this trip to complete their education." ("Two Iloilo Girls to Make World Tour Unchaperoned," 1924, p. 31). His only stipulation was that they send him letters of their travel with detailed statements of their expenses. Aside from the usual destinations that many society girls visited such as Paris, Rome, Los Angeles, and New York, they would also find themselves wandering off-beaten paths such as Havana, Cuba ("Cuba Seen Through Eyes of Filipino Girl Globe Trotter," 1925) and Dublin ("Dublin Irishman Sighs for Philippines," 1926). Their proud father shared their impressions of the places they visited through the letters they sent in periodicals. After their return from their two-year round-the-world trip, their youngest sister, Fanny de la Rama, who worked as secretary to their father while they were away, was also given the same privilege and took a more extended five-year trip ("Fanny Will Follow Foot-Steps of Her Much Traveled Sisters" 1926.).

5 Coddiwomple: To Travel in a Purposeful Manner Towards a Vague Destination

Reading the narratives in the periodicals, not all who traveled do so to enjoy leisurely pursuits. It was clear that the Filipina traveled for serious purposes. Some traveled to represent the country's political interests and its women, handle business matters, attend conferences, and do further studies. Mrs. Sofia de Veyra, the wife of resident commissioner Jaime C. de Veyra, was very active in the fight for women's suffrage and women's education, whether she was in the country or Washington DC accompanying her husband. In a letter to the Alumni Association of the Philippine Normal School from Washington DC, Mrs. de Veyra advised the young Filipina in the country's regeneration. She considered herself entitled to share her thoughts on the matter, stating that "Having thus seen more of the world and having more years on my shoulders," she hoped to counsel the youth concerning the tasks of the women of the land (de Veyra, 1919, p. 7). Due to her many activities, she was bestowed with the title of being "The Little Mother of Them All" ("The Little Mother," 1920, p. 23). Mrs. de Veyra delivered lectures to several associations educating the American public about the Philippines (Castillejo, 1920). She was the official delegate to several conventions, such as the 1922 Pan American Conference and the National League of Women Voters (Villa, 1922a). She even became the special guest to crack the champagne bottle in a warship destroyer named "Jose Rizal" (Salazar, 1919). She also attended various receptions for her and her husband in the United States, including one at the White House given by Mrs. Warren G. Harding (Villa, 1922b). Included in this affair were several Filipinas, including Mrs. Aurora Quezon (First Lady of the Philippines from 1935 to 1944), who also accompanied her husband Manuel L. Quezon in various parliamentary missions. She even represented him in various socials and significant events such as the Olympic games in Japan, where she was photographed with several members of Manila's Four Hundred ("Society Seen at Games," 1925).

Dr. Maria Paz Mendoza-Guazon campaigned with Judge Jose Abad Santos under the Philippine Educational Mission by enumerating the Filipina's activities in various professional fields ("Judge Santos' "Big Bertha" Fired," 1926). She also utilized her personal resources to inform Americans about the Filipino people ("You Represent 11,000,000 Filipinos," 1926). Encarnacion Alzona, a well-known suffragist and historian, would be in and out of international conferences concerning the Philippines and educational matters (Alzona, 1927).

Some women mixed business with pleasure as they accompanied their husbands in their work, like the wives of the politicians who were part of the various Philippine Parliamentary Missions ("Another Presentation of Philippine Parliamentary Mission," 1922; *Damas Filipinas de la Segunda Mision en la Casa Blanca*, 1922). Mrs. Andrea del Rosario Aguinaldo, the wife of the well-known businessman and owner of the biggest department store in Manila, Mr. Leopoldo R. Aguinaldo, usually joined her husband in his foreign travels to gain new ideas for their department store L.R. Aguinaldo ("National Affairs: Personalities," 1932). Mrs. Juan Moran, an army officer's wife, accompanied her husband Lt. Moran to the United States and, due to this, lived in three American posts ("Social Life in an Army Post," 1932). Mrs. J.H. Onas, whose husband was working onboard a United States navy patrol on the Yangtze river, was even given the honor by General Lou Kin-chang to review his troops ("Filipino Lady Invited to Review Chinese Troops," 1925). While Visayas' socialites Doña Maria Lopez (the richest women in Iloilo and Negros), Mrs. Ana Ledesma Vda. De Lopez, Miss Rosario Lopez, Mrs. Salvador Araneta, Miss Fanny Ledesma, and Mrs. Albino Santos did not only fly from Iloilo to Manila through the Iloilo-Negros Air Express company, but they were also board of directors and stockholders to this new travel business enterprise ("Women Pioneers in a New Business Enterprise," 1933; Gonzales & Ramos, 1933).

Most of the women featured in periodicals were able to travel to the United States as part of the government's *pensionado* program. The *pensionado* program that started in 1903 sent Filipino students to various US universities for training, further studies, and to acquaint them with American institutions, customs, and ideals (Lim, 1929). Periodicals enthusiastically documented their experiences, impressions, and achievements. Well-known women such as Honoria Acosta, Maria Paz Mendoza-Guazon, Encarnacion Alzona, Enriqueta Macaraig, Tarhata Kiram, Carmen Aguinaldo, and Maria Kalaw, to name a few, were part of this prestigious group. It was in the frame of doing further studies that they had the opportunity to widen their horizons within the university's confines and the world outside it. Not just day tourists, they were travelers who had a chance to undertake higher learning in the most prestigious universities such as Harvard, Johns Hopkins, and Columbia. They were able to see America's sights and sounds, and they were given a chance to have a deeper understanding of the culture through first-hand experiences in their daily lives as students. They were also given opportunities to travel outside the US, as one news article stated, "Philippine government students in the US desiring to return to the island via Europe will be allowed an extension of two months in order to enable them to see some countries in Europe" ("The News of the Week," 1923, p. 9). *Pensionadas* like Rosa Militar and Ines S. Villa became the Filipino students' voices abroad as they became contributing writers to magazines at home. Many *pensionadas* were able to meet prominent personages one can only dream of meeting. Consuelo Valdez met President Harding (Valdez, 1923a). Honoria Acosta was able to meet President Roosevelt, while the Vanderbilts provided her and other students with food and presents during the holidays ("Reminiscences of a Government 'Pensionada,'" 1932). Pilar Herrera, whose specialty was chemical research, had the rare opportunity to meet Marie Curie ("The Foremost Filipina Scholar Today," 1921). Josefa Abaya was among those selected to have dinner with the Rockefellers and the Carnegies ("Josefa Abaya Dined with Rockefellers & Carnegies," 1923).

Once in a while, those coming from the middle and lower classes get to be featured for their travels due to their work. Miss Patrocinio Sales, part of the staff of traveling demonstrators under the Food Preservation Division of the Bureau of Science, was able to visit "practically all parts of the Philippines" ("Be a Demonstrator and See the Philippines!" 1932, p. 38). Home demonstration agents Misses Natividad Brodet and Presentacion Atienza had the opportunity to travel to the United States to get new ideas. ("2 Filipino Girls in US to Teach Local Folk to Make Better Homes", 1934). The local branch of Marshall, Field, and Company sent Raquel Bartolome and Urbana Cruz on an 18-month tour in 64 American cities to demonstrate how dainty undergarments were made in the Philippines ("Embroidery Workers Invade United States," 1922). Nurses connected to the American Red Cross were able to service Filipino laborers in Hawaii plantations ("Two Nurses Trained for Service," 1922). Miss Fortunata Ugtong, who was part of the delegation to aid Japan's earthquake victims, was chosen as the representative to meet with Prince Hirohito due to her cheerful and helpful personality despite the discomforts of the voyage to Japan ("The Pollyanna of the Japanese Relief Expedition," 1923). Aside from these lucky women, those in the entertainment industry were usually featured when they performed in other countries. Many were singers such as Luisa Tapales and Jovita Fuentes. Singer Isabel Sanchez was even able to appear in a leading role before King Alfonso of Spain (McCulloch Dick, 1926). Actresses such as Lena Jacobs, Vitang Escobar, and Dimples Cooper related their stories as they tried their luck in the theatre and film industry outside the country.

6 Numinous: Feeling Both Fearful and Awed by What Is Before You

Travel during those times, as written in periodicals, sounded idyllic and romantic. However, once in a while, the reader was given a peek of the travails of traveling. Behind the glamour were significant challenges, especially for first-timers or those whose timing was rather unfortunate. A journal supposedly written by Miss Josefa Jara, who became one of the most well known social workers of her time, vividly captured the misery of sea travel. It all started on a positive note with good humor and delicious meals until the ship met an angry sea. Everything went downhill after that as she experienced a worst-case of seasickness, to the point that she called her companion to provide instructions concerning who would get her personal effects if she died on the ship (Morente, 1919). The Philippine delegation for the YMCA convention had a challenging time acclimatizing to the frigid weather they encountered in Shanghai. Even bundled up with woolen suits, heavy underwear, socks, overcoat, gloves, mufflers, felt hat, high leather shoes, rubbers, they still felt the cold in their bones and through chattering teeth prayed for the hot season they will be going back home to (Romero, 1922). Travelers like Senator Celestino Rodriguez and his wife, who had access to the finest chefs and high-class hotels, slowly lost weight as they toured the US. They found the dishes "tasted insipid, that they weren't seasoned enough." Their saving grace was a Chinese *chop-suey* restaurant they found ("Didn't Like Chow" in America," 1921, p. 2). Even those who visited Paris flocked to Spanish and Chinese restaurants after leaving the steamships they boarded looking for the familiar tastes readily available at home (Villanueva Jr., 1929a).

Nevertheless, these difficulties can be considered trivial compared to those experiences abroad that brought some to the deep end. In an article entitled "Brought Back Mad" (1933, pp. 6, 59, 62–63), four women were brought back to the Philippines from several mental hospitals in California. All of them left the country to seek their fortune or continue their studies in the United States. Instead, they found themselves feeling lost in "a strange country, an indifferent and sometimes prejudiced alien society, a climate that is none too favorable, unemployment, and starvation" ("Brought Back Mad," 1933, p. 6). Faced with these difficulties and tragic events, some of them gave in to insanity. This scenario may be an extreme one, but this was also a reality for certain Filipinas traveling to look for a better life but had unfortunate luck instead.

7 Traveler's Gaze: To Survey Her Object and Assess It Within a Particular Frame

The international Filipina travelers related the sights they have seen, the differences between manners, customs, and personalities of the people, especially the women in other countries, new technologies not yet available in the Philippines, and the differences in clothing, weather, and food. They related the many first experiences they had, whether seeing a new place or trying out the subway. The first Filipino sent to the United States for temperance work, Consuelo Valdez's (1923a) story captured the excitement of seeing snow for the first time while on a train on her way back to Ohio:

> As I looked out of the window, I saw some white stuff on the houses and all over the ground. I suspected it was snow, but I decided to ask for information…I chose a kind looking old man, who I thought would not laugh at my ignorance. I approached him quite shyly and said, "Pardon me, sir, can you tell me what the white stuff on the ground is?" He looked at me for a minute and then said, "Don't you know? That's snow" (pp. 28–29).

Pensionadas, on their return home, were always asked about their impressions. They compared and contrasted the Philippines to the places they have visited and related the differences between the Filipina and American women. Filipinas represented the country when they traveled because most people in other countries were unfamiliar with the Philippines. Many Americans did not know where it was, who lived there, and what life was like. Due to the expositions Americans and other foreigners have seen, most thought that Filipinos were uncouth and hung from tree to tree like monkeys. Solita Garduño's first experiences in the National Training School of the Young Women's Christian Association was to hear a confession from her next-door neighbor who thought that, "Filipinos were savages running wild and naked through the woods and living up in the trees like apes," (Garduño, 1926, pp. 6–7). So her neighbor was on the alert during their subway ride to Columbia to see if she might break out into "some queer tricks or forget my civilized manners at the excitement of the rush and noise of this suffocating underground thoroughfare" (Garduño, 1926, pp. 6–7).

Many of those who traveled inadvertently became unofficial representatives of the country. From the periodicals' narratives and images, the Filipina's traveling persona was exoticized, and her Oriental image was emphasized. The Oriental-Occidental concept was pervasive. Descriptors such as the "little brown sister," "oriental charm," and "from the East" were relatively common. The anonymous writer who interviewed the *pensionadas* Carmen Aguinaldo - the daughter of Emilio Aguinaldo, and Princess Tarhata Kiram - the niece of the Sultan of Sulu, used the idea of the "exotic East" in the description of the two ladies;

> Their voices had the soft cadences of old Spain and the languor of the South in their timbre. Slim and brown, eyes that fire has breathed into radiance, and there you have a picture of maids from the Inner city of Manila, where the romance of Spain mingles with Saxon modernity that they so applaud and emulate. ("On a Princess and a Maid from the Philippines," 1920, pp. 5–6).

On the other hand, Maria Lanzar described the Filipina specifically the *pensionada* as an "Oriental with an Occidental outlook," which made the American girl think of her as sufficiently Occidental to be able to appreciate the peculiarities of an American girl while being accepted by her Oriental peers as one of them from the East (San Martin, 1928a, p. 3, 33, 40). Miss Lanzar's awareness of this dichotomy may also be emphasized by the fact that she was one of the recipients of the Barbour Scholarship Fund for Oriental Women. Most of the Filipina travelers' narratives straddled the Oriental/Occidental, traditional/modern conceptions. She had the "exotic" qualities of those coming from the East, had the old-fashioned and conservative image of Maria Clara.[2] However, she was also modern, independent, cosmopolitan, and educated, who were equal and, at times, even better than their peers in other countries. Most came back with a bit more polish, sporting the newest trends abroad like *pensionadas* coming back with bobbed hair or society girls such as Pacita de los Reyes who "electrified her friends with her new hair-do. She had her hair put up in little rolls all around and up on top of her head, with bangs to boot" (Grau, 1936b, pp. 20–21). She also brought with her a collection of new gowns that she wore in Manila's various events (Grau, 1936a).

The Filipiniana dress,[3] aside from being used by the Filipina suffragist as a form of representation of power, was also donned by Filipinas abroad to change misinformed ideas propagated by foreign newspapers picturing the Filipino people as "half-civilized, half-dressed, or even as having tails" (Villa, 1922b, p. 7). Filipinas proudly wore the Filipiniana costume during official events and special occasions such as the official White House reception hosted by Mrs. Harding, who fell in love

---

[2] Maria Clara is the heroine in Jose Rizal's *Noli Me Tangere*. Her name and image have become synonymous to the traditional and feminine ideal in the Philippines, but there are others who consider her as a weak and obsolete idea of what a Filipina should be.

[3] The Filipiniana dress pertained to here is the *Mestiza* dress. It consists of a blouse, a long skirt, and a *panuelo* or kerchief. This dress is usually worn during formal occasions.

with the exquisiteness of the dress (Villa, 1922b). During her attendance at the Women's International Peace League, a Swedish periodical put Miss Josefa Llanes front and center. Her handle on economic problems, and her "quaint and dainty native dress that made her look like a fairy" created a good impression on her peers ("Swedish Paper Takes Notice of Filipino Girl," 1924, p. 30). More often than not, the Filipiniana dress was a source of pride for the Filipina traveler. Still, an exception would be the ladies in Shanghai who resisted wearing the native costume because they did not like being called "Mango Ladies" (Navas, 1921, p. 2). However, Navas (1921) felt that the Filipino ladies should feel flattered since the mango was the most selected and expensive fruit in Shanghai during that time. Navas (1921, p. 2, 4) pointed out that, "Mango Lady is simply the foreigner's euphemistic way of expressing his compliments to and admiration of the sweetness and the eliteness, if I may use the word, of the Filipina in native costume."

8 Passport: An Official Document Certifying the Holder's Identity and Citizenship

As they traverse the world outside, their presence in the public sphere and their conscious or inadvertent representation of the country proved that in their opportunity to travel, they showed that women had agency by breaking the stereotypes and perceptions concerning the Filipino in various ways. The classmates and professors of Ms. Emilia Malabanan at Miami University in Oxford, Ohio, in the beginning, talked to her slowly and used only rudimentary language, thinking she might have a hard time understanding them. They were all surprised when Miss Malabanan received one of the highest grades in English ("Pensionada Gives America Some Surprises," 1920). At the beginning of their career in Europe as Cho-Cho-san in "Madame Butterfly," Jovita Fuentes and Isang Tapales were advertised as Japanese girls. Many bitterly criticized them for allowing this to happen, but as they gained success, they were able to present themselves as Filipinas ("Why Fuentes and Tapales are 'Japanese,'" 1927; Villanueva, Jr., 1930; Yotoko, 1930). The Filipina abroad was usually mistaken for Japanese such as Miss Consuelo Valdez when she was a delegate to the World and National Conventions of the Woman's Christian Temperance Union. She was able to set the record straight with grace and panache (Valdez, 1923a). Although her patience was tried during her visit to Chautauqua, New York, as she received a comment, "Philippines? Oh yes. You belong to us," to which she calmly corrected the speaker (Valdez, 1923b, pp. 4–6).

9 Lakbay: Travel, Voyage, Journey

For one to understand the present, one needs to have a deeper understanding of its past. Through the power of the periodical, this chapter addressed important topics that have been left by the academic wayside - tourism history and women's history. The unearthing of another hidden layer of the story of the Filipina helped in the telling of the story of Philippine tourism history as well. Most of the topics on tourism scholarship have been about contemporary issues. If ever mentioned, its history is simply referred to in a couple of sentences or a paragraph at most. This is due to the lack of historical research on this topic. This chapter hopefully contributed to add to both fields of scholarship.

As pointed out by Yang, Khoo-Lattimore, and Arcodia (2017, p. 1010), there have been investigations on western female travelers, but "existing tourism research has rarely referred to Asian female travellers from the past," and that historical scholarship on the topic was listed as an urgent task "for building a critical tourism scholarship in Asia." The study of the Filipina traveler from the past gives a deeper understanding of gender performances and women's agency to Filipina female travelers in the present. Providing the necessary details of the past creates a more nuanced understanding of the Filipina's travel experiences, travel identities, and travel behaviors. It challenges the stereotyped and prejudiced ideas about women and travel. The dearth of literature offers a huge opportunity for new scholarship to interrogate the past with the present.

Barbara Korte (2012) stated that travel had a liberating effect for women and redefined gendered space. In her exploration of the world, whether it be right at her very doorstep or into some mysterious part of the globe, the intrepid Filipina traveler showed her agency and influence. She sailed through the seas, climbed mountains, rode airplanes, ventured into new spaces, pursued higher learning, fought for the country's freedom, and embraced new experiences. For good or ill, they represented the Philippines when the world was somewhat unfamiliar with the country and its people. Through the eyes of the Filipina traveler, the story of the visitor and the visited became visible. Their photos captured the impressions, experiences, sights they have seen, and the people they met. They became the social observers and storytellers to those who were preparing their sojourn or dreamers who aspired to one day have a chance to lay their eyes on foreign lands. From staying at home, the world opened up to her and became her oyster. In the process, she brought a broader context and a more nuanced perspective to the story of the Filipina.

References

2 Filipino Girls in US to Teach Local Folk to Make Better Homes. (1934, February 4). *The Sunday Tribune*, p. 3.
A Page for the Young Reader. (1913, May 17). *Philippines Free Press*, p. 10.
All Aboard for Baguio. (1929, March 9). *Graphic*, p. 1.

Alzona, E. (1927, January 9). Internationalism in Education. *The Sunday Tribune Magazine*, p. 13.
Another Presentation of "Philippine Parliamentary Mission". (1922, July 29). *Philippines Free Press*, p. 6.
Barangay Goes Picnicking, Fishing, in Native Style. (1938, January 31). *Foto News*, pp. 44–46.
Be a Demonstrator and See the Philippines! (1932, October 19). *Graphic*, pp. 38 & 49.
Before You Go Shopping. (1933, March 23). *Graphic*, p. 42.
Big Filipino Picnic Held in California. (1920, September 18). *Philippines Free Press*, p. 2.
Brought Back Mad. (1933, February 16). *Graphic*, pp. 6, 59, 62–63.
Capital Society Moves Center to Cooler Place. (1931, March 29). *The Sunday Tribune*, p. 23.
Castillejo, J. (1920, April 1). Mrs. de Veyra and Miss Dwyer Educating the American Public on Things Philippine. *The Citizen*, p. 9.
Cuba Seen Through the Eyes of Filipino Girl Globe Trotter. (1925, March 14). *Philippines Free Press*, p. 14.
Daughters of Vicente Madrigal Leaving for French Finishing School. (1931, April 16). *The Sunday Tribune*, p. 5.
Damas Filipinas de la Segunda Mision en la Casa Blanca. (1922, August 19). *Philippines Free Press*, p. 32.
De Veyra, S. (1919, May 23). From Washington Come Words of Advice for Women. *The Citizen*, p. 7–8.
Despedida | Definition of Despedida by Oxford Dictionary on Lexico.com also meaning of Despedida. (n.d.). Retrieved October 26, 2020, from https://www.lexico.com/definition/despedida
Didn't Like "Chow" in America. (1921, November 19). *Philippines Free Press*, p. 2.
Director and Mrs. Kalaw Entertain at Despedida Tea Yesterday. (1931, April 16). *The Tribune*, p. 5.
Dublin Irishman Sighs for Philippines. (1926, March 13). *Philippines Free Press*, p. 24.
Embroidery Workers Invade United States. (1922, November 4). *Philippines Free Press*, p. 2.
Enjoy Baguio's Balmy Breezes. (1931, April 16). *The Sunday Tribune*, p. 6.
Fanny Will Follow Foot-Steps of Her Much-Traveled Sisters. (1926, April 24). *Philippines Free Press*, p. 26.
Fashion: Summertime Means Swimming, New Bathing Suits. (1938, February 28). *Foto News*, pp. 42–43.
Filipino Lady Invited to Review Chinese Troops. (1925, September 19). *Philippines Free Press*, pp. 4–5.
Filipino Picnic in Japan. (1916, July 1). *Philippines Free Press*, p. 10.
Filipino Women Grace Exposition. (1931, July 8). *The Tribune*, p. 3.
"Floating University" Visit Manila. (1926, December 4). *Philippines Free Press*, pp. 2 & 26.
Foto News Editor Joins Kalaw Picnic for College Newsmen. (1938). *Foto News*, pp. 30–33.
Garduno, S. (1926, July 3). We Are Your Nieces By Forcible Adoption. Philippines Free Press, pp. 6–7.
Gonzales, A., & Ramos, J. (1933, February 9). Manila to Iloilo in Three Hours. *Graphic*, pp. 6–7, 59.
Grau, C. (1936a, January 10). The Higher Life. *The National Review*, pp. 26–27.
Grau, C. (1936b, February 28). The Higher Life. *The National Review*, pp. 20–21.
Hernandez, M. (1919, October 30). Breezes from Chicago. *The Citizen*, pp. 10 & 13.
Ilongos in Manila Celebrate Annual Reunion. (1926). *Philippines Free Press*, p. 41.
Josefa Abaya Dined with Rockefellers & Carnegies. (1923, November 10). *Philippines Free Press*, pp. 4–5.
Judge Santos' "Big Bertha" Fired. (1926, July 17). *Philippines Free Press*, pp. 6–8.
Korte, B. (2012). Travel writing in "The English Woman's Journal" (1858–1864): An area of leisure in the context of women's work. *Victorian Periodicals Review*, 45, 158–174.
Lim, R. (1929, April 20). Pampered Pensionados. *Graphic*, pp. 6–7, 43, 47.
Making the Most of Vacation. (1928, March 3). *Philippines Free Press*, pp. 14–16.
Manila Browses on Sunday. (1938, May 1). *Foto News*, pp. 3–4.

Manila Railroad Company. (1914, November 7). *Philippines Free Press*, p. 29.
Manila Railroad Company. (1932, December 15). *Graphic*, p. 39.
McCulloch Dick, H. (1926, August 7). A Filipino Girl Who Sang Before King Alfonso. *Philippines Free Press,* pp. 2, 4, 25.
McKee, A. (2005). *The public sphere: An introduction*. Cambridge University Press.
Members of Smart Set are Already in Baguio. (1928, April 14). *Graphic*, pp. 20–21.
Mindano, Luzon and Visayas United. (1923, February 17). *Philippines Free Press*, p. 14.
Miss Pamintuan to Go to Europe. (1931, February 14). *The Sunday Tribune*, p. 6.
Montalban, V. (1928, June 9). Antipolo: A Study in Evolution. *Graphic*, p. 14, 31.
Morente, P. (1919, November 13). A Diary of Sea Voyage. *The Citizen,* pp. 3–4, 10.
Most Travelled Filipino Women. (1927, July 2). *Philippines Free Press,* pp. 4, 27.
Mrs. Arambulo Welcomed Back. (1933, May 18). *Graphic*, p. 62.
National Affairs: Personalities. (1932, September 28). *Graphic News Supplement*, p. 9.
Navas, R. (1921, March 26). *Philippines Free Press,* pp. 2 & 4.
On a Princess and a Maid from the Philippines. (1920, January 8). *The Citizen*, pp. 5–6.
On With the Dust. (1928, March 31). *Graphic,* p. 1.
Pacific Mail S.S. Co. (1915, May 29). *Philippines Free Press*, p. 23.
Pensionada Gives America Some Surprises. (1920, February 5). *The Citizen*, p. 5.
Philippine Aerial Taxicab Co. (1931, February 22). *The Sunday Tribune*, p. 2.
Red Cross Summer Camp in Nagcarlan. (1923, April 28). *Philippines Free Press,* p. 6.
Reminiscences of a Government 'Pensionada.' (1932, October 12). *Graphic*, pp. 38, 60.
Romero, J. (1922, April 22). With Philippine Delegation Bound for Peking. *Philippines Free Press,* pp. 20–21.
Salazar, J. (1919, February 8). When Mrs. De Veyra Cracked the Champagne Bottle. *Philippines Free Press,* pp. 2 & 4.
San Martin, M. (1928a, August 11). The Times is Not Yet. *Graphic,* pp. 3, 33, 40.
San Martin, M. (1928b, December 22). Motive Power a La Mode. *Graphic,* pp. 42–43.
Smith, Bell & Co's. (1915, April 17). *Philippines Free Press,* p. 18.
Social Life in an Army Post. (1932, October 26). *Graphic,* pp. 38 & 46.
Society Girl to Tour the World. (1931, February 8). *The Sunday Tribune*, p. 23.
Society Seen at Games. (1925, May 30). *Philippines Free Press*, p. 41.
Some Suggestions for Making You Fresh and Dainty During the Hot Summer Days. (1933, March 30). *Graphic,* p. 42.
Swedish Paper Takes Notice of Filipino Girl. (1924, August 9). *Philippines Free Press*, p. 30.
The Floating Centro Escolarina. (1928, March 3). *Graphic,* p. 2.
The Foremost Filipina Scholar Today. (1921, September 3). *Philippines Free Press,* pp. 3 & 6.
The Little Mother of Them All. (1920, March 6). *Philippines Free Press*, p. 23.
The News of the Week. (1923, April 21). *Philippines Free Press*, p. 9.
The Pollyanna of the Japanese Relief Expedition. (1923, November 10). *Philippines Free Press,* p. 21.
These Farm Trained Girls From Negros Can Make City Society Girls Sit Up. (1925, January 24). *Philippines Free Press,* pp. 2 & 7.
To Baguio Kid, to Baguio! Leave the Oven. (1919, April 25). *The Citizen,* p. 13.
Traveling Through Europe and America with Three Society Girls. (1931, July 15). *The Tribune*, p. 5.
Two Iloilo Girls to Make World Tour Unchaperoned. (1924, April 26). *Philippines Free Press*, p. 31.
Two Nurses Trained for Service. (1922, December 23). *Philippines Free Press,* p. 20.
United States Lines. (1925, February 7). *Philippines Free Press,* p. 19.
Vacation Days! (1922, March 25). *Philippines Free Press*, p. 1.
Vacation Make-up. (1937, April 8). *Graphic,* pp. 34 & 38.
Valdez, C. (1923a, January 20). My Washington Trip. *Philippines Free Press,* pp. 28–29.
Valdez, C. (1923b, November 17). Sightseeing in America. *Philippines Free Press,* pp. 4–6.
Villa, I. (1922a, October 7). *Philippines Free Press,* pp. 18 & 23.
Villa, I. (1922b, August 12). *Philippines Free Press,* p. 7.

Villanueva, F., Jr. (1929a, September 7). *Philippines Free Press,* pp. 2–3, 40.
Villanueva, F., Jr. (1929b, September 14). *Philippines Free Press,* p. 41.
Villanueva, F., Jr. (1929c, October 13). *Philippines Free Press,* pp. A–C.
Villanueva, F., Jr. (1930, August 9). *Philippines Free Press,* p. 26.
What to Do During Your Vacation. (1933, March 30). *Graphic,* pp. 37 & 50.
Why Fuentes and Tapales are Japanese. (1927, April 2). *Philippines Free Press,* p. 12.
Why Go to Baguio. (1935, November 1). *The Philippines Herald Year Book,* p. 134.
Women Pioneers in a New Business Enterprise. (1933, February 23). *Graphic,* pp. 39 & 60.
Yang, E. C. L., Khoo-Lattimore, C., & Arcodia, C. (2017). A narrative review of Asian female travellers: Looking into the future through the past. *Current Issues in Tourism, 20*(10), 1008–1027. https://doi.org/10.1080/13683500.2016.1208741
Yotoko, G. (1930, August 30). Anecdotes About Jovita Fuentes. *Philippines Free Press,* p. 32.
You Represent 11,000,000 Filipinos. (1926, September 4). *Philippines Free Press,* pp. 6–7.

Katherine G. Lacson is an Assistant Professor at the Department of History at Ateneo de Manila University, Quezon City, Philippines. She holds a PhD in History from the University of Cote d'Azur, France. Her research interests include Philippine History, Women's History, Visual History, and Business History. She is currently working on a book manuscript about representations of *Manileña* women during the American period in the Philippines.

Brian C. Gozun was the Dean of the Ramon V. del Rosario College of Business at De La Salle University Manila from 2010 to 2019. He completed his Ph.D. in Social Systems Analysis at the National Graduate Institute for Policy Studies in Tokyo, Japan, and undertook his post-doctoral fellowship at the Universitat Ramon Llull in Barcelona, Spain. His research works focused on entrepreneurship, systems analysis, structural equation modeling, sustainable transport, and content analysis. He was a full professor at the Decision Sciences and Innovation Department of DLSU.

Part IV
The Researcher's (Reflexive) Gaze

Significance of the Carabaos in Harvest Festivals in the Philippines

Peter Jerome B. Del Rosario

Abstract Recent research suggests that urbanization of festival sites to invite more tourists reduces local spaces into backdrops of festival events and puts nonhuman animals into the periphery. This chapter focuses on how harvest festivals become venues for the inclusion of carabaos in the face of urbanization and rural development in the Philippines. Historical analysis of selected reports from the Philippine Agricultural Review (1908–1922) and a comparative case study of harvest festivals which were held in predominantly agricultural and heavily industrial localities were conducted. Results reveal that Filipino farmers still relied on the carabaos due to sociocultural significance and geographic reasons despite the animal's exclusion from the introduction of agricultural machineries. This deep entanglement was expressed in the harvest festivals, which creatively used the carabaos as temporary bearers of images pertaining to the locality's cultural heritage and agro-industries amidst rapid urbanization. The relevance of the carabaos in the localities' religious and farming history was highly emphasized in the more agricultural festival sites; however, issues on the ethical treatment of the carabaos were observable. It is concluded that carabaos are highly celebrated in festivals regardless of the locality's main land use. A need to review some practices concerning the carabaos is recommended to the festival organizers.

Keywords Festivals · Carabao · Rural development · Agriculture · Industries

1 Introduction

Festivals are indispensable tools in tourism, economic development, and place marketing (Getz, 2010). However, tangible and intangible cultural heritage are put into periphery in the process of transforming a place into tourist and destination sites.

P. J. B. Del Rosario (✉)
Department of Social Forestry and Forest Governance, College of Forestry and Natural Resources, University of the Philippines Los Baños (UPLB), Los Baños, Laguna, Philippines
e-mail: pbdelrosario@up.edu.ph

This is because festival sites are built with mostly commercial establishments (e.g., parks, cafes, and bars) for an urban appeal in order to invite more tourists which, although unintentional, reduces local spaces into mere backdrops of festival events devoid of sociocultural narratives (Perry et al., 2020). These developments further exclude nonhuman animals because these are usually centered on humans and the landscape that the latter occupy.

In the context of agricultural development in the Philippines, it is the carabao as a farm animal which had colonial histories of exclusion in the face of agricultural mechanization. During the American Occupation of the Philippines, the country experienced the surge of the rinderpest disease which heavily affected the carabaos and the farming industry. According to Moberly (1908), the rinderpest disease is very contagious that it led to thousands of dead cattle and carabaos in the Philippines. After the disease outbreak, modernization of agriculture was initiated by the US Bureau of Agriculture where Filipinos were introduced with the concepts of cooperative organization and agricultural education (Cretcher, 1915). Mechanical technologies (e.g., windmills, steam engines, tractors, and trucks) were also recommended by the American Government to replace farm animals so that the farmers may expect a more bountiful harvest from high-yielding seeds (Binswanger, 1984). These recommendations for agricultural development, however, unintendedly othered the carabao in the farming history of the Philippines. Still, the Filipinos resorted to use the carabaos in rice farming and celebrated the farm animal every May through harvest festivals.

This book chapter aims to analyze the significance of carabaos in harvest festivals in the Philippines. First, this study employs historical analysis to understand the reasons why the Filipinos continued to rely on the carabaos during the colonial period. Second, it attempts to understand how the Filipinos' reliance on the carabaos was represented in the visual displays of harvest festivals with different land use purposes. Specifically, two festival sites having dominant agricultural land use allocations, and another two with predominantly residential/industrial area uses, were selected for this study. Through comparative analysis, the similarities and differences of how carabaos are celebrated in these study sites are discussed. Particularly, comparative analysis was performed to analyze if the major land use of a festival site influences how the carabaos are celebrated, as well as to understand whether these farm animals are either being included or excluded in the context of urbanization or rural development of the localities.

2 Methodology

This study is divided into two parts: a historical analysis of the deep entanglement between the Filipinos and the carabaos (Sect. 3), and a comparative case study of harvest festivals in the Philippines (Sect. 4). The historical analysis was designed the set the context of the study. Studies which discuss the Filipino-carabao relationship (e.g., Wendt, 1998; Ludovice, 2018; Camba, 2019) and agricultural mechanization during the colonial period (e.g., Binswanger, 1984; Balisacan & Fuwa, 2007; Doeppers, 2010) were gathered and analyzed in order to understand the Filipinos' continual reliance on the carabaos as a farming animal. How this relationship was challenged during the colonial rule was also investigated by gathering historical records from the Philippine Agricultural Review (1908–1922) and Worcester's (1899) book titled, *The Philippine Islands and Their People*. These sources were subjected to historical analysis, a qualitative research method designed to critique and triangulate historical information by situating it within other texts in order to widen the understanding of a social phenomenon (Kipping et al., 2014). In the analysis, the historical texts are categorized into the following themes which guided the discussion: economic benefits provided by the carabaos, Western critiques on the utility of the carabaos as a farming animal, proposals for agricultural mechanization, and the resistance of the Filipinos against the methods to suppress the rinderpest disease.

This approach was followed by the analysis of the selected harvest festivals using a comparative case study approach. The case study approach, as defined by Creswell et al. (2007), is designed to explore a single or multiple case over time through a detailed, in-depth data collection involving multiple sources of information, and reports a description of the case or case-based themes in an analytic approach. In an attempt to understand how carabaos are represented and included as a nonhuman animal in highly agricultural and primarily industrial harvest festival sites, this study employed a comparative case study research. In total, four harvest festival sites were purposively selected in the study (Table 1). Lucban in Quezon and Pulilan in Bulacan were selected for having majority of their land use allocation as agricultural, while Vigan in Ilocos Sur and Pavia in Iloilo were chosen because of their predominantly industrial land area. Also, the selected festival sites have two common elements in their festival events – the carabaos and harvests are both celebrated in their holding.

Each festival site's biophysical information based on publicly available documents was first discussed in order to expound on the geographic location of the harvest festivals. This method was conducted to emphasize how each festival site

Table 1 Location, land area, and land use allocation of the selected harvest festivals

Festival sites	Festival name	Land area (in has)	Main land use
Pulilan, Bulacan	Kneeling Carabao Festival	3,975.000[a]	71.86% agricultural; 26.12% urban[e]
Lucban, Quezon	San Isidro Labrador Festival	15,415.000[b]	54.49% agricultural; 26.22% forest[b]
Vigan, Ilocos	Karbo Festival	2,886.085[c]	44.44% residential (cottage industries); 33.94% agricultural[c]
Pavia, Iloilo	Carabao Carroza Festival	2,715.000[d]	43.92% industrial; 19.53% agricultural[f]

Sources: [a]Pulilan CLUP 2013–2020; [b]Lucban CLUP 2014–2024: [c]Vigan CLUP 2010–2020; [d]PSGC-PSA, 2008; [e]Pulilan Socio-Econ Plan 2016; [f]Pavia CLUP 2002–2011

was either primarily agricultural or industrial, before proceeding on describing the festivals' holding. The festivals were documented through field observations and informal conversations that I have conducted during the festivals' holding in the years 2016 and 2017. It should be noted that it is difficult to generalize the results of this study to all harvest festivals in the Philippines. As Creswell et al. (2007) explained, case study research is only true for the subjects and settings being studied, a limitation that applies in this study.

3 History of Filipinos' Deep Entanglements with the Carabaos

In the pre-Hispanic Philippines, the carabao was first used as a ritual animal rather than a farm assistant (Ludovice, 2018). During the Hispanic period, the Spaniards introduced irrigation in the rice field which allowed the carabaos to be harnessed with plow and harrow for farming (Aguilar, 2008). Due to their sheer strength to go through the muddy rice fields, the carabaos were considered as the most effective farming utility and were thus domesticated as draft animals (Ludovice, 2018). In traditional Filipino rice farming systems, the carabaos therefore provided draft power which range from land preparation to harvesting (Balisacan & Fuwa, 2007).

The carabaos were therefore instrumental to the Filipino farmers who became rich, as the farm animal was used in exporting rice, sugar, tobacco, and other cash crops during the cash-crop economy introduced by the Spaniards (Blount, 1912; Ludovice, 2018).

During the American period, the farming system of the Filipinos was heavily criticized. Dean C. Worcester, the then secretary of US Insular Government in the Philippines, discriminated the country's farming system, specifically the use of carabaos in the field. In his 1899 book titled, *The Philippine Island and Their People,* he expressed that it is uncomfortable to ride the carabaos and that they were unreliable means of conveyance. He added that the horses could even go further in places where the carabao could not and described the latter as lazy and sluggish because of their usual tendency for impromptu mud bath than working under the sun. He further noted that carabaos die easily when overworked. It can be argued that this perspective on the backwardness of the Philippine agriculture lies on the success of Western agriculture which capitalizes on mechanization. Western mechanical technologies (e.g., windmills, steam engines, tractors, and trucks) are highly recommended to substitute for animals when the farmers expect bountiful harvest from high-yielding seeds (Binswanger, 1984). However, such technologies are only most profitable when the labor is scarce in a particular locale or when the farmer-investor belongs to rich societies with large capital stocks to afford mechanization (Camba, 2019). For Klock (1995), these colonial agricultural recommendations were intended for the Americans to take control over the agricultural areas and facilitate land sales. As Camba (2019) revealed, the US government partnered with agribusiness industries and the Filipino-landed elites to utilize "state power, customary land relations, and commodity-specific characteristics to appropriate vast amounts of unpaid work (p. 1)" among the agrarian classes. Furthermore, these large-scale farm and plantation using agricultural machineries are not suitable to the usually small landholdings of the majority Filipino farmers (e.g., Klock, 1995; Camba, 2019), which has led small Filipino farmers to continually depend on the carabaos in farming or rent one from their landlord (Camba, 2019). For Klock (1995), this also indicated the American's oversimplified understanding of the rural Filipino peoples' situation and their customary land practices.

The major obstacle with the use of the carabaos in rice farming was experienced during the rinderpest disease which attacked a number of cattle and carabaos in the Philippines. Youngberg (1922) noted that the American Government decided to pay the farmers who will deliver to them their sick animals; however, the monetary incentive did not help as the owners preferred the quarantine of their carabaos for sentimental reasons. He added that Filipino farmers attempted to hide their sick animals from the authorities and only reported that their carabaos were sick when the beasts were on the verge of death. Specifically, he revealed that the farmers of Siquijor and Rizal even wept bitterly when their sick animals were taken away and shot. Decker (1912) also revealed a specific case from the farmers of Balaoan, La Union who preferred for their carabaos to die in their backyard than to be separated from them. Ward (1911) noted that the carabao being regarded as a family pet made it difficult for the farmers to report them when infected. Despite such challenges, the farming industry of the Philippines which heavily relied on the carabaos continued to survive. Balisacan and Fuwa (2007) implied that despite the continuous agricultural mechanization in the Philippines and across Asia in the contemporary period, the Filipino farmers continually depended on the carabaos.

These historical accounts suggest that there is a deep entanglement between the Filipinos and the carabaos. From a ritual animal into a farming assistant, the carabaos have provided sociocultural significance and economic benefits to the Filipinos up to the present times. The sentimental reasons of the Filipino farmers to hide their carabaos or wait for them to die with the rinderpest disease also suggest an emotional attachment to their family pet. This deep entanglement, in the present, can also be observable through harvest festivals in the Philippines which celebrates the carabaos.

4 Carabaos in Philippine Harvest Festivals

4.1 Representation of Carabaos in Predominantly Agricultural Festival Sites

Two predominantly agricultural sites were identified in this study: Lucban in Quezon and Pulilan in Bulacan. Located at the foot of Mount Banahaw, Lucban's comprehensive land use plan (CLUP) in 2015 revealed that its land area is 15,415 ha with rolling terrain and scattered slopes, which makes the use of carabaos in the local agriculture possible in the area. Among the five land uses in Lucban (i.e., built-up and residential, agricultural, protected forest reserve or watershed, agro-industrial areas, and agroforestry areas), agricultural areas occupied majority of the land (8399.63 ha or 54% of the total land area) while the least were the residential areas (399.34 ha) and agro-industrial areas (211.40 ha). The municipality's major crops are coconut and rice while the secondary crops are high value crops such as root crops, leafy vegetables, and fruit trees (Lucban CLUP, 2015). Rice fields covered 730.88 ha in irrigated areas and 487.87 ha in rainfed areas. Most farm households in Lucban were also engaged in livestock (e.g., carabaos, hogs, goats, and horses) and poultry raising. Carabaos were utilized as work animals in preparing the farm and carrying heavy loads of farming produce where vehicles are unavailable (Lucban CLUP, 2015).

During the 2015 San Isidro (Saint Isidore) Pahiyas Festival in Lucban, I observed that the houses along the festival route were adorned with agricultural produce (e.g., *palay* or unthreshed rice stalks, fruits, and vegetables), edible and non-edible manufactured products (e.g., *longganisa* or native sausage, *kiping,* and weaved baskets and hats), and religious sculptures of Saint Isidore. The religious sculpture of Saint Isidore is also coupled with additional characters, such as a man kneeling on his left-hand side (i.e., the landowner who was mean to the lowly farmer Isidore) and an angel with a carabao on his right-hand side (i.e., together, substitutes for Isidore in his farming activities whenever he decides to attend the mass). It can be suggested that the inclusion of the carabao in these sculptures indicate the religious significance of the carabaos in the life of the farmers.

A notable observation was a slogan in the Pahiyas Festival (Fig. 1) showing, "*Kalabaw Ko, Kaagapay Ko*" (i.e., My carabao is my assistant) as backdrop of a makeshift carabao replica. It can be suggested that this slogan implies the continual reliance of Lucban farmers on the carabaos. Aside from the displays outside the houses in the festival, I noticed that the carabaos were also celebrated through a competition titled, *Bikas Gayak* (i.e., well-adorned), where carabaos are put on spotlight for their hard work in the rice fields. In the competition (Fig. 2), the carabaos were attached with small nipa huts adorned with agricultural produce and paraded in the festival route in front of the residents and tourists, a festival element to celebrate the contribution of the carabaos in their farming history.

Pulilan is a municipality located in the center of Bulacan. Its total land area is 3975 ha and is composed of 19 barangays (Pulilan CLUP, 2013–2020). Like most

Fig. 1 One of the houses during the 2015 San Isidro Pahiyas Festival showing a slogan "Kalabaw Ko, Kaagapay Ko". (Source: Del Rosario et al., 2017)

Fig. 2 The Bikas Gayak Competition where carabaos are shown pulling nipa huts designed with produce (Source: Del Rosario, 2017)

of the areas in Central Luzon, Pulilan's land is mostly characterized by flat terrain wherein the majority is agricultural (71.86% or about 2856 has; Pulilan SEP, 2016). Cultivation of high value crops also takes place in Pulilan where all barangays are involved in rice production, particularly of irrigated rice (Pulilan LGU, 2010). Like in Lucban, carabaos are frequently used in rice farming in Pulilan.

Similar with the Pahiyas Festival in Lucban, the Kneeling Carabao Festival in Pulilan displayed images of local agriculture and highlighted the carabaos. Celebrated every 14th or 15th of May, the Kneeling Carabao Festival is one of the highly attended festivals in the Philippines due to the impressive capability of the carabaos to pull large floats containing the bountiful harvests of each barangay. Its grand parade is an indexical symbol of the agricultural industry of Pulilan, Bulacan which consists of the farmers, his carabao, and the bountiful harvest. The festival was also popular because of the carabaos' ability to genuflect upon the farmer's instructions or whenever it gets near the local parish. Hundreds of carabaos were shaved, decorated with garland, and were trained to kneel in front of the Parish Church of San Isidro Labrador (Pulilan LGU, 2007). During the parade, each barangay showcased a huge float which resembled a typical nipa hut being pulled by the carabaos (Fig. 3).

While the festival was rooted from the celebration of the feast of Saint Isidore, an economic perspective suggests that the inclusion of the carabaos in the festival as well as their training to kneel during the parade could have been motivated by the additional income that can be earned by their farmer-owners. During an informal conversation, I have learned that each carabao could be rented for PhP 5000 (USD 100). Meanwhile, those which were not rented by sponsors but still participated in the festival were given PhP 1000 (USD 20) instead of gift packs (Manuel, 2015).

Fig. 3 Float of Brgy. Dulong Malabon which resembled a nipa hut bearing agricultural produce during the 2015 Kneeling Carabao Festival in Pulilan, Bulacan. (Source: Del Rosario et al., 2017)

The income earned during this festival cannot be earned for a whole day of farm work, therefore, suggesting that the carabaos continually help in providing the farmers with income on and off the farm.

In the 2015 Kneeling Carabao Festival, majority of the floats featured mini nipa huts designed with harvested crops such as unthreshed rice, lady fingers, corn, banana, eggplant, string beans, tomatoes, watermelon, and betel nut. The decorations also included ornamentals such as marigold, sunflower, and snake plant. In terms of the produce displayed outside the church, a conversational interview revealed that some of the produce and products displayed along the houses were imported from Lucban, especially the *kiping* (i.e., leaf-shaped wafer made of glutinous rice). In fact, the display outside the San Isidro Labrador Church in Pulilan, Bulacan were similar with the adornments used in the San Isidro Pahiyas Festival in Lucban, Quezon. Most of the displays in the local church were unthreshed rice, pineapple, water gourd, and radish in the bottom of the windows, while the arch was designed with *kiping*.

The commercial sponsors of the Kneeling Carabao Festival (e.g., bank, pawnshop, mall, private resort, cellphone and telecommunication company, motor company, and drug store) were also given spotlight in the parade. Specifically, the commercial floats of the festival's sponsors are pulled by the carabaos wearing clothes and costumes that signify the company. The commercial floats, while similarly representing the nipa hut of the barangay floats, were also adorned with the sponsors' posters, freebies, and the pictures of their celebrity endorsers. I also noticed that 20 commercial floats joined the Kneeling Carabao Festival which outnumbered the 14 barangay floats during the grand parade. Figure 4 shows an example of a commercial float during the 2015 Kneeling Carabao Festival which

Fig. 4 A 'commercial' float during the 2015 Kneeling Carabao Festival in Pulilan, Bulacan. (Source: Del Rosario et al., 2017)

interestingly shows an ice cream cart being pulled by the carabao, in contrast with the more traditional floats paraded by each barangay.

4.2 Representation of Carabaos in Predominantly Industrial Festival Sites

The predominantly industrial sites chosen for this study are Vigan City in Ilocos Sur and Pavia in Iloilo. Vigan City is generally plain with a total land area of 2886.09 ha (Vigan CLUP, 2010). According to the municipality's comprehensive land use plan (2010), Vigan is also described as an "island with three rivers" because it is bounded by Abra, Govantes, and Mestizo Rivers which isolate it from the rest of the province. This abundance of water sources, plain topography, and fertile land makes Vigan very suitable for agriculture and carabao-raising (Vigan CLUP, 2010). In 2006, more than half (53.44% or 1542.33 has) of Vigan's land area was devoted to agriculture. However, agricultural lands decreased due to the conversion of agricultural land to residential and commercial uses, which led to agriculture only occupying 33.94% (979.54 has) of the municipality as of 2012 (Vigan CLUP, 2010).

Despite the decreasing agricultural areas, the municipal government of Vigan still celebrated the importance of its agricultural industry and the carabaos (locally called *karbo*) through its Karbo Festival which was launched in 2005 (Dumlao, 2006). This festival is a sub-festival under the general name, Viva Vigan Festival of the Arts. In Karbo Festival, the body of the carabao is made as canvas for a theme-based painting (Fig. 5). The carabaos are then attached to a sled locally called *pasagad* which is also designed based on the annual theme. In 2016, this one-day competition was held at Plaza Salcedo and the carabaos were paraded through the town plaza. Water based paints were used for the carabao painting and *pasagad* designing competition.

The theme of the 2016 competition was *Pamana ng Nakaraan, Yaman ng Kasalukuyan* which pertains to the "cultural heritage of the municipality is today's treasure." The winner of the competition painted many tangible heritage in Vigan such as the local church, earthen pots and jars, capiz windows, and the local *biga-biga* plant from which Vigan got its name. There is also an indication of intangible heritage in the painting by including an elderly praying just above the illustration of the local church, showing the religiosity of the locals. Here, it can be analyzed that the farm animals served as temporary bearers of images pertaining to the Vigan's cultural heritage. This activity therefore enables the carabaos to connect to the cultural narratives of the town, which suggest that they were not displaced in the municipality despite its continuous efforts to industrialize.

Pavia, a municipality in Iloilo, is totally flat with no coastal areas and measures of 2715 ha overall (Pavia CLUP, 2002). The comprehensive land use plan (2002–2011) of the municipality also revealed that the main land use categories in Pavia are industrial (43.92% or 1192.43 has) and residential (26.56% or 721.04 has)

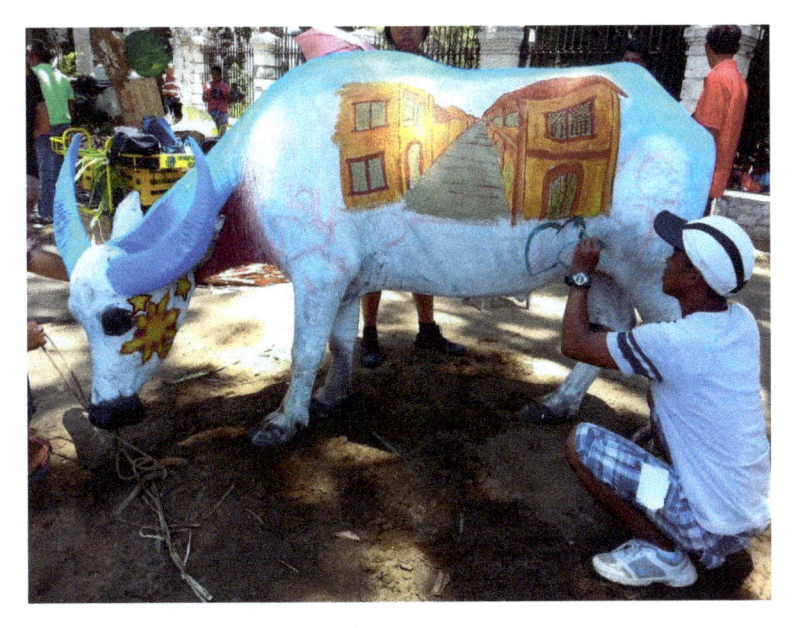

Fig. 5 A local artist in Vigan is painting the Calle Crisologo on the body of a carabao during the competition proper. (Source: Del Rosario et al., 2017)

while only 19.53% (530.24 has) is devoted to agriculture. Industrialization in Pavia boomed in the 1980s when the residents and investors from outside the town established manufacturing plants due to the municipality's strategic marketing location in Iloilo. The municipality have also actively campaigned to invite industrial investors to the municipality. The municipality was successful and was declared the Regional Agro-Industrial Center of Western Visayas in 1988 (Gumana, n.d.). Agricultural areas produce rice, vegetables, high-value commercial crops, and ornamental plants. In terms of livestock, local residents still raise carabaos, cattle, swine, goat, and ducks (Pavia CLUP, 2002). In their celebration of the Carabao Carroza Festival, such agricultural produce and the carabaos were still highlighted. According to Galang-Bumanlag (2011), the festival was intended mainly to honor the carabao and consisted of three main attractions: the carabao-carroza parade, the carabao-carroza race, and the search for carabao-carroza festival queen.

In the 2016 Carabao Carroza Festival, I observed that the *carrozas* are designed with a mix of agricultural produce, papier-mache, baskets, pots, and other manufactured products (Fig. 6). The *carrozas* were then attached to the carabaos with costumes matching the design of the former. Inside each *carroza* is the barangay's muse in gowns and makeup for a separate beauty pageant competition. It is also noticeable that most barangays used the back of the *carrozas* as canvas of their artworks which communicated images of the local culture and livelihood. For example, a *carroza* was seen to illustrate a woman guiding a younger boy in pottery making, a prominent cottage industry in the municipality. Other *carrozas* featured miniature furniture as well as products made from bamboo. These designs, as well

Fig. 6 A carroza is designed with a big basket of produce with a slogan above it pertaining to quality jobs that can be provided by the municipality. (Source: Del Rosario et al., 2017)

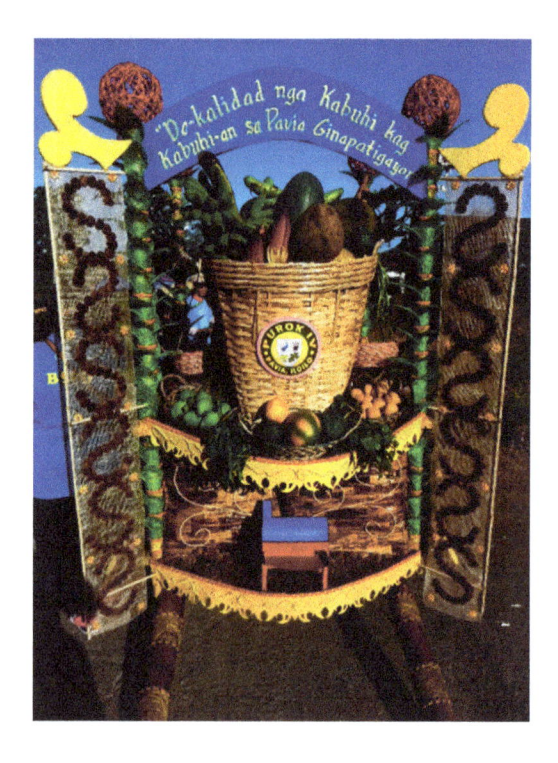

as the slogan "*De Kalidad na Trabaho, Ari sa Pavia*" (i.e., Quality Jobs are Possible at Pavia) aimed to highlight both the municipality's cottage and manufacturing industry and industrial service. While the municipality of Pavia is primarily occupied by agro-industries, symbols pertaining to the manufactured agriculture-based products are still present in the designs of the carrozas pulled by the carabaos. Similar with the case of the Vigan, it can be concluded that the carabaos in Pavia have not lost their place in this predominantly industrial municipality.

5 Conclusion and Recommendations

This book chapter analyzed the significance of carabaos in Philippine harvest festivals amidst ongoing urbanization or rural development. Festival sites with predominantly agricultural and industrial land use allocation were purposively selected as case studies to provide a comparative view of the carabao representations. First, this study situated that the deep entanglement between the Filipinos and the carabaos as indicated in the precolonial and colonial historical narratives made the farm animal an important nonhuman species in the lives of the Filipino farmers. This connection was also found to be reflected in the selected harvest festivals in the Philippines, as observed in the inclusion of the farmers and the carabaos in the events' main activities and displays.

The study suggests that the festivals are venues through which the carabaos can find belongingness in localities experiencing urbanization and rural development. While agricultural lands where carabaos work are being increasingly replaced with industrial and residential areas, the farm animal's contribution is still widely recognized as in the case of the predominantly industrial sites: Vigan City and Pavia. This could be because agriculture is the secondary and tertiary land use of the two municipalities; hence, the carabaos' importance in farm activities were still highly regarded in these localities. How the carabaos were used in both Karbo Festival and the Carabao Carroza Festival also suggest that the farm animals can become symbol-bearers of the municipalities' tangible and intangible cultural heritage and agro-industrial development.

While the carabaos are at the center of the festivals in predominantly agricultural locations, there were some observations that need to be considered. In the case of Pahiyas Festival, the *Bikas Gayak* parade wherein the commercial sponsors had given away freebies to spectators could make the farm animals barely noticed during the festival. In the Kneeling Carabao Festival, a careful guideline on how some carabaos were forced to kneel by tapping their knees with a stick (as they have been trained) must be reconsidered, too. This is because while the event placed the carabao in the spotlight, they were also put in danger during the preparation and on the actual day of the parade. Such observations were rooted from the fact that these festivals are highly attended by local and foreign tourists.

It is suggested for future research to look for harvest festivals in localities with extremely industrial land use allocation and very low to little agricultural areas. Future researchers can also employ other lenses in analyzing the carabaos' inclusion or exclusion in the face of urbanization and rural development outside festivals. For example, how the carabaos are being utilized as a dairy animal instead of working in the farm can be studied in relation to decreasing agricultural areas in the locality. Lastly, the carabao can be analyzed as a postcolonial animal in future discussions related to this study, to address the need to continually produce local histories where the roles and representations of animals in the colonial and postcolonial history are endowed with political and cultural contexts (e.g., Armstrong, 2002).

Acknowledgments This interpretive study includes the author's preliminary findings for his doctoral dissertation focused on the carabaos in colonial and postcolonial Philippines, as well as his personal reflections and observations as the project leader of a commissioned research titled "Social imageability and socio-cultural, economic, and biophysical contexts of selected Philippine carabao festivals" under the Philippine Carabao Center (PCC). The author expresses his gratitude to PCC for this research involvement which sparked his interest in the wide realm of carabao studies in the Philippines.

References

Aguilar, F. V. Jr. (2008). Rice in the Filipino diet and culture. *PIDS Research Paper Series No. 2008-03*. Philippine Institute for Development Studies.

Armstrong, P. (2002). The postcolonial animal. *Society & Animals, 10*(4), 413–419.

Balisacan, A., & Fuwa, N. (2007). Challenges and policy options for agricultural development: Overview and synthesis. In A. Balisacan & N. Fuwa (Eds.), *Reasserting the rural development agenda: Lessons learned and emerging challenges in Asia* (pp. 1–32). SEARCA and ISEAS.

Binswanger, H. P. (1984). Agricultural mechanization: A comparative historical perspective. *The World Bank Research Observer, 1*(1), 27–56.

Blount, J. H. (1912). *The American occupation of the Philippines, 1898–1912*. The Knickbocker Press.

Camba, A. A. (2019). The food regime in late colonial Philippines: Pathways of appropriation and unpaid work. *Journal of Agrarian Change, 19*(1), 101–121.

Creswell, J. W., Hanson, W. E., Clark Plano, V. L., & Morales, A. (2007). Qualitative research designs: Selection and implementation. *The Counseling Psychologist, 35*(2), 236–264.

Cretcher, M. (1915). A year of agricultural organization in the Philippines. *The Philippine Agricultural Review, 8*(3), 226–232.

Decker, C. H. (1912). Rinderpest in the Amburayan river valley. *The Philippine Agricultural Review, 6*(8), 392–394.

Del Rosario, P. J. B. (2017). *Hermeneutic analysis of the San Isidro Pahiyas Festival in Lucban, Quezon as a development communication medium*. [Unpublished master's thesis]. College of Development Communication, UP Los Baños.

Del Rosario, P. J. B., Montes, A. R. J., Fajardo, A. R., & Battad, L. G. (2017). *Social imageability and socio-cultural, economic, and biophysical contexts of selected Carabao festivals in the Philippines*. Philippine Carabao Center - UPLB.

Doeppers, D. F. (2010). Fighting rinderpest in the Philippines, 1886–1941. In K. Brown & D. Gilfoyle (Eds.), *Healing the herds: Disease, livestock economics, and the globalization of veterinary medicine* (pp. 108–128). Ohio University Press.

Dumlao, A. (2006). Carabaos take center stage in Ilocos festivals. *Philippine Star*. Retrieved on February 11, 2022 at https://www.philstar.com/nation/2006/05/24/338314/carabaos-take-center-stage-ilocos-festivals

Galang-Bumanlag, R. (2011). Pahiyas festival: A mix of Lucban's carabao-cart parade and grand decoration. *PCC Newsletter, 10*(2), 24–27.

Getz, D. (2010). The nature and scope of festival studies. *International Journal of Event Management Research, 5*(1), 1–47. ISSN: 1838-0681.

Gumana, B. J. (n.d.). *Pavia: Industrial boom town of Iloilo and Western Visayas*. Retrieved from https://municipalityofpavia.wordpress.com/pavias-pride/ last March 25, 2022.

Kipping, M., Wadhmani, R. D., & Bucheli, M. (2014). Analyzing and intepreting historical sources: A basic methodology. In M. Bucheli & R. D. Wadhmani (Eds.), *Organizations in time: History, theory, and methods* (pp. 305–329). Oxford University Press.

Klock, J. S. (1995). Agricultural and forest policies of the American colonial regime in Ifugao Territory, Luzon, Philippines, 1901–1945. *Philippine Quarterly of Culture and Society, 23*(1), 3–19.

Ludovice, N. P. P. (2018). The Carabao and the encounter of the law in nineteenth-century Philippines. *Society & Animals, 26*(1), 1–20.

Manuel, K. (2015). Pulileños celebrate the Kneeling Carabao Festival. Retrieved from http://bulatlat.com/main/2015/05/15/pulilenos-celebrate-the-kneeling-carabao-festival/. Last 18 Jan 2017.

Moberly, D. G. (1908). Common dangerous communicable diseases of domestic animals in the Philippine Islands. *The Philippine Agricultural Review, 1*(3), 110–119.

Municipal Planning and Development Office of Lucban, Quezon. (2014). *Socio-economic indicators of Lucban in 2014*.

Municipality of Lucban, Quezon. (2015). *Comprehensive land use plan of Lucban, Quezon 2014–2024.*
Municipality of Pavia, Iloilo. (2002). *CLUP 2002–2011.*
Municipality of Pulilan, Bulacan. (2007). *Pulilan Carabao festival.* Retrieved from www.bulacan.gov.ph/tourism/touristspot.ph. Last 18 Jan 2017.
Municipality of Pulilan, Bulacan. (2009). *Comprehensive land use plan of the Municipality of Pulilan, Bulacan.*
Municipality of Pulilan, Bulacan. (2010). Rice production, by barangay. Retrieved from https://www.pulilan.gov.ph/agriculture.php. Last 18 Jan 2017.
Municipality of Pulilan, Bulacan. (2013). *Comprehensive land use plan of Pulilan 2013–2020.*
Municipality of Pulilan, Bulacan. (2016). *Socio-economic plan of the Municipality of Pulilan, Bulacan.*
Municipality of Vigan, Ilocos Sur. (2010). *Comprehensive land use plan of Vigan 2010–2020.*
Perry, B., Ager, L., & Sitas, R. (2020). Cultural heritage entanglements: Festivals as integrative sites for sustainable urban development. *International Journal of Heritage Studies, 26*(6), 603–618. https://doi.org/10.1080/13527258.2019.1578987
Philippine Statistics Authority. (2008). *Philippine standard geographic code for the Municipality of Pavia.* Retrieved from http://nap.psa.gov.ph/. Last 8 Feb 2017.
Ward, A. R. (1911). The rinderpest problem. *The Philippine Agriculture Review, 4*(7), 333–343.
Wendt, R. (1998). Philippine fiesta and colonial culture. *Philippine Studies, 46*(1), 3–23.
Worcester, D. (1899). *The Philippine Islands and their people.* Macmillan and Co., Ltd.
Youngberg, S. (1922). A brief history of rinderpest in the Philippine Islands. *The Philippine Agricultural Review, 15*(3), 205–217.

Peter Jerome B. Del Rosario is an Assistant Professor of the Department of Social Forestry and Forest Governance, College of Forestry and Natural Resources (CFNR), University of the Philippines Los Baños (UPLB). He was given the CFNR Outstanding Teacher Award in the Social Sciences (Junior Category) in 2018 for using adult-based, experiential, and blended learning in teaching social forestry and forestry extension. He is a graduate of BS (cum laude) and MS Development Communication in UPLB and is currently taking PhD Philippine Studies in UP Diliman. His research interests include tourism and festival studies, postcolonial and cultural studies, and resistance studies in the Philippines.

Interpreting the Meanings of Carabao Festivals in the Philippines: A Multi-method Study

Peter Jerome B. Del Rosario, Anna Reylene J. Montes, and Liza G. Battad

Abstract This chapter aims to examine the meanings of selected carabao festivals in the Philippines. A research framework proposing how such meanings can be interpreted through the interplay of published festival images, visitor experience, and festival contexts was operationalized. Based on this framework, a multi-method qualitative research approach composed of visual methods, field observations, document review, and small group discussions was employed. We found that images of agriculture, the residents' artistry, traditional games, and communal practices were core themes common across all festival images produced by the Philippine Carabao Center. The analysis revealed deeper meanings of the carabao festivals. First, we interpret that such festivals mainly symbolize agriculture and the farming community. Second, these are potential vehicle for communicating sociocultural and developmental topics to the tourists and visitors. Lastly, these festivals offer farmers increased income opportunity by connecting them to the local market. We recommend future researchers to study how some biophysical, cultural, and economic issues are masked behind the favorable images of carabao festivals in the Philippines.

Keywords Carabao festivals · Festival image · Farming community · Tourism · Visual methodologies

---

P. J. B. Del Rosario (✉)
Department of Social Forestry and Forest Governance, College of Forestry and Natural Resources, University of the Philippines Los Baños (UPLB), Los Baños, Laguna, Philippines
e-mail: pbdelrosario@up.edu.ph

A. R. J. Montes
Philippine Carabao Center, University of the Philippines Los Baños (UPLB), Los Baños, Laguna, Philippines

L. G. Battad
Philippine Council for Agriculture and Fisheries, Department of Agriculture, Quezon City, Philippines

1 Introduction

Travel information authorities invite local and foreign tourists to various destinations through the creation of a destination image: the aggregation of the impressions and ideas that visitors mostly associate with a destination (Crompton, 1979). This 'projected image of a destination' is used to market tourist sites to potential visitors through carefully crafted photographs (Picazo & Moreno-Gil, 2017). Recent studies, however, reveal that such destination images are only facade of the actual condition of the community especially those of the poor and marginalized (e.g., Antolihao, 2014; Manongsong, 2015).

Experiencing tourist destinations and festival sites is not reliant only on the projected destination images alone, but also on the individuals' lived experiences. Palmer (2009), for example, revealed that tourists' individual backgrounds shape their subjective experiences of a destination. The researcher's voice and emotional reactions should be taken into consideration too, as these influence their thinking in the field and later during data analysis (Rose, 1990), thereby emphasizing the need for reflexivity during the research process (Hammersley & Atkinson, 1995).

In this study, we aim to interpret the meanings of selected carabao festivals in the Philippines by looking at a concept related to destination images, namely, Stokols' (1981) social imageability, which is defined as the capability of a place to evoke vivid community-held meanings among its users and occupants (e.g., tourists and residents). In order to address how destination images mask the actual condition of host communities, we will follow Lopes' (2011) recommendation to analyze how various contexts (e.g., political, social, and economic) of tourist sites shape the destination images that people may experience in their actual visit. In visiting the festival sites and attending these events, we will also employ reflexivity (e.g., Palmer, 2009) in our interpretation of the festival images. We argue that interpreting the meanings of these carabao festivals can be understood through the interplay of the following constructs: the published (projected) festival images; festival sites' biophysical, economic, and sociocultural contexts; and the tourist-researchers' subjective experiences of these events. This is because analyzing the interplay of these three constructs can help in understanding the commonalities and contradictions of the published festival images and our experiences during the on-site visits. We acknowledge that our subjective experiences as tourist-researchers and cultural and institutional insiders may influence the meanings that we attached in our interpretations of carabao festivals in the Philippines.

2 Research Framework, Methodology and Methods

A research framework (Fig. 1) was operationalized to enhance our understanding of the meanings of the carabao festivals. This framework shows the interplay of three dimensions, namely:

Fig. 1 Research framework used for interpreting the meanings of carabao festivals

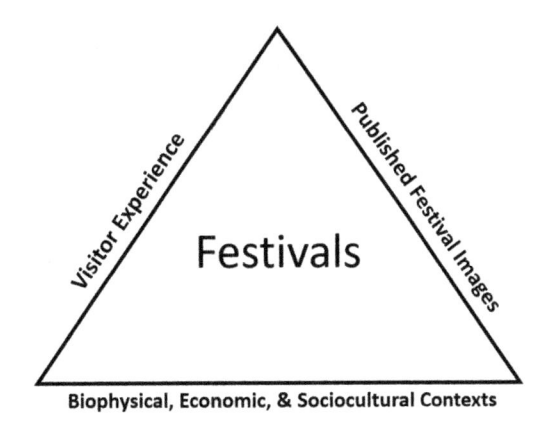

[Triangular diagram with "Festivals" at center, labeled sides: "Visitor Experience", "Published Festival Images", and base: "Biophysical, Economic, & Sociocultural Contexts"]

- published festival images – the projected images found on books, magazines, and other forms of mass media.
- visitor experience – in this study, drawn from the researchers' (as tourists) experiences of attending the festivals.
- festival contexts – the biophysical, economic, and socio-cultural contexts of the festivals, including their origin and histories.

A multi-method qualitative research approach composed of visual methods, field observations, document review, and small group discussions was employed to examine each of these dimensions (Fig. 2).

2.1 Visual Methods

Following previous tourism and festival studies (e.g., Rakic & Chambers, 2009 on tourism in Crete, Greece; Morales, 2011 on Aguman Sanduk Festival in Minalin, Pampanga; Del Rosario, 2019 on Pahiyas Festival in Lucban, Quezon), visual methods were employed to analyze the published festival images for this study. Visual and thematic analysis of the published festival images from the PCC's coffee table book and newsletter were particularly performed (Fig. 2). These publications were provided to us by the PCC to give us an understanding of the basic information about the festivals and the images that could be seen during their holding.

In visual analysis, the image's internal narrative (e.g., content, story provided by the image) and external narrative (e.g., social relations within which the image is embedded at any moment of viewing) can be analyzed (Banks, 2001). Using Pink's (2006) visual methodology, three key areas could be examined: (1) the context in which the image is produced; (2) the content of the image; and (3) the contexts and subjectivities through which the images are viewed. Aiming to better understand the internal and external narratives of the festival images from the PCC Newsletter, we analyzed the images' denotation (e.g., literal description of each photograph), and

VISUAL AND THEMATIC ANALYSIS OF FESTIVAL IMAGES	FIELD VISIT AND OBSERVATIONS	DOCUMENT REVIEW	SMALL GROUP DISCUSSION
o Accessing the PCC publications o Analyzing the images' denotation o Identifying the core themes of the festival images o Reading the general description of each carabao festival	o Visiting the festival sites o Conducting ethnographic photography and ethnographic videotaking o Observing the behavior of residents and spectators during the festival o Conversational interviews o Writing field notes	o Accessing the locality's comprehensive land use plan, socioeconomic plan, or provincial development plan o Analyzing the biophysical, economic, and sociocultural information of the localities	o Transferring important keywords from our field notes into meta cards o Thematizing our field notes o Discussing each festival meanings, including the clarity and contradiction of the festival images

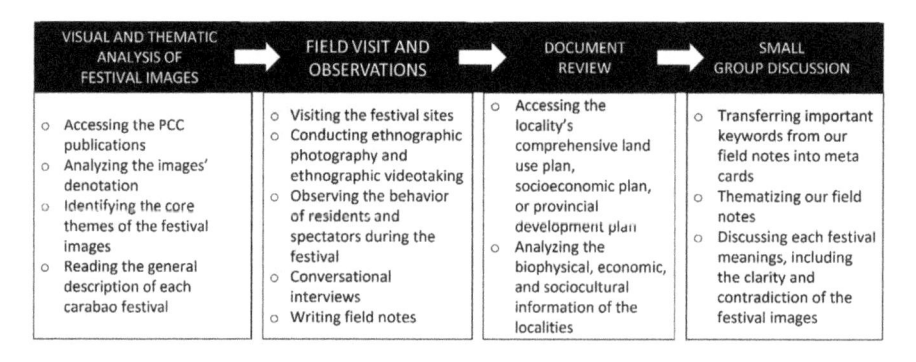

Fig. 2 Schematic diagram of the study's methodology

identified the core themes that were common across all the photographs provided by PCC in the two publications. Further, we analyzed both the general description of each carabao festival and the relevant sociocultural information provided by the authors of each article in the PCC newsletter. This approach has also provided us preliminary ideas of the possible festival contexts within which the photographs were situated, prior to our visits to the festival sites.

2.2 Field Observations

We attended the nine carabao festivals in the Philippines between May 2015 and September 2016 (Table 1). These festivals were chosen by the PCC, the funding institution for this research, as the festival activities centered on carabaos. During our visits to the festivals, we performed field observation techniques which included photographing, video recording, direct observations of residents and attendees, informal conversations, and field note taking.

Festival visits included the documentation of the festival images through a process called ethnographic photography and ethnographic video-taking (MacDougall, 1997). Data collection, including photographing and video recording, focused on documenting the preparation and official holding of the festival, particularly its grand parade. In addition, we documented specific activities during the festival that differed from what was described in the PCC publications. Using an observer-as-participant approach (Creswell, 2013), observational data included describing participant behavior of those who watched the festival parades and/or partook in other on-site activities. This included observing how participants followed the protocols set by the festival organizers (e.g., crowd control), and how they interacted with one another during the festival. In addition, informal interviews with some key informants (i.e., residents) were also conducted to give us more information on the festivals and validate our observations during the field visits.

Table 1 Location and name of carabao festivals studied, and date of attendance

Location (town, province)	Main livelihood	Name of festival	Date attended
Pulilan, Bulacan	Agriculture (farming and fishing)	Kneeling Carabao Festival	14 May 2015
Angono, Rizal	Industrial (services and manufacturing)	San Isidro Labrador Festival	15 May 2015
Lucban, Quezon	Agriculture (agriculture and cottage industry)	San Isidro Pahiyas Festival	15 May 2015
Catigbian, Bohol	Agriculture (farming)	Katigbawan Festival	17–18 June 2015
Carigara, Leyte	Agriculture (farming and fishing)	Turugpo Festival	26 March 2016
Pavia, Iloilo	Industrial (commercial establishments)	Carabao-Carroza Festival	3 May 2016
Vigan, Ilocos Sur	Industrial (commercial establishments)	Viva Vigan Festival of the Arts	6–7 May 2016
San Jose, Nueva Ecija	Agriculture (farming and merchandising)	Gatas ng Kalabaw Festival	10 August 2016
San Agustin, Isabela	Agriculture (farming)	Nuang Festival	28 September 2016

To improve the trustworthiness of the observation data, we reflected on our lived experiences and positionalities which shaped our interpretations of the festivals (Ellis, 2007). Mr. Del Rosario is an assistant professor in the University of the Philippines (UP) Los Baños. He is interested with how festivals as folk media can be used to communicate development topics, as most communication practitioners prefer to use mainstream mass media channels. He believes that folk media such as festivals are closer to the culture of the locality and can be instrumental for communicating developmental topics. In this research, he used this lens to identify what festival images related to carabaos, agriculture, and other developmental topics are observable in the festival sites.

The second and third authors work at the PCC, which is the funding agency for this research. As a government agency, PCC is mandated to conserve, propagate, and promote the carabao as a source of milk, meat, draft, and hide to benefit the rural farmers for poverty alleviation and food security. This research is also funded in order to understand how the carabao festivals can be instrumentalized to reach out local farmers. Ms. Montes, a Senior Science Research Specialist of PCC at UP Los Baños (UPLB), is the head of its Carabao-based Enterprise Development Section. In this study, she provided necessary information on the potential of the carabaos for enterprise development and the role of PCC in each locality. She used this lens to identify what local livelihoods related to the carabaos and agriculture were observable in the festival sites. Meanwhile, Dr. Battad is a Doctor of Philosophy in Community Development graduate from UPLB and was the head of the PCC's National Headquarters and Gene Pool at the time of this study. As an expert in economics and community development, she helped in analyzing the biophysical and economic condition of the locale and how these influenced the festival images in the festival sites. Their expertise on carabao enterprise and economics provided insights on how the carabao festivals become a venue for expressing the value of the livestock industry and agriculture to the local communities.

2.3 Document Review

Document review was performed to uncover the biophysical, sociocultural, and economic contexts of the festivals (Fig. 2). This included analyzing the comprehensive land use plan (CLUP), socioeconomic plan (SEP), and provincial development plan (PDP) of each festival site. In the analysis, we identified the municipality's major land uses and livelihood sources, and how these relate to the holding of the carabao festivals.

2.4 Small Group Discussions and Data Synthesis

Finally, we revisited our field notes to create general observations on meta cards which were organized around themes during a series of small group discussions (Fig. 2). At this stage, we compared the PCC images of the festivals to our documented experiences during the festival visits. Through this constant comparison of data, we identified major themes that reflect the meanings of the nine carabao festivals (see Sect. 6):

- Carabao festivals mainly symbolize agriculture and the farming community.
- Carabao festivals are potential vehicles or medium to communicate sociocultural, economic, and developmental topics to tourists and the locales.
- Carabao festivals offer farmers an increased income opportunity and connection to the local market.

3 Festival Images of Carabao Festivals in the Philippines

The two PCC publications showed the images of each carabao festival location that any tourist would expect upon their visit. Generally, all the photographs in PCC's coffee table book highlighted the carabaos as the festivals' center of attention. Similar images were shown in the PCC newsletter, coupled with more information about the locality and the festival's history. Table 2 summarizes the festival images associated with each carabao festival.

Upon the visual and thematic analysis of the festival images, we identified four core themes. The first theme referred to *images of agriculture* (Fig. 3) which mainly

Table 2 Description of festival images shown in the PCC publications

Festival	Description	Photographs provided by the Philippine Carabao Center
Kneeling Carabao Festival in Pulilan Bulacan	It features carabaos that can kneel in front of the San Isidro Local Parish	Two kneeling carabaos with its body painted in apple-green; another carabao pulling a sled designed with produce; spectators standing on both sides of the road to witness the performance; façade of the local parish where the carabaos genuflect
San Isidro Pahiyas Festival in Lucban, Quezon	Celebrated in honor of Saint Isidore and features houses covered with colorful produce on its façade	Carabaos attached with small sleds resembling nipa huts that were decorated with produce; carabaos passing in front of the local parish; the festival route showing houses designed with colorful produce, unthreshed *palay,* and *kiping* (i.e., leaf-shaped rice wafer made from glutinous rice); spectators on each side of the road watching the carabao parade
Carabao Carroza Festival in Pavia, Iloilo	It features carabaos pulling carrozas or large chariot-like sleds where ladies in fineries (i.e., attire and accessories) were seated	Carabaos dressed with cloth and woven mat that is designed matching the carroza's; the materials used in building and designing the carroza are bamboo, cardboard, and indigenous materials (e.g. coconut husks and fruit seeds); different ladies who served as muses in each barangay riding on the carroza; carabao race
Gatas ng Kalabaw Festival in Nueva Ecija	Celebrates the carabaos' importance as provider of dairy products	Carabao race featuring farmers in two-wheeled chariot-like sleds
Nuang Festival in San Agustin, Isabela	Celebrates the crossbred carabaos given by the PCC to the farmers of the municipality	Carabao parade where farmers were shown riding and maneuvering the carabaos on the national road; a close-up shot of carabao adorned with crown made of betel nuts; a carabao dressed in pink cloth
Katigbawan Festival in Catigbian, Bohol	Celebrates the municipality's three important cultural heritage: (1) *katigbi*, an ornamental plant with flowers shaped like rosary beads; (2) *tigbaw* or caves; and (3) *bawan* or carabaos	Carabaos costumed with colored fabrics or cloth; carabao wearing a golden yellow ruffled dress that is paired with a colored umbrella as its headdress; farmers riding their carabaos during the parade; a carabao kneeling on the ground
San Isidro Labrador Festival in Angono, Rizal	Celebrates the life of Saint Isidore and the artistry of its residents through a carabao parade	Carabao heads made of papier-mâché which were attached to a big four-wheeled wagon that served as the carabao's body; life-size version of Angono's *higantes* or giant mascots

(continued)

Table 2 (continued)

Festival	Description	Photographs provided by the Philippine Carabao Center
Turugpo Festival in Carigara, Leyte	Features a carabao joust inside an open-air arena	Carabaos locking horns inside an arena; a crowd of residents and tourists standing behind the fences made of bamboo surrounding the arena; little children crouching under the bamboo fence in front of the older audiences; *palosebo,* a native Filipino game
Karbo Festival in Vigan, Ilocos Sur	Features the carabaos that were used as canvas for painting artworks pertaining to the festival's theme	A carabao painted with an underwater scenery; another carabao painted with a caricature of a young boy on a backdrop of colorful rice fields and mountains; sleds designed with a miniature nipa hut; spectators taking photographs of the painting competition

Fig. 3 Sample image pertaining to agriculture, particularly the carabaos and produce. (Source: Galang-Bumanlag, 2011)

feature the carabaos and the bountiful harvests. In the local parade of the first six festivals, carabaos were shown pulling sleds of different sizes, the smallest of which are the ones in Karbo Festival while the largest are the floats/*carrozas* in the Kneeling Carabao Festival. Such sleds had varying designs which pertain to local agriculture. Those of the Pahiyas Festival and Kneeling Carabao Festival looked like nipa huts adorned with produce (e.g., vegetables) which we interpreted as a reference to the Filipino folk song *Bahay Kubo* (i.e., native hut).

The second theme described *local artistry, resourcefulness, and creativity,* including images of decorated carabao costumes and their sleds (Fig. 4). In the

Fig. 4 Photograph showing the residents' creativity in designing the carrozas during the Carabao Carroza Festival. (Source: PCC, 2012)

Carabao Carroza Festival, the carrozas were made of bamboo, cardboards, and woven mats that were turned into carriages for the festival muses. The carabaos were also portrayed differently in the publications. In the Katigbawan Festival, the carabaos were clothed for purposes of a carabao pageant. The residents of Angono, Rizal even created carabaos made of papier-mâché in the San Isidro Festival to feature local artistry. Perhaps the most novel among the incorporation of the carabaos in the festival are those in Karbo Festival where carabaos are painted.

Traditional games are captured in the third theme. Carabao race was shown in Gatas ng Kalabaw Festival and Carabao Carroza Festival. The latter (Fig. 5) holding the race as it is rooted in their history of a communal celebration in the Agusan riverbed (Del Rosario et al., 2017). Interestingly, *palosebo* was held in Turugpo Festival where boys were seen climbing a bamboo pole to get the prize on top while spectators watch from below.

The fourth theme refers to *communal practices* (Fig. 6). The tradition of *turugpo*, a term which evolved from *tugpo/togpo* which means matchmaking, has been practiced in the municipality since the colonial period (Marcelo, 2011). Although this practice was originally done for resistance against the colonizers, the tradition persisted until today as a form of entertainment during the Holy Week (Del Rosario et al., 2017). The other communal practice implied in the photographs is

Fig. 5 The carabao race during the Carabao Carroza Festival. (Source: PCC, 2012)

Fig. 6 Photographs showing the carabao joust and the spectators during the Turugpo Festival. (Source: PCC, 2012)

pagpapahiyas, the local term of Lucban residents for putting produce on the façade of the houses in an artistic way during the Pahiyas Festival. This tradition started in the 1500s during the Hispanic period, although the term was only coined by Fernando C. Nañawa in 1968 (Nañawa, 2009).

4 Field Observations on the Festival Sites

To strengthen our understanding of the festival images we used researcher observations in the field. The Carabao Carroza Festival (Fig. 7) began in early morning in Brgy. Ungka-I where we saw the barangay captains and their residents putting up costumes for the carabaos and setting up their carrozas. We also observed some *bakla* (i.e., Filipino term for gay men) fixing the muses' dresses or gowns as the latter were seated on the carroza before and during the parade. For us, such a situation implies social inclusion of the LGBTQI community in the festival although they were in the backstage of this event. A case related to this was Morales' (2011) study on how heterosexual men initially cross-dressed to portray pregnant women in the local parade of the Aguman Sanduk Festival, to gradually welcome the gay men who now portray as the wives of the heterosexual men in its more recent holdings.

The Gatas ng Kalabaw Festival in Nueva Ecija also started with a parade where the residents were dressed in Western cowboy and cowgirl attire, followed by the members of the Philippine Army, Bureau of Fire Protection, Homeowners Association, and various dairy cooperatives and associations. This presence of cooperative associations is indicative of the intention of the Gatas ng Kalabaw Festival to provide a venue where community and other local organizations could sell their carabao-based products in its trade fair. This trade fair (Fig. 8) was initiated by the Department of Trade and Industry in partnership with the peoples'

Fig. 7 Photograph of a carroza during the Carabao Carroza Festival

Fig. 8 The trade fair during the Gatas ng Kalabaw Festival in San Jose City, Nueva Ecija

organizations. We consider this being done to promote PCC's crossbred and dairy carabaos among smallholder farmers who can invest later on for possible entrepreneurial opportunities.

Compared with Gatas ng Kalabaw Festival, which ironically did not have any carabao in their parade, the Pahiyas Festival featured the farmers and their carabaos (Fig. 9) along with the local officials, and some muses and escorts of each barangay wearing traditional Filipino costumes. There were also local competitions that gave the residents additional sources of income such as the best food cart contest featuring *pancit habhab* or native pasta, the best native gown contest called *Parikitan*, the most gaily decorated cart in the *Bikas Gayak Competition*, and the *Pahiyas Timpalak Competition* where houses are adorned with colorful mix of produce, *kiping,* and Christmas lights. We view these competitions have added variety to the holding of the festival compared to a typical fiesta setting focusing only on a single parade.

In the Kneeling Carabao Festival (Fig. 10), members of the Philippine National Police (PNP), the Federation of Senior Citizens, and some TV celebrities joined the parade, with the latter gaining the attention of the spectators who went beyond the boundary set by the policemen in the roadside for purposes of crowd control. With a narrow highway and an estimate of 800,000 spectators as revealed in our interview with a policeman, it became difficult for the festival organizers to control the crowd who went near the carabaos and the floats to take photographs. For Cañete (2016), this heavy focus on the carabao parade overshadowed the religious aspect of the

Fig. 9 Photograph of the farmers guiding their carabao during the Bikas Gayak parade in the Pahiyas Festival in Lucban, Quezon

Fig. 10 Photograph of a barangay float during the Kneeling Carabao Festival in Pulilan, Bulacan

festival, which is to offer gratitude to Saint Isidore, the patron saint of the farmers. Here, we view that the introduction of new elements (e.g., TV celebrities) could influence the contemporary holding of these festivals, and potentially, their meanings for attendees.

Out of all the carabao festivals that we attended, Katigbawan Festival (Fig. 11) featured the highest number of crossbred carabaos as each farmer in 22 barangays of Catigbian, Bohol are required by PCC to join the parade for accounting purposes.

Fig. 11 The carabao parade during the Katigbawan Festival in Catigbian, Bohol

The cooperatives and interested business sectors were also asked by the LGU to attend the parade, with the latter serving as resource speakers for the seminar on livestock entrepreneurship among the local farmers after the activity. We observed that aside from holding communal traditions, the festival was used as a venue for marketing and establishing business networks for smallholder farmers. We find this in line with Getz's (2010) statement that festivals could be used as tools for economic development while enlivening tourism.

Meanwhile, the Karbo Festival which is a sub-festival under the week-long Viva Vigan Festival of the Arts had a small parade of the carabaos after the painting competition and announcement of winners. The event started in the morning where the carabaos were painted with different images (Fig. 12) pertaining to the theme (e.g., Vigan's cultural heritage is today's treasure). Therefore, the artists painted different heritage sites such as its local parish and Calle Crisologo where vintage houses during the Hispanic period were still built. There were also paintings that emphasized Vigan as one of the 7 New Wonder Cities of the World and a UNESCO World Heritage Site. Seeing this practice of painting the carabaos gave us a different perspective on how such farm animal could become a canvas of artistic expressions. This, according to former mayor Ferdinand Medina, is intended to promote the carabao both as the national animal and as an artistic medium (Dumlao, 2006).

Interestingly, Nuang Festival featured the carabaos' utility as a dairy animal and source of meat. After the parade in the morning, the male members of the community were seen preparing the ingredients and cooking food on giant cooking pans called *kawa* (large woks). The farmers were also observed dressing up their carabaos with creative designs (e.g., a dress made connected anahaw leaves) for the Best Dressed Carabao and Dam competition (Fig. 13). Since the carabaos in the Nuang Festival are all PCC's crossbreds, some farmers participated in the carabao milking

Fig. 12 The painting competition in the Karbo Festival during the week-long Viva Vigan Festival of the Arts

Fig. 13 The carabao (with its farmer-owner) who won the best dressed competition during the Nuang Festival in San Agustin, Isabela

competition. Moreover, the cooks of each barangay were preparing their meal courses that would be added for the 1001 carabao recipe that is compiled by the tourism office. This emphasis on using carabao as source of meat and milk in the municipality imply its utility beyond farming activities. We also interpret that focusing on the carabaos' potential for enterprise appears as the municipality's way of inviting private companies to invest in the festival by engaging the farmers for other livelihood opportunities, such as those in the Gatas ng Kalabaw Festival for its trade fair and the Katigbawan Festival for its auction market.

The parade of the remaining festivals, however, do not have any aspects that were different from the ones written by the PCC. The San Isidro Labrador Festival in Angono, Rizal only had its small parade in the early morning as its major holding. It featured a simple and short parade of the carabao replicas made of papier-mâché. The festival organizer that we spoke to said that the parade was very short and rather led us to the place where the papier mâché were stored. During our conversation, we discovered that only four carabaos were present in the parade. Such a short parade suggests that the festival is a minor event in the municipality, considering that they have a more grandiose holding of another festival namely, the Higantes Festival. We also view that the fact having only four carabaos in the festival is connected with the very low agricultural land area in Angono.

To complement our observations and experiences, and further enrich our interpretations of the festival meanings, we unpacked the biophysical, economic, and social-cultural contexts of the festival sites in the next section.

5 Biophysical, Economic, and Sociocultural Contexts of the Carabao Festivals

Most festival sites were generally flat except in Carigara, Leyte and Lucban, Quezon which are hilly, explaining why the sleds in Pahiyas Festival are small when compared to those of Kneeling Carabao Festival. Meanwhile, the flat topography of the other festival sites enabled the carabaos to parade and pull huge floats and carrozas.

The history of Angono's land use change showed that the municipality suffered a rapid conversion of its agricultural lands into residential subdivision projects as seen in its land use allocation. Currently, the majority (40.35% or 928.05 has) of Angono's land use is devoted to residential areas (Angono CLUP, 2016). Due to the increase in population and migration of outsiders to Angono, subdivisions and other business establishments were built in the municipality. This led to a major decrease in farming areas and consequently, the loss of carabao in the communities. Consequently, this intensified the cause of holding the San Isidro Labrador Festival. For the municipal mayor, the festival was a good way to help the youth realize the importance of agriculture while promoting artistry; thus, a fusion of art-based tourism and ecotourism in the area (Marcelo, 2011).

Meanwhile, Catigbian in Bohol was able to emphasize the importance of inviting traders and local business owners to buy different livestock animals in the town through its auction market (Goyagoy, 2011) despite having less than half of its land use allocation intended for agriculture (4955.49 has or 43.85% as per Catigbian

CDP, 2013). This enabled a win-win situation for the farmers and the LGU to make the locality famous because of the festival while promoting additional sources of income among the farmers.

As expected, the municipalities with the majority of their land use devoted for agricultural purposes showed realistic images of agriculture. For example, 54% (8399.63 has) of the total land use in Lucban, Quezon is devoted in agriculture (Lucban CLUP, 2015) which enabled the local residents to display abundant produce in the facade of their houses and include real carabaos in its grand parade. The municipality of Pulilan, Bulacan also had its major total land area devoted for agriculture (2856.44 has or 72%; Pulilan CLUP, 2013), although our visit in 2015 showed that there were more commercial floats which featured lesser produce. However, this was taken as an opportunity by the farmers to gain PHP 5000 to PHP 10,000 (approximately USD100 to USD200) depending on the carabaos' ability to kneel and pull larger floats. In a way, this festival became a strategic event to showcase its cultural heritage while enabling the farmers to gain additional income.

While the aforementioned municipalities managed to display abundant agriculture in their festival's holding, we found that these festival sites highlighted more of their industrial land use. In the Carabao Carroza Festival, replicas of Pavia's signature industrial products (e.g., ceramic products and furniture) were added as adornments in each carroza. This is because the majority of Pavia's land use is intended for industrial purposes (43.92% or 1192.43 has; Pavia CLUP, 2002). Meanwhile, the Karbo Festival in Vigan, Ilocos Sur displayed rich cultural heritage and artistry. In a more urban setting, the holding of the Karbo Festival reminisced local agriculture mainly through the painting on the carabaos and the designs of the sleds. This is because the majority of the locality's land use is residential (44.44% or 1282.59 has) rather than agricultural (Vigan CLUP, 2010).

Compared with the former festivals that highlighted either the agricultural or industrial characteristics of the municipality where it is held, the Turugpo Festival in Carigara, Leyte highlighted its sociocultural heritage because of its heavy colonial roots. The municipality's history illustrates that the carabao joust was a form of the colonial Filipinos' resistance against the Spanish friars during the Holy Week (Marcelo, 2011). Currently, the holding of the festival does not have traces of resistance, but a festive celebration and local tourism motivated the residents to continue its holding. In terms of showcasing Carigara's agriculture in the festival's holding, there were booths and stalls selling local cuisines and delicacies. In terms of Nueva Ecija's Gatas ng Kalabaw Festival and Isabela's Nuang Festival, the benefits of the carabaos as a source of income and nutritious milk was more emphasized in the holding considering that the municipalities are recipients of PCC's programs.

6 Meanings of the Carabao Festivals

Upon analysis of the carabao festivals in different approaches, we interpreted three themes that capture the meanings of the carabao festivals in the Philippines. First, carabao festivals symbolize agriculture and the farming community. Despite the hardships involved in agricultural activities and its decreasing productivity, the carabao festivities showcase the locals' celebration of their resources and their eagerness and excitement to spend a day of break from their ordinary activities. Sadly, it also conveys a misrepresentation of the reality of farming that it is always fun and joyous with bountiful harvests and prosperous farmers. Therefore, the carabao festivals imply the farmers' deliberate attempts to produce images of farming life that is free from the hardships and difficulty that they encounter on a daily basis.

Considering that some festival sites such as Angono suffered a rapid conversion of their agricultural lands and decreased the number of their carabaos, the celebration of the San Isidro Labrador Festival is but an attempt to relive the farming life, even if temporarily. In fact, even the use of carabao replicas made of papier-mâché in an artful distortion of the images of the carabaos. However, we suggest that this portrays the capability of the festival to provide nostalgia among the local people about agriculture and farming life. A similar interpretation was proposed by Gado-Gonzales, et al. (2017), as they revealed that the use of carrozas attached to the carabaos during the festival is a way to recall the times when it is used frequently by farmers, compared today that the carabaos are now replaced with mechanical hand tractors called, *kuliglig*.

Second, we interpret that the carabao festivals also carry with them sociocultural topics about the community. How the 40-year-old *kabawan* or auction market was institutionalized through the creation of the Katigbawan Festival in Catigbian, Bohol is an example of how tourists could learn about the municipality's trading activities and economic history. Vigan's Karbo Festival also carried with them messages about the city's cultural heritage, landmarks, and environmental advocacies which make the festival a venue to communicate development topics – a finding similar with what Del Rosario (2019) revealed about the Pahiyas Festival of Lucban, Quezon. Lastly, Turugpo Festival also bears with it the potential of communicating cultural heritage through the carabao joust.

Third, we posit that the carabao festivals serve as venues for farmers to increase income opportunities; hence, proving that festivals act as mediums to reach the market. This was shown through the auction market in Katigbawan Festival, the trade fair in Gatas ng Kalabaw Festival, and the promotion of PCC's intensified crossbreeding program in the Nuang Festival. The carabaos in the festival served as a symbol of Filipino characteristics such as being strong, sturdy, hardworking, steady, fun-loving, grateful, and uncomplaining. The local term "*kayod kalabaw*" (working as hard as the carabaos) is therefore literally and figuratively communicated through the festival. While the carabaos pull carts or carrozas, transport humans and agricultural produce, and joust with other carabaos, the farmers were also shown exerting additional efforts to prepare their carabaos for the festival aside from the daily burden of farm work. This also shows how the farmers and their carabaos were inseparable as communicated in one of the slogans shown in a house in Pahiyas Festival, saying *"Kalabaw Ko, Kaagapay Ko"* (My carabao is my companion). This indicates the deep entanglement between the carabaos and the farmers which has been studied in previous research (e.g., Dela Cruz, 2016; Ludovice; 2018; Camba, 2019).

7 Conclusions

This book chapter aimed to unpack the meanings of carabao festivals in the Philippines using a multi-method qualitative approach. We conclude that the carabao festivals explored in this chapter depict idyllic and idealized harvest scenes in rural Philippines. Indeed, the vibrant colors seen in the published festival images and our field visits contribute greatly to making the festivals evocative and memorable. Interestingly, the carabao festivals also showed images promoting commercial and non-agricultural commodities such as that of the Kneeling Carabao and Pahiyas Festival. However, such images do not oppose but rather elaborate the meanings of carabao festivals. These images, although seemingly contradictory, actually enhance the festivals' power to evoke emotions and memories among the residents and tourists as these make the festivals more spectacular. Although the festivals clearly communicated images of farming life and agriculture, the hodgepodge of images also reflected the Filipinos' *halo-halo* culture. Using the *halo-halo*[1] metaphor, we suggest that a carabao festival is said to be composed of a set of images, symbolisms, and activities that appear differentiated when scrutinized but blend beautifully when mixed together.

The carabao festivals, therefore, reflect an interworking of several ideologies of different institutions in a festival site. The local and national government offices which set the rules and regulations of the holding, the local parish which represents the Catholic religion and Saint Isidore, and the farming community all work together to display such images in the festival. In conclusion, the images of the carabao, agriculture, and community in the carabao festivals can be seen as an assemblage of images, or a chain of associated meanings that constitute a complex cultural system.

This study has implications on the use of multiple methods in tourism and festival studies. While visual images are always used as secondary and complementary texts to aid the observational data of researchers, this study showed that images could undergo rigorous analysis and be substantiated through analyzing the contexts where it was produced – a challenge on festival studies that was raised by Pernecky and Rakic (2019). Such methodology has been explored in earlier festival studies (e.g., Rakic & Chambers, 2009; Morales, 2011; Del Rosario, 2019) but the

---

[1] Filipino dessert made of mixed sweetened beans, fruits, and shaved ice drizzled with condensed milk.

biophysical and economic contexts that shaped the festivals' holdings have not been merged yet in their analysis. While our observations have added texture to the meanings of the carabao festivals, we acknowledge that this source of information has been limited by our subjective experiences of the festivals. We suggest future studies to delve deeper into the experiences of visitors to carabao festivals.

Focusing on festival images also had implications on how the Philippines is viewed in the international arena. That some festival sites had decreasing agricultural lands, and that the farmers heavily rely on additional income during the festivals imply how harvest festivals in the country were able to mask biophysical and economic issues in order to provide a favorable image. Thus, this study challenges researchers to look at how issues of class, power, and inequality are hidden behind carefully crafted festival images that tourists and outsiders receive on the surface.

References

Antolihao, L. (2014). From fiesta to festival: Tourism and cultural politics in the Philippines. *Kyoto Review of Southeast Asia 1*(15). Retrieved last July 24, 2020 from https://kyotoreview.org/about-us/

Banks, M. (2001). *Visual methods in social research*. Sage.

Camba, A. A. (2019). The food regime in late colonial Philippines: Pathways of appropriation and unpaid work. *Journal of Agrarian Change, 19*(1), 101–121.

Cañete, R. R. (2016). Performing faith, celebrating plenty, conserving tradition: The case of the Carabao festival of Pulilan, Bulacan, The Philippines. In N. Duangwises & L. D. Skar (Eds.), *The folk performing arts in ASEAN*. Princess Maha Chakri Sirindhorn Anthropology Centre.

Creswell, J. W. (2013). *Qualitative inquiry and research design: Choosing among five approaches* (3rd ed.). Sage.

Crompton, J. L. (1979). Motivations for pleasure vacations. *Annals of Tourism Research, 6*(4), 408–424.

Del Rosario, P. J. B. (2019). Hermeneutic analysis of the San Isidro Pahiyas festival as development communication medium in Lucban, Quezon, Philippines. *Journal of Hospitality and Tourism Insights, 2*(2), 203–220. https://doi.org/10.1108/JHTI-01-2019-0002

Del Rosario, P. J. B., Montes, A. R. J., Fajardo, A. R., & Battad, L. G. (2017). *Social imageability and socio-cultural, economic, and biophysical contexts of selected Carabao festivals in the Philippines*. Philippine Carabao Center - UPLB.

Dela Cruz, A. R. D. (2016). Epizootics and the colonial legacies of the United States in Philippine veterinary science. *International Review of Environmental History, 2*(1), 143–172.

Dumlao, A. (2006). Carabaos take center stage in Ilocos festivals. *Philippine Star*. Retrieved on February 11, 2022 at https://www.philstar.com/nation/2006/05/24/338314/carabaos-take-center-stage-ilocos-festivals

Ellis, C. (2007). Telling secrets, revealing lives: Relational ethics in research with intimate others. *Qualitative Inquiry, 13*(1), 3–29.

Gado-Gonzales, C. L. B., Manuel, F. G. E., Gandeza, H. U., & Gonzales-Esmero, D. B. (2017). Rice festivals as means of agricultural extension? *Philippine Journal of Crop Science, 42*, 147–148.

Galang-Bumanlag, R. G. (2011). Pahiyas festival: A mix of Lucban's carabao-cart parade and grand decoration. *PCC Newsletter, 10*(2), 24–27.

Getz, D. (2010). The nature and scope of festival studies. *International Journal of Event Management Research, 5*(1), 1–47. ISSN: 1838-0681.

Goyagoy, J. G. (2011). In Katigbawan festival: Hail, hail, the king and queen of Carabaos. *PCC Newsletter, 10*(2), 20–21. ISSN: 1655-2496.

Hammersley, M., & Atkinson, P. (1995). *Ethnography. Principles and practice* (2nd ed.). Routledge.

Lopes, S. D. F. (2011). Destination image: Origins, developments and implications. *Revista de Turismo y Patrimonio Cultural, 9*(2), 305–315.

Ludovice, N. P. P. (2018). The Carabao and the encounter of the law in nineteenth-century Philippines. *Society & Animals, 26*(1), 1–20.

MacDougall, D. (1997). The visual in anthropology. In M. Banks & H. Morphy (Eds.), *Rethinking visual anthropology* (pp. 276–295). Yale University Press.

Manongsong, R.D. (2015). *Tinig ng mga nag-aagawan: Magkakaibang Pananaw ukol sa mga Usaping Pangkaunlaran-Pagkalinangan sa Agawan Festival ng Sariaya, Quezo*. [Unpublished BS thesis]. College of Development Communication, University of the Philippines Los Baños, Laguna.

Marcelo, K. E. M. (2011). Turugpo festival: A tradition of Carabao joust in Leyte. *PCC Newsletter, 10*(2), 18–19. ISSN: 1655-2496.

Morales, J.Z. (2011). *Aguman Sanduk: The meanings of cross-dressing performances in a Kapampangan festival* [Unpublished MA thesis]. University of the Philippines Diliman, Quezon City.

Municipality of Angono, Rizal. (2016). *Comprehensive development plan of Angono, Rizal 2016–2026*.

Municipality of Catigbian, Bohol. (2013). *Comprehensive development plan 2013–2019*.

Municipality of Lucban, Quezon. (2015). *Comprehensive land use plan of Lucban, Quezon 2014–2024*.

Municipality of Pavia, Iloilo. (2002). *CLUP 2002–2011*.

Municipality of Pulilan, Bulacan. (2013). *Comprehensive land use plan of Pulilan 2013–2020*.

Municipality of Vigan, Ilocos Sur. (2010). *Comprehensive land use plan of Vigan 2010–2020*.

Nañawa, F.C. (2009). *History of the Pahiyas, untold story*. Retrieved from https://pahiyasfestival.com/history-of-the-pahiyas-the-untold-story/. Last 5 Sept 2020.

Palmer, C. (2009). Reflections on the practice of ethnography in heritage tourism. In M. L. S. Sorensen & J. Carman (Eds.), *Heritage Studies* (pp. 123–139). Methods and Approaches, Routledge.

Pernecky, T., & Rakic, T. (2019). Visual methods in event studies. *Event Management, 23*(1), 179–190.

Philippine Carabao Center. (2012). *Carabao Festivals* (Coffee table book). Philippine Carabao Center.

Picazo, P., & Moreno-Gil, S. (2017). Analysis of the projected image of tourism destinations on photograps: A literature review to prepare for the future. *Journal of Vacation Marketing, 25*(1), 3–24.

Pink, S. (2006). *The future of visual anthropology: Engaging the senses*. Routledge.

Rakic, T., & Chambers, D. (2009). Innovative techniques in tourism research: An exploration of visual methods and academic filmmaking. *International Journal of Tourism Research, 12*(4), 379–389.

Rose, D. (1990). *Living the ethnographic life*. Sage.

Stokols, D. (1981). Group X place transactions: Some neglected issues in psychological research on settings. In D. Magnusson (Ed.), *Towards a psychology of situations: An interactional perspective* (pp. 393–415). Lawrence Erlbaum.

Peter Jerome B. Del Rosario is an Assistant Professor of the Department of Social Forestry and Forest Governance, College of Forestry and Natural Resources (CFNR), University of the Philippines Los Baños (UPLB). He was given the CFNR Outstanding Teacher Award in the Social Sciences (Junior Category) in 2018 for using adult-based, experiential, and blended learning in teaching social forestry and forestry extension. He is a graduate of BS (cum laude) and MS Development Communication in UPLB and is currently taking PhD Philippine Studies in UP Diliman. His research interests include tourism and festival studies, postcolonial and cultural studies, and resistance studies in the Philippines.

Anna Reylene J. Montes is a Senior Science Research Specialist of the Department of Agriculture - Philippine Carabao Center (DA-PCC) at UPLB. She is Regional Coordinator and Focal for Regions IV-A, IV-B, and V on Carabao-based Enterprise Development Program, Milk Feeding, Carabao-based Business Improvement Network, and Coconut-Carabao Development Projects. She was awarded as the National Outstanding Development Officer by the DA-PCC in 2018 and as Lingkod Bayan by Civil Service Commission, Region IV-A in 2021. She is a Bachelor of Science in Development Communication and Master of Management in Development Management graduate in UPLB. She was a developer and editor of various local and international technology manuals.

Liza G. Battad is the Assistant Secretary for Regulation of the Department of Agriculture for Regulations, the Executive Director of the Philippine Carabao Center (PCC), and OIC-Executive Director of the Philippine Council for Agriculture and Fisheries. She was recognized for her meritorious ingenuity in empowering marginalized sectors as active agriculture value chain players. She was the 2022 Golden Wheel Awardee on Growing Local Economy by the Rotary Club District 3780, the 2021 College of Public Affairs Distinguished Alumni by the UP Alumni Association, Inc., and the Natatanging Kawani ng PCC in 2002. She graduated BS Agricultural Economics at Pampanga Agricultural College. She obtained her Masters in Agribusiness Management in 1994 and Ph.D. in Community Development in 2006 at UPLB as PhilRice and BAR-NARDSAF Scholar, respectively.

Researching Luzon Island's Pancit Culinary Heritage: Cultural Mapping and Stakeholders' Perspective

Jame Monren T. Mercado and Avi Ben P. Andalecio

Abstract This chapter examines how the Filipino noodle dish known as *pancit* made a hallmark on Filipino cuisine and established a firm relationship on Filipino culture and heritage. The researchers traveled within and across the biggest island group of the Philippine archipelago in search of different varieties of *pancit* both highlighting the significance through exhaustive culinary mapping and probing into stakeholders' perspectives. This funded research project by the National Commission for Culture and the Arts (NCCA) paved the way for the completion of the country's most comprehensive research on culinary studies. The findings suggested that there were also achievable solutions for the sustainability of *pancit* as a symbol of Filipino communities in the Luzon island. Another perspective suggested that the significance of *pancit* goes beyond the cultural domain. The analysis provided support for the premise that *pancit's* significance is congruent to the participant communities' economic needs, history, and environment, to mention a few. However, *pancit's* cultural significance, in order to be protected, must be disseminated to younger generations for its sustainability.

Keywords Culinary mapping · Heritage · Luzon Island · Pancit · Philippines · Stakeholders' perspectives

J. M. T. Mercado (✉)
College of Tourism and Hospitality Management, Research Center for Social Sciences and Education, The Graduate School – Center for Conservation of Cultural Property and Environment in the Tropics, University of Santo Tomas, City of Manila, Philippines
e-mail: jtmercado@ust.edu.ph

A. B. P. Andalecio
College of Tourism and Hospitality Management & The Graduate School, University of Santo Tomas, City of Manila, Philippines
e-mail: apandalecio@ust.edu.ph

1 Introduction

Noodles are perhaps one of the most popular staples around the world; from East to West, there are multitudinous dishes from different regions. Asia, with its range of rich cultural diversity, is remarkably the epicenter where one can find the best variety of noodle dishes that astounded the culinary world by storm (Schlotter & Spielmann-Rome, 2015). Since then, noodle dishes have spread to different annals of gastronomic mainstays, from posh European restaurants to small and humble eateries on Asian alleys. *Pancit* is a Filipino noodle dish flavored with seafood and/or meat and/ or vegetables (Sta. Maria & Koh, 2019; Tayag & Quioc, 2012; Fernandez, 2000). Classic memories from family gatherings to typical school-day recess would be accompanied by a snack, with the most common Filipino carbohydrate source next to rice, *pancit* (Mercado & Andalecio, 2020). It can be eaten and enjoyed as a main dish, consumed with rice or even used as a sandwich filling. For instance, in Tuguegarao City, Cagayan, *pancit batil batong* is a staple food, which, according to our interviews, can be a replacement for rice as a source of carbohydrates for the entire day. Hence, locals devour this dish any time of the day (see Fig. 1).

Some of the most influential traders in Asia were the Chinese (Scott, 1994). The Chinese sailed from mainland China to the Philippine archipelago and brought noodles to their provincial trade partners (Sta. Maria, 2006). It then was acculturated into dishes reflecting the authentic and classic Filipino style of cooking. The Chinese relationship with the Filipinos dates back to the tenth or eleventh century, but it is estimated that undocumented trade may have started even two centuries earlier (Fernandez, 2000). Ultimately, a bond was forged through cultural exchange of

Fig. 1 Figural representation of *pancit batil-patong* of triangle *panciteria* in Tuguegarao City, Cagayan, Philippines. In the culinary culture of the *Cagayanons*, *batil* means "*to beat something like egg*" and *patong* is translated as "*putting something on top*". Normally, they topped the noodles with cooked ground *Carabao* (Water Buffalo) *Meat*. (Photo from the authors)

food, thus, becoming the focal point of influence of the early Chinese traders with the Filipinos (Neuman, 2018; Go, 2005; Scott, 1994; Fox, 1967; Wernstedt & Spencer, 1967).

Pancit in the Philippines has a number of variations based on its regional identity (Mercado & Andalecio, 2020). *Pancit*, is enjoyed in nearly every Filipino household and considered by many a comfort food (Tayag, 2012); it has come to represent natural and cultural abundances of the country and is widely featured in festivals or local town *fiestas* (or festivals). *Pancit* truly is a symbol of Filipinos which established a firm connection to the richness of their faith, culture, and heritage (Fernandez, 1988).

Scientific and academic approaches applied in documenting heritage and culture are already an immediate need for different countries and localities (NCCA, 2019; Cook & Taylor, 2013). These approaches strengthen the awareness of the community and serve as a basis for conservation, safeguarding, and development programs and projects. These can also promote sustainability, specifically on balancing the significance of a community's cultural heritage and progressive urbanization and development (Zerrudo, 2008). In culinary heritage, specifically in the Philippines, different institutions and individuals are implementing culinary mapping projects to sustainably develop communities through culinary heritage tourism (Santiago-Tiopes, 2020; Garcia, 2020). Safeguarding through documentation and interpretation of the culinary tradition is also an urgent need for communities, especially for traditions that are currently practiced and sustained (Mercado & Zerrudo, 2018). It is important to analyze the significance of a culinary tradition of a community. This contributes to the story and importance of the community and how food evolves and develops as part of the heritage of the people (Mercado & Andalecio, 2020).

This chapter narrates the conceptualization and implementation of the research project entitled, "*Ysla de Panciteria*[1]: A Preliminary Study on the Culinary Heritage Significance of *Pancit* using the Heritage Documentation Approach – The Case of Luzon Island, Philippines", funded by the National Commission for Culture and the Arts (NCCA) in 2019. Specifically, this chapter attempts to:

- establish the significance of cultural heritage mapping tool in the documentation of a community's *pancit* culinary significance (Sect. 2);
- share the general scope of our research process and methods through a framework (Sect. 3);
- discuss the process of researcher–stakeholder collaboration and communication (Sect. 4); and
- highlight different issues and constraints on *pancit* culinary heritage safeguarding and our experiences during the conduct of the research fieldwork (Sect. 4).

---

[1] When a pancitero or the person who cooks pancit for a living settled in a more permanent space, the place came to be called as panciteria (with the Spanish suffix -ria added to a noun, to mean a place where one can have such an item, i.e., cervezeria, panaderia, chocolateria, etc.). One went to a panciteria for comida China or Chinese food, and likewise, to a karinderia for Filipino fare (Tayag, 2012).

2 Ang Paglalakbay tungo sa Ysla de Panciteria (A Journey Towards the Island of Panciteria): An Overview

Different varieties of *pancit* in the Philippines are present nowadays from Luzon, Visayas, and Mindanao. The developments from the varieties were based on how it is being indigenized by the community, the regional context, and cultural significance (Mercado & Andalecio, 2020). The *Ysla de Panciteria* project aims to explicate the culinary heritage significances in Luzon Island, Philippines using the heritage documentation approach. We documented 101 *pancit* dishes from 8 regions, 20 provinces, 27 cities, and 26 municipalities (Mercado & Andalecio, 2020). In the findings, we identified that localities having the highest number of *pancit* dishes have significant historical background on early Chinese trading and commerce (Ramos, 2018; Gliane et al., 2015; Chu, 2010; O'Brian, 1993). Based on the research, the areas having the highest number of *pancit* dishes are the National Capital Region, specifically in the City of Manila, the province of Cavite, particularly in the municipality of Tanza, and the province of Camarines Sur, notably in the municipality of Nabua (Mercado & Andalecio, 2020). Table 1 presents the *Ysla de Panciteria* list of documented *pancit* dishes.

Table 1 Tabular representation of the *Ysla de Panciteria Pancit* documentation

Geographical region of Luzon Island	Province	City/municipality	*Pancit* dish
Region 1: *Ilocandia*/Ilocos Region	Ilocos Norte	City of Batac	*Miki*
		Laoag City	*Hibol*
			Pancit Lusay
	Ilocos Sur	Vigan City	*Pancit Musiko*
Region 2: Northern Philippines/Cagayan Valley	Cagayan	Aparri	*Miki Nilad-dit*
		Tuguegarao City	*Pancit Batil Patong*
			Sinanta
	Isabela	Cabagan	*Pancit Cabagan*
Region CAR: Cordillera Administrative Region	Abra	Bangued	*Abra Miki*
Region 3: Central Luzon	Bataan	Balanga City	*Pancit Cupang*
		Morong	*Hu Tieu*
		Orani	*Pancit Palabok*
		Orion	*Pancit Luglug*
			Spabok
	Bulacan	Bocaue	*Batchoy Tagalog*
			Pancit Alanganin
		Hagonoy	*Pancit Hagonoy*
		Marilao	*Pancit Marilao*
		City of Meycauayan	*Pancit (This is it Pancit!)*
		Sta. Maria	*Pancit Papaya*
	Nueva Ecija	City of San Jose	*Pancit Kanin*
	Pampanga	Angeles City	*Pancit Luglug*
	Tarlac	Anao	*Pancit Anao*

(continued)

Table 1 (continued)

Geographical region of Luzon Island	Province	City/municipality	*Pancit* dish
Region NCR: National Capital Region		City of Manila	*Alimango Sotanghon*
			Beef Hofan
			Beef Lamien
			Bihon Soup
			Cha Misua with Quail Egg
			Chami
			Chuan Tsai
			Duck Misua with Chinese Herb Soup
			He Ma Mi
			Hong Kong Style Crispy Noodles
			Instant Pancit Canton
			Kiam Tsai
			Lobihon
			Lomisua
			Ma Chi On
			Maki Mi
			Miki Bihon Soup
			Miki Bihon
			Misuaco
			Owwa Misua
			Pancit Canton Lo Han Chay
			Pancit Canton
			Pancit Satae Mi Guisado
			Pata Bihon
			Shui Jiao Mian
			Sizzling Noodles
			Sotanghon Guisado
			Tomato Bihon
			Tostado Bihon
			Vegetarian Cha Misua
			Zha Jiang Mian
		Makati City	*Pancit Puti*
		Malabon City	*Pancit Labong*
			Pancit Malabon Puti
			Pancit Malabon
		Marikina City	*Pancit Pinagulong*
		Muntinlupa City	*Mami*
			Pancit Malabon
			Pancit Palabok
		Pasay City	*Pancit Palabok*
			Pata Bihon
		Pasig City	*The Original Pancit with Chicharon*
		Quezon City	*Beef Pares Mami*
			The Original Mami
		City of San Juan	*Pancit San Juan*

(continued)

Table 1 (continued)

Geographical region of Luzon Island	Province	City/municipality	*Pancit* dish
Region 4A: Southern *Tagalog* – *CaLaBaRzon*	Batangas	Batangas City	*Pancit Tikyano*
		Lipa City	*Lomi*
			Miki Guisado
		Taal	*Pancit ni Mang Biko*
	Cavite	Cavite City and Kawit	*Pancit Henoy*
		Cavite City	*Almondigas*
			Pancit choko en su tinta
			Pancit Palabok
			Pancit Puso
			Pansate
		Rosario and Cavite City	*Pancit Kilawin*
		Tanza	*Calandracas*
			Pancit Estacion
		Tanza and Trece Martires City	*Pancit Estacion Negra*
	Laguna	Pagsanjan	*Pancit Ulam*
		San Pablo City	*Pancit Kalabuko*
		City of San Pedro	*Pancit Maciang*
		City of Santa Rosa	*Pancit Grade 1*
		Paete and Pagsanjan	*Mikelo*
	Quezon	Lucban	*Pancit Habhab*
		Lucena City	*Chami*
	Rizal	Angono	*Laksa*
		Morong	*Pancit Palengke*
Region 4A: Southern *Tagalog* – *MiMaRoPa*	Marinduque	Boac	*Pancit Canton*
		Santa Cruz	*Miki Guisado*
	Palawan	Puerto Princesa	*Chao Long*
	Romblon	Odiongan	*Kumo*
Region 5: *Bicolandia/Bicol Region*	Albay	Daraga	*Pancit Bicol Express*
	Camarines Sur	Bato	*Pancit Bato*
		Nabua	*Pancit Bato with Kinalas*
			Pancit Inulas
		Naga City	*Pancit Log Log*
			Pancit Kinalas

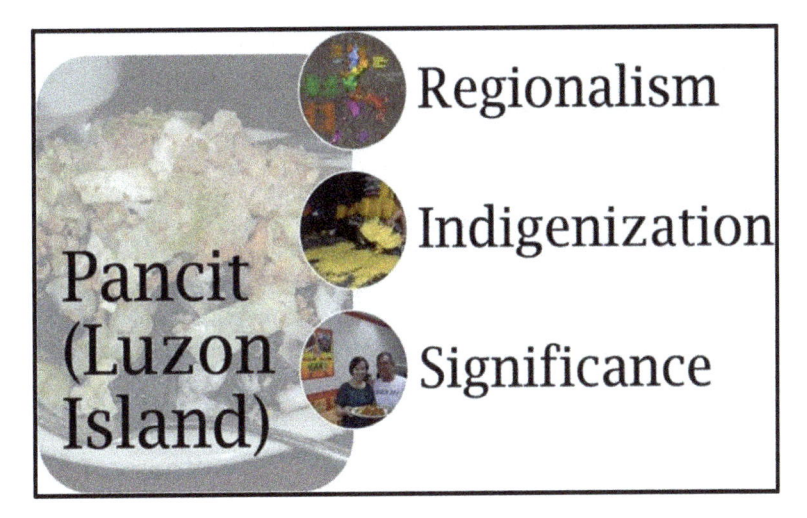

Fig. 2 The Luzon Island *Pancit* culinary heritage conceptual framework. (Source: Mercado & Andalecio, 2020)

As part of the research process, we identified the different culinary characteristics of *pancit* based on the community practices. We identified the raw ingredients and the environment, selling points, cooking equipment and tools, process of cooking, consumption, and recycling and disposal of waste. From the concept of Luzon's *pancit* culinary characteristics and significance of the community, we conceptualized the Luzon Island *pancit* Culinary Heritage Conceptual Framework (see Fig. 2; Mercado & Andalecio, 2020).

In the process of coordination and openness of the community, it was either the primary stakeholders (e.g., LGUs and NGOs) who determined and communicated with the subject *panciterias* or we, as the researchers, were the ones who coordinated directly to the owners of the *panciterias*. From what we experienced, owners were cooperative and readily agreed to join as key informants of the research project. Aside from sharing the story of their culinary heritage, it was also one way of promoting their businesses on this kind of academic platform. However, there were also restrictions highlighted by the key informants during the process of the in-depth interview and on-site observation.

This framework recognizes how *pancit* in Luzon has developed through regionalism or unique regional cultural and heritage identity. The culinary tradition was also influenced by the different resources available in the area, which makes *pancit* an indigenized food of the community. Once the community integrates it to their everyday lifestyle, different values and significant aspects are developed. The significant aspects identified are historical, culinary, aesthetic, agricultural, economic, health, social, and symbolical means. All of these contribute to the culinary identity and value of *pancit* culinary tradition as one of the unique intangible cultural heritages of the community. The next section discusses the research design and methods (i.e., culinary heritage mapping) we employed in our Luzon Island *pancit* culinary heritage mapping.

3 *Kwentong Pamayanan at Panlasa (Stories of Community and Taste):* Behind the Culinary Heritage Mapping of Luzon Island *Pancit*

In understanding the significance and value of *pancit* to the community, we utilized cultural heritage mapping as our research approach for the project. Cultural mapping is a research technique of systematic documentation and identification of natural and cultural heritage of a place and its related community (Cook & Taylor, 2013; NCCA, 2019). It can be used for documenting different types of heritage, such as tangible movable, tangible immovable, natural landscape, natural flora and fauna, intangible, and personality.

In the Luzon Island *pancit* project, we utilized the mapping tool for culinary heritage developed by the University of Santo Tomas Graduate School – Center for Conservation of Cultural Property and the Environment in the Tropics (UST GS-CCCPET, 2017). The mapping tool was based on the UNESCO 2003 Convention, Australia International Council on Monuments and Sites (ICOMOS) Burra Charter (2013), Getty Conservation Institute (GCI) Planning Process Methodology (The J. Paul Getty Trust, 2002), Republic Act No. 10066 or the National Cultural Heritage Act of 2009 (Congress of the Philippines, 2009), and the Culinary Mapping Dimensions (Sta. Maria, 2016). The mapping tool on culinary heritage highlighted different information, such as a food's primary identity (name of the food), associated persons and communities, characteristics (raw ingredients, selling points, materials and equipment, process of cooking, consumption, and recycling and disposal of waste), significance (historical, culinary, aesthetic, agricultural, economic, health, social, and symbolical), safeguarding protocols, and the use of the mapping output after the documentation (UST GS-CCCPET, 2017). In the process of our Luzon Island *pancit* culinary mapping, we employed this tool following three general steps, namely: researching available archival and documentary evidence; observing and documenting *pancit* dishes and their related culinary culture in different areas; and analysing findings.

Through these processes, we conceptualized the *Ysla de Panciteria* Research Methodological Framework (see Fig. 3) which details how we conducted and implemented the research project through the use of different materials and methods. The framework shows the utilization of culinary mapping (archival and documentary; and observation and interview) and stakeholders perspectives (local government and community) in collecting and determining relevant information for our research project.

We started with examining and assessing different archival and documentary evidence. This step provided us an idea on what types of *pancit* dishes are being cooked in different regions, provinces, cities, and municipalities. The presence of different references is crucial in providing us different information on localities and their culinary culture on *pancit*. Some of these references were journal articles and books authored by Filipino and foreign writers, government documents and tourism promotional paraphernalia, academic *vlogs*, newspaper clippings (print and online),

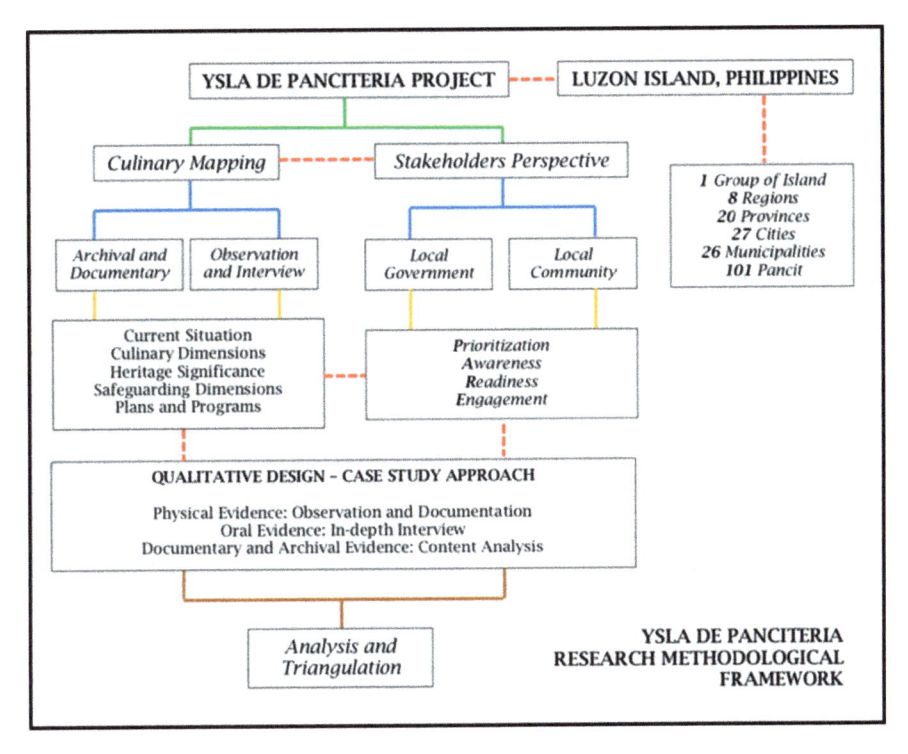

Fig. 3 Figural representation of the *Ysla de Panciteria* methodological framework. (Conceptualized by the authors)

travel shows available in mass and social media platforms, commercial magazines, and other related documents. During this process, we also identified people in the locality to serve as our contact persons, who could potentially assist us during fieldwork. Contact persons could be tourism and cultural officers in the local government unit (LGU), local researchers and historians, non-government organizations (NGO), *panciteria*[1] owners, community leaders, and other related informants. Communication letters were sent to potential contact persons for ethical consideration and proper coordination. Before the actual fieldwork, oral orientations with the key informants were performed to provide discussions on the purpose and significance of the study. Consent forms were also provided to systematically document the approval of their participation in the study.

In the fieldwork, we conducted our on-site observations by visiting different local *panciterias* offering notable *pancit* dishes. The basic criteria of the subject must be *pancit* dishes that are existing, emerging, and potentially known in the community or the study site. We comprehensively documented their process of preparation, cooking, and consumption through photo and video documentation (see Fig. 4). If we would like to clarify something and ask questions, we were implementing in-depth interviews to the key informants. This allowed us to create open discussions and exchanges of ideas, guided by the mapping template. Voice

Fig. 4 Figural representation of an example of our on-site observation and documentation. In the photo, Constantine Poblete, the Son of Agnes Bautista-Poblete (Owner, Cantina de Tita A. in Cavite City), was cooking *Almondigas*, a Noodle Soup made from *Miswa* and Meatballs. (Photo from the authors)

recorders were also utilized to document the conversations. All modes of documentation were discussed with the key informants. We sought their consent for data privacy and intellectual property rights provision.

After the process of data collection, we analyzed the collected information by triangulating the data coming from the on-site observation and in-depth interviews using the mapping tool.

4 *"Cooking"* the Story of *Pancit* through the Stakeholders' Perspective: Local Governments and Communities

In the field of culinary safeguarding, the data suggests that policymakers have a significant role when it comes to decision-making, as these individuals are critical stakeholders who constitutionally and personally benefit through historical past and its preservation. This project revealed the situation and reality of both the state of governance and the communities vis-à-vis heritage conservation.

Food is a communal heritage (Kapelari et al. 2020; Mercado & Andalecio, 2020). It provides culinary stories and experiences of the community and its related environment. Such stories and experiences differ among members of the community, especially the owners of *panciterias* and personalities known for cooking their *pancit* culinary tradition. Previous research has indicated differences in experiences in terms of coordination, approval and orientation of heritage (Lee, 2015). Thus, the local government and its community must be cognizant in building relationships and policy in order to best uphold cultural heritage.

The data from this study revealed five significant aspects of determining the stakeholders' perspectives, namely: *prioritization and political will, knowledge and awareness, readiness and openness,* and *engagement and participation.* These realizations throughout our research fieldwork revealed the issues and constraints that affect the overall effectiveness in the execution of programs and projects set by the stakeholders. The process of researcher-stakeholder collaboration highlights these key aspects as an outcome of a scholarly process which in turn reveals the different issues and constraints on *pancit* culinary safeguarding. Each aspect is discussed individually in the following sections.

4.1 Prioritization and Political Will

We visited 53 LGUs (i.e., towns and municipalities) all over Luzon and witnessed the efforts made by a good number of local executives with their cultural and tourism and related offices. Politicians, as the primary policy-makers in the Philippines, play an important role in culinary safeguarding. Sheer political will of the people in power can yield developments on advocacy movements mostly lobbied by non-state actors. A number of examples taken from the results of this research project will give a contextual understanding on how significant prioritization is to all levels of the government from the national to the local context. However, the majority of the LGUs and their exercise of local autonomy as enshrined in the constitution, greatly influences the quality of culinary safeguarding efforts (see Fig. 5).

After observing the localized projects of each LGU, we drew comparisons according to the degree of appreciation and awareness they have with their local *pancit* dish. The DATA/INTERVIEWS showed that many in positions of local authority prioritized socio-economic needs and had little knowledge and awareness, if any, on heritage safeguarding is or at least a background on its significance. We view that knowledge and awareness are key in understanding why these local executives continue to regard or disregard the significance of the culinary safeguarding in their jurisdiction as these variables influence their decision making. The findings demonstrated that, currently, LGUs felt that the majority of the politicians follow a capitalistic approach, vesting only in interests that result in direct economic growth. There were, however, some politicians who were described as thinking beyond only economic growth. We view it that the technocratic and the non-traditional approach of these politicians had helped the efforts of conservation groups to fight for culinary safeguarding in general.

Unfortunately, heritage safeguarding, especially on intangible cultural heritage, has always been neglected by policy-makers because of the lack of the basic

Fig. 5 Photo of Mr. Desiderio Lattao, Owner of Felicitas Fastfood Restaurant in Cabagan, Isabela. He is a member of the community who benefited from their LGU's ordinance focusing on the recognition and protection of their town's *pancit cabagan*. (Photo from the authors)

qualities that they must possess such as political will through knowledge, awareness, readiness, and openness, as previously discussed. The majority of the LGUs are struggling with the negative effects of local politics and other priorities not aligned with the principles of sustainability beginning with the system and political climate until prioritization of plans. Having outlined all these challenges, it is absolutely difficult for conservation groups to penetrate the political spectrum without any support from the LGU. The term of a local chief executive (e.g. mayor) is good for only three years (maximum of three terms or 9 years upon re-election) and not to mention the culture and nature of creating and implementing policies in both national and local scene which only focuses on short-term to medium-term development plans.

In the Philippines, LGUs have often neglected the importance of having long-term plans for their jurisdiction because of the political and electoral systems. Hope, however, is still present if, regardless of the political affiliation of the succeeding management, will sustain and continue the plans made up by the outgoing administration. This will bring us back to the questions of prioritization and political will, level of knowledge and awareness, degree of openness and readiness, and lastly, the willingness of the LGU to engage and participate as the primary mover.

4.2 Knowledge and Awareness

Knowledge and sense of awareness play a vital role for the decision making processes of policy-makers. As such, their levels of knowledge and sense of awareness ultimately steer their LGUs' approaches, based on their a-priori or a-posteriori plans or policies. We found that most of the local executives in Luzon had no prior background on safeguarding, let alone heritage management. Qualifications for the tourism officer's position mostly depend on trust, confidence, and nepotism; thus, defeating the very purpose of what bureaucracy is (Rocamora & Aguiling, 2020).

Most of the LGUs have no tourism offices and are normally placed under the Planning and Development Office. This office is responsible for the overall developmental affairs of the LGU, which concentrates on different industries and social services provided to the community. This kind of administrative structure is not an ideal model for serious heritage conservation advocacies because decisions basically come from people who lack formal qualifications for heritage management and tourism product development. Although almost the entire key informant pool had college degrees and post-graduate qualifications, most of the inquiries raised by the researchers resulted to lack of proper knowledge and awareness on heritage conservation; thus, supporting the result of the mapping method we completed. Through our interviews of local executives, we found a level of awareness on culinary safeguarding, as one of the aspects that respects sustainable approaches for future generations, is evident in a good number of LGUs.

4.3 Readiness and Openness

While, both knowledge and awareness play an important role in leadership, the readiness and openness of governments are also important. We define the practice of anticipatory approaches as anticipating what is likely to happen in the future. In the context of this study, we suggest this practice must also be applied to culinary safeguarding. We suggest that leaders must be willing to learn and re-learn the socio-cultural aspect of development, which is often overlooked and misunderstood, replacing a reactive approach with a proactive approach. Although we observed a sufficient number of public servants who have adopted a proactive leadership approach, a majority of the LGUs continue to practice traditional politics and governance which lacks the anticipatory measures on key aspects of public administration, specifically, in addressing heritage issues and concerns.

We found out that readiness and openness, as practiced by a number of LGUs in the project, have paved the way for exemplifying good practice of governance or as the Department of the Interior and Local Government (DILG) puts it, worthy of receiving the Seal of Good Local Governance (SGLG).[2] This program is a good way of encouraging more LGUs to perform better and achieve more positive outcomes especially on heritage conservation and other sustainable development practices in their jurisdiction's cultural properties.

An example of good practice was demonstrated by the LGU of Cabagan in Isabela. There, the LGU created and implemented an ordinance that protects their very own *Pancit Cabagan*. In doing so, they declared the dish as one of the intangible cultural heritage and symbol of the town which makes provision for better tourism growth and cultural awareness (see Fig. 6). Based on the personal accounts that we documented, we found out that through the initiated of the Cabagan LGU, significant positive results were realized, such as people empowerment through local noodle industry development.

Aside from the government as the primary stakeholder, another important player is the local communities as the bearers of the culinary tradition. Most of the

Fig. 6 Photo from left to right, Mr. Avi Ben P. Andalecio (co-author of the research project), Mrs. Pacita Chua-Lattao and Mr. Desiderio Lattao (restaurant owners) Mr. Jame Monren T. Mercado (lead researcher of the research project), with the Tourism Officer of Cabagan, Isabela, Ms. Joylyn T. Bulan. (Photo from the authors)

---

[2] The Seal of Good Local Governance (SGLG) assesses Local Government Units (LGUs) on whether they attain minimum governance standards, specifically on "good fiscal or financial administration or financial sustainability, disaster preparedness, social protection and sensitivity program, health compliance and responsiveness, sustainable education, business friendliness and competitiveness, safety, peace and order, environmental management, tourism, heritage development, culture and arts, and youth development" (Congress of the Philippines, 2019).

members of the community had to limit the information they shared. Information, such as raw ingredients, process of cooking, and presentation, were generalized since it is considered as their "trade secret" within their business operation or familial culinary culture. This is a concern by the community due to potential commercial consumption and degrading its substance as a traditional familial food. Although we discussed the overview and the objectives of the study thoroughly to them, they wanted to keep it within their premises. Also, for some, they experienced or heard cases of people joining or participating in studies related to food. However, they were not recognized and at some point, used the information to put up their businesses on food and beverage. This case on restrictions is normal in documenting culinary heritage, especially if it is being used as a commercial or trade product for public consumption (Mercado & Zerrudo, 2018, 2019). Nevertheless, they answered all questions as much as possible.

4.4 Engagement and Participation

The willingness of the LGUs to prioritize heritage conservation and willingness of the local community to participate are crucial elements to promote sustainability. Policy-makers are critical stakeholders who constitutionally and personally benefit from the historical past and its preservation. The past often influences the present-day identities and behaviours associated with the cultural properties of the jurisdiction. Based on our fieldwork, the towns of Cabagan in the province of Isabela; the entire province of Bataan; the towns of Bocaue and Marilao in Bulacan province; San Jose City in Nueva Ecija province; Lipa City in Batangas province; San Pablo City in Laguna province; the town of Lucban in Quezon province; Puerto Princesa City in Palawan; and the town of Daraga in Albay province are worth noting for their outstanding works on recognizing their respective *pancit* dishes by means of recognition for their local cooks, restaurant owners and establishments. Furthermore, they created ordinances and policies to protect local communities' cultural properties. Thus, it is commendable what these LGUs have exemplified to propagate and promote the value and significance of their heritage which the future generation will benefit and learn from. These LGUs and their local communities have chosen to engage and be part of something that would showcase their cultural uniqueness and identity. By engaging and participating in conservation efforts as stated by the informants during our interviews, we believe they have secured their future and their identity as manifested by their culture and heritage.

The local community's pride and hospitality are the things that we noticed during our fieldwork (see Fig. 7). Participants were accommodating and repeatedly offered us complimentary food and beverages. They felt that such actions showcased their hospitality and pride promoting and safeguarding their unique *pancit* tradition. By keeping their guests comfortable and satisfied, they hope guests will return to experience their culinary traditions, strengthening the industry as well as promoting their *pancit* tradition.

Fig. 7 Figural representation of the example of our in-depth interview with the community. In the photo, Mr. Dindo Montenegro, a *Taaleño* and Local Historian, shared the Culinary Significance of *Pancit ni Mang Biko* or *Pancit Sabsab*, which can be located at the Taal Public Market. (Photo from the authors)

Our research indicates that communities will work to ensure that the significance of their *pancit* culinary heritage is being communicated and promoted. While documenting each of their *pancit* versions, they expressed pride when sharing its story and how it affects their communal lifestyle. We also observed their passion in safeguarding the culinary tradition through government-led programs and project (e.g., festivals and events), community participation (e.g., joining in different culinary competitions), and advocacies initiated by non-government organizations (e.g., research and promotions). Although communities use *pancit* for livelihood purposes, they always highlighted the significance of transmitting their culinary tradition from generation to generation with many answers on safeguarding focused on teaching and assigning tasks for their sons/daughters/grandchildren.

5 Conclusions

The aim of this chapter is to narrate our experiences on conceptualizing and implementing the *Ysla de Panciteria* project. We provided findings from both primary and secondary sources and our personal observations throughout the project. The *Ysla de Panciteria* Project was more than a research project; it was an experience that we will never forget. By travelling through Luzon, the biggest island group of the

Philippines with its eight regions, 20 provinces, 27 cities, and 26 municipalities we documented 101 *pancit* dishes. In doing so, we were able to meet wonderful people and discover the things which opened our awareness and fuelled our own Filipino heritage appreciation and sense of pride.

Through rigorous culinary mapping and examination of the stakeholders' perspectives, we unravelled the wonders of this staple noodle dish. Delving through archives and documents of culinary historians, observing the old and new ways and methods of the preparation, cooking, and eating *pancit,* we uncovered unique attributes of the dish from one province to another. The documentation of the experiences of local governments and communities regarding their challenges and success stories demonstrated the importance of conservation of culture and heritage as well as stakeholder cooperation. We propose that solutions to the issues could be achieved and approached by *assessing the current situation, culinary dimensions, heritage significance, safeguarding dimensions, and collaborating on ideas on plans and programs* for the common good of their communities through *prioritization, awareness, readiness, and engagement.*

We have experienced so much in this project up to the point of being extremely excited on starting the second leg for the remainder of the island groups of the Philippines (i.e., Visayas and Mindanao) that has been post-poned as a result of the COVID-19 pandemic. However, we are optimistic to return to the road to complete a project for the entire country and hopefully open new doors of opportunity for collaborations with local governments and communities and join them in their advocacies in safeguarding the intangible cultural heritage treasures in their own backyards. This will ultimately fulfil our advocacy to protect and save the identity of Filipinos, one dish at a time.

Revisiting section three of this chapter gave us idea about the importance of a scholarly process and shared important technical insights for academicians and policy-makers to collaborate for a holistic process of evidence-based policy making by revisiting a locality's current situation, reviewing the culinary dimensions, discovering heritage significance and safeguarding dimensions, and its transition into plans and programs. The technicality we discussed aims to share ideas and knowledge so that local researchers, academicians and LGUs can create projects to address key-issues on culinary cultural heritage. Knowledge and awareness are essential for the implementation of policies of LGUs. Similarly, policy-makers must have the readiness and openness to adapt to change and accept trends in the world of governance especially in facing challenges in their jurisdictions.

Ultimately, the academic contributions of this project will aid researchers and academicians in the technical processes of understanding the cultural heritage of local cuisines. As the trend on heritage and conservation grows, we call for our current and future policymakers to make radical changes to uphold culinary heritages in the Philippines, and elsewhere. From the meticulous process of cooking, selling, and consumption (Sta. Maria, 2016), we were amazed, and at the same time, concerned by the results of year-long delving into the sustainability of communal shared traditions of *Pancit* making as an industry, to the complexity of the statutory milieu of national and local governance. All thanks to this legendary culinary delight that all Filipinos love, the *pancit.*

Acknowledgments This paper is an academic narrative of our experiences and observations during the conduct of the research titled: "*Ysla de Panciteria*: A Preliminary Study on the Culinary Heritage Significance of *Pancit* using the Heritage Documentation Approach – The Case of Luzon Island, Philippines". The research project was funded under the National Commission for Culture and the Arts (NCCA) Research Awards 2019 for an Individual Category. We would like also to express our gratitude to Asst. Prof. Maria Regina Policarpio-Arriero, MA from the University of Santo Tomas Department of English, for proofreading this chapter.

References

Australia ICOMOS. (2013). The Burra Charter: The Australia ICOMOS charter for places of cultural significance. *Australia International Council on Monuments and Sites*. https://australia.icomos.org/wp-content/uploads/The-Burra-Charter-2013-Adopted-31.10.2013.pdf. Accessed 22 Sept 2020.

Chu, R. (2010). *Chinese and Chinese mestizos of Manila: Family, identity and culture 1860s–1930s*. UST Publishing House.

Congress of the Philippines. (2009). Republic Act No. 10066: National Cultural Heritage Act of 2009. *Official Gazette*. https://www.officialgazette.gov.ph/2010/03/26/republic-act-no-10066/. Accessed 27 Sept 2020.

Congress of the Philippines. (2019). Republic Act No. 11292: The Seal of Good Local Governance Act of 2019. *Official Gazette*. https://www.officialgazette.gov.ph/downloads/2019/04apr/20190412-RA-11292-RRD.pdf. Accessed 06 Dec 2020.

Cook, I., & Taylor, K. (2013). A contemporary guide to cultural mapping: An ASEAN – Australia perspective. *Association of Southeast Asian Nations*. https://www.asean.org/wp-content/uploads/images/2013/resources/publication/Contemporary%20Guide%20to%20Cultural%20Mapping%20Rev%20X.pdf. Accessed 27 Sept 2020.

Fernandez, D. G. (1988). Culture ingested: Notes on the indigenization of Philippine food. *Philippine Studies, 36*(1), 219–232.

Fernandez, D. G. (2000). *Palayok: Philippine food through time, on site, in the pot*. Bookmark.

Fox, R. (1967). The archaeological record of Chinese influences in the Philippines. *Philippine Studies, 15*(1), 41–62.

Garcia, C. (2020, November 06). Food tourism 1010: Cultural food mapping and experiences [Video]. *Facebook*. https://www.facebook.com/wofexuniversity/videos/273438264082344/

Gliane, N., Delupio, N., Kahiwat, J., & Comedis, E. (2015). Pancit Malabon: Malabon Heritage. Presented in the DLSU Research Congress 2015. De La Salle University, City of Manila, Philippines. https://www.dlsu.edu.ph/wp-content/uploads/pdf/conferences/research-congress-proceedings/2015/LCCS/003LCS_Gliane_NGM.pdf. Accessed 22 Sept 2020.

Go, J. (2005). Ma'I in Chinese records – Mindoro or Bai? An examination of a historical puzzle. *Philippine Studies, 53*(1), 119–138.

Kapelari, S., Alexopoulos, G., Moussouri, T., Sagmeister, K. J., & Stampfer, F. (2020). Food heritage makes a difference: The importance of cultural knowledge for improving education for sustainable food choices. *Sustainability, 15*(1509). https://doi.org/10.3390/su12041509

Lee, S. (2015). Working with policy-makers for integrating heritage science research into political priorities. *Studies in Conservation, 60*(2), 48–56. https://doi.org/10.1080/00393630.2015.1117865

Mercado, J. M. T., & Andalecio, A. B. P. (2020). Ysla de Panciteria: A preliminary study on the culinary heritage significance of Pancit using the heritage documentation approach – The case of Luzon Island, Philippines. *Journal of Ethnic Foods, 7*(19), 1–25. https://doi.org/10.1186/s42779-020-00057-1

Mercado, J. M. T., & Zerrudo, E. B. (2018). Pamanang Kulinarya: Developing a safeguarding plan for culinary heritage using the statement of significance – The case of Lomi in Lipa City, Batangas, Philippines. *SPAFA Journal., 2*, 1–33. https://doi.org/10.26721/spafajournal.v2i0.584

Mercado, J. M. T., & Zerrudo, E. B. (2019). Rekado ng Kwento: The culinary heritage significance of Lomi in Lipa City, Batangas, Philippines. *Journal of Philippine Tourism and Hospitality Studies, 1*(1), 1–16.

NCCA. (2019). Cultural mapping toolkit: A guide for participatory cultural mapping in local communities. *National Commission for Culture and the Arts*. https://ncca.gov.ph/about-ncca-3/ncca-cultural-mapping-program/. Accessed 27 Sept 2020.

Neuman, N. (2018). On the engagement with social theory in food studies: Cultural symbols and social practices. *Food, Culture & Society, 22*(1), 78–94.

O'Brian, J. J. (1993). *The historical and cultural heritage of the Bikol people*. Ateneo de Naga University.

Ramos, G. (2018). *Republic of taste: The untold stories of Cavite cuisine*. Ige Ramos Design Studios.

Rocamora, J. T., & Aguiling, H. M. (2020). Competencies of tourism officers in the Philippines: Toward a development of competency model for managing destinations in public governance. *Review of Integrative Business and Economics Research., 9*(3), 20–66.

Santiago-Tiopes, K. R. (2020, November 26). Keynote speech: Food and farm tourism initiatives of Department of Tourism [Video]. *YouTube*. https://www.youtube.com/watch?v=eB4uZPh3gAk&feature=emb_logo

Schlotter, K., & Spielmann-Rome, E. (2015). *Culinary China a celebration of food and tradition*. H.F Ullmann Publishing GmbH.

Scott, W. (1994). *Barangay: Sixteenth-century Philippine culture and society*. Ateneo de Manila University Press.

Sta. Maria, F. P. (2006). *The governor-general's kitchen: Philippine culinary vignettes and period recipes 1521–1935*. Anvil Publishing.

Sta. Maria, F. P. (2016). *What kids should know about Filipino food*. Adarna House.

Sta. Maria, F. P., & Koh, B. (2019). *Kain Na!: An illustration guide to Philippine food*. RPD Publications.

Tayag, C. (2012, May 10). Long live the pancit!. *PhilStar Global*. https://www.philstar.com/lifestyle/food-and-leisure/2012/05/10/805030/long-live-pancit. Accessed 3 Dec 2020.

Tayag, C., & Quioc, M. (2012). *Linamnam: Eating One's way around the Philippines*. Anvil Publishing.

The J. Paul Getty Trust. (2002). Assessing the values of cultural heritage. *Getty Conservation Institute*. https://www.getty.edu/conservation/publications_resources/pdf_publications/pdf/assessing.pdf. Accessed 27 Sept 2020.

UST GS-CCCPET. (2017). *Mapping template for culinary heritage* [Unpublished Document]. The Graduate School – Center for Conservation of Cultural Property and the Environment in the Tropics, University of Santo Tomas, City of Manila, Philippines.

Wernstedt, F., & Spencer, J. (1967). *The Philippine island world: A physical, cultural and regional geography*. University of California Press.

Zerrudo, E. B. (2008). *Pamanaraan: Writings on Philippine cultural heritage management*. UST Publishing House.

Jame Monren T. Mercado is an Academic Staff at the College of Tourism and Hospitality Management, University of Santo Tomas, Manila. In the same University, he is a Faculty Research Associate under the Research Center for Social Sciences and Education and an Associate Researcher of The Graduate School – Center for Conservation of Cultural Property and Environment in the Tropics. He is currently a Member of the Board of Directors, Philippine Association of Researchers for Tourism and Hospitality, Inc. and an Associate Member under Division VIII (Social Sciences), Department of Science and Technology – National Research Council of the Philippines.

Avi Ben P. Andalecio is an Academic Staff at the College of Tourism and Hospitality Management of the University of Santo Tomas in Manila. His research interests revolve on Sustainable Tourism, Special Interest Tourism, Public Administration, and Public Policy. He has presented and published several researches in the Philippines and abroad. Some of his major recognitions include the National Commission for Culture and the Arts Research Grant Recipient 2019 as a Co-Author. He also serves as the current Secretary for Central Manila of the Philippine Association of Researchers for Tourism and Hospitality, Inc.

Tourism in the Philippine Society: Conclusions and Looking Forward

Richard S. Aquino and Brooke A. Porter

Abstract This edited book uncovered some of the contemporary tourism issues in the Philippines, explored through the perspectives of communities, hosts, tourists (local and foreign), and Filipino scholars. This concluding chapter revisits the contributions from each chapter organized through thematic analysis. Particularly, key findings from the contributions are discussed as they inform two broad themes, namely, the *tourism orientation of hosts* and *guests' orientation of the Philippines*. Implications for furthering knowledge of tourism within the context of Filipino society are outlined.

Keywords Filipino culture · Tourism management · Hospitality studies · Critical tourism studies · Philippines

1 The Aims and Contributions of the Book

The primary aim of this edited volume was to compile scholarly inquiries on contemporary tourism phenomena in the context of Filipino culture and society. Structured mainly within the different versions of *gaze* in tourism studies, this aim was achieved by curating contributions that examine issues occurring in various forms and settings of tourism in the Philippines. The contributions showcased the diversity of the Filipino culture and society in examining some of the understudied phenomena in Philippine tourism, such as festivals (chapters "Exploring Residents' Perceptions of Tourism in a Pilgrimage Destination: The Case of Our Lady of Peñafrancia in Naga City, Philippines", "Significance of the Carabaos in Harvest

---

R. S. Aquino (✉)
University of Canterbury, Christchurch, Canterbury, New Zealand
e-mail: richard.aquino@canterbury.ac.nz

B. A. Porter
Auckland University of Technology, Auckland, Auckland, New Zealand

Coral Triangle Conservancy, Taguig, Philippines
e-mail: bporter@aut.ac.nz

Festivals in the Philippines", and "Interpreting the Meanings of Carabao Festivals in the Philippines: A Multi-method Study"), community-based tourism (chapter "Community-Based Tourism: An Analysis of Ugong Rock Adventures Stakeholders' Social Capital in Facilitating Community Participation"), slum tourism (chapter "Strolling Between Shanties: Tourists' Perceptions and Experiences of Manila's Slums"), culinary heritage conservation (chapter "Researching Luzon Island's Pancit Culinary Heritage: Cultural Mapping and Stakeholders' Perspective"), religious events (chapter "Exploring Residents' Perceptions of Tourism in a Pilgrimage Destination: The Case of Our Lady of Peñafrancia in Naga City, Philippines"), travel during the colonial era (chapter "The Traveling Filipina in Periodicals (1898–1938)"), and more contemporary settings such as travelling in the Philippines during the COVID-19 pandemic (chapter "Home Away from Home: Foreign Vloggers' Gaze of the Philippines During the COVID-19 Pandemic").

Moreover, this edited volume has provided a platform for Filipino scholars to convey their perspectives in understanding local tourism issues. This aim was achieved through collaborating with new, emerging, and senior Filipino academics coming from varied disciplinary backgrounds. The Philippine-centric contributions presented multiple researcher positionalities that underpinned the knowledge creation process and the insights offered in each chapter. Revisiting each chapter revealed several implications that were categorized according to their knowledge contributions, particularly on the *tourism orientation of hosts* and *guests' orientation of the Philippines*.

1.1 Tourism Orientation of Hosts

In the Philippines, the policies and initiatives set forth by governmental agencies are argued to influence the tourism orientation of service providers and host communities. While such initiatives may be translated into the creation of tourism experiences by the host communities (Alejandria-Gonzalez, 2016), the tourism orientation of hosts can also be formed by their knowledge and awareness of tourism (e.g., Porter et al., 2018), as well as, their perceptions of tourism impacts (Aquino, 2020). Part II – *The Host Gaze* – has put forward contributions that inform the tourism orientation of some Filipino host communities. Specifically, chapters under this theme (chapters "Exploring Residents' Perceptions of Tourism in a Pilgrimage Destination: The Case of Our Lady of Peñafrancia in Naga City, Philippines" and "Community-Based Tourism: An Analysis of Ugong Rock Adventures Stakeholders' Social Capital in Facilitating Community Participation") highlighted the economic nature of tourism, as the host communities under these studies alluded to the financial benefits they receive from engaging in tourism. However, nuances were also evident in these chapters' findings.

In exploring residents' perceptions of pilgrimage-induced tourism in Naga City, Bagadion and Capistrano (chapter "Exploring Residents' Perceptions of Tourism in a Pilgrimage Destination: The Case of Our Lady of Peñafrancia in Naga City,

Philippines") signalled the potential negative impacts of tourism on the purpose of holding the Our Lady of Peñafrancia festivities that are integral in the faith and spirituality of the residents. Excessive commercialization through tourism was implied to potentially compromise the very nature of the pilgrimage for the community. In the case of the Ugong Rock Adventures located in Palawan, Delas Alas, Pagador, and Capistrano (chapter "Community-Based Tourism: An Analysis of Ugong Rock Adventures Stakeholders' Social Capital in Facilitating Community Participation") showed that participation in this community-based tourism project was driven by residents' social capital, more specifically, by the Filipino value of *bayanihan* (i.e., cooperative action founded on the principle of mutual effort). These authors further stressed the role cultural norms and shared values have in forming tourism orientations.

Beyond the concept of host gaze, other chapters also provided some insights into the tourism orientation of hosts. For example, Del Rosario's (chapter "Significance of the Carabaos in Harvest Festivals in the Philippines") analysis of Philippine harvest festivals argued that the carabao acts as a symbol that links the traditional holding of the events with their modern-day celebrations. Adding to this inference, it can also be suggested that traditional rituals and symbols could be adapted to the communities' evolving practices and touristic orientations of holding these festivals. While in chapter "Researching Luzon Island's Pancit Culinary Heritage: Cultural Mapping and Stakeholders' Perspective", Mercado and Andalecio's fieldwork highlighted that communities' sense of pride in their culinary heritage inspires the desire to safeguard culinary traditions through festivals, events, and tourism projects.

1.2 Guests' Orientation of the Philippines

The orientations of guests visiting places in the Philippines were also captured in the contributions. Guests' tourism orientations can be shaped by several individual factors and practices (such as the tourist gaze), but also by the artefacts projected to them by service providers (Alejandria-Gonzalez, 2016) and the tourism experiences that they co-create with host communities. Analyzing stranded travel vloggers' content on Youtube, Badilla, Carvajal, C.F. Castro, and M.P. Castro (chapter "Home Away from Home: Foreign Vloggers' Gaze of the Philippines During the COVID-19 Pandemic") showed that destination characteristics, food experiences, local authorities' handling of the COVID-19 pandemic, and Filipino qualities influenced these visitors' images of the country. Their findings revealed Filipinos' "friendly, helpful, hospitable, laidback, and easy-going" attitude in touristic interactions in a pandemic setting, traits that are consistent with the Filipino brand of hospitality.

Baquillas and Gozun (chapter "Strolling Between Shanties: Tourists' Perceptions and Experiences of Manila's Slums") provided insights into the images of an urban community experiencing poverty by drawing from online data generated by tourists engaging in slum tourism in Manila. Their findings emphasized that the affective component (e.g., feelings and emotions) of the visitors' experiences provided deeper insights into this atypical tourism activity, and tour participants' image of the tourism activity and locations. Specifically, the tourism experience was revealed to evoke positive emotions emphasizing the eye-opening nature of the tour, subsequently encouraging guests to reflect on their experiences.

Del Rosario, Montes, and Battad (chapter "Interpreting the Meanings of Carabao Festivals in the Philippines: A Multi-method Study") provided insights into the images of agricultural communities in the Philippines, by assuming the role of tourists (the researchers as the "guests") in visiting and unpacking the meanings of selected carabao festivals. Through an insider lens coupled with other methodological approaches, these authors argued that while the carabao festivals' projected images have shown some images of farming life in the Philippines, these do not fully represent the current hardships experienced by the agricultural sector. Nonetheless, the festivals showed the deep entanglements between the carabaos and Filipino farmers.

2 Concluding Thoughts and Future Research Suggestions

Individuals' desire to see and experience others' way of life is a fundamental driver of tourism. Similarly, the tangible and intangible manifestations of culture make up one integral capital for communities engaged in this industry. Regardless of their role, tourism actors' (hosts or guests) cultural norms likewise shape their interactions with one another and their consumption of tourism experiences. This edited volume has shown how the diversity of the Filipino culture and society shapes the tourism phenomena co-created by host communities and guests to and within the country. The contributions offered insights into the realities of tourism in Philippine host communities through the various academic lenses employed by Filipino academics. In doing so, the chapters add to the burgeoning knowledge on contemporary Asian tourism. While the contributions delved into important issues, an exhaustive exploration of the facets of culture, society, and tourism in the Philippines was not presented in this volume. Nonetheless, this limitation offers opportunities for future research.

There is a strong need for scholarly investigations of how Filipino cultural values and norms are embedded in the creation of tourism experiences. Some of the contributions alluded to these cultural values gazed upon by visitors (e.g., hospitality) and community members (e.g., *bayanihan*) occurring on the surface of tourism-related social exchanges. Critical analyses are needed, particularly on the utilization of cultural values in branding the hospitality of the Filipino people (e.g., the Department of Tourism's programme, *The Filipino Brand of Service Excellence*). Future studies should dig deeper into the role of these norms and values, for example, by employing concepts of cultural complexity, Filipino social psychology, and critical ethnographic methods (e.g., Dela Santa & Tiatco, 2019; Ooi, 2019). Decolonial and indigenous approaches are also strongly encouraged in examining these topics.

As a population of a low-income country where tourism is an integral part of its economy, Filipinos are commonly framed as hosts engaging in tourism as a livelihood activity, in many tourism studies (e.g., Gier et al., 2017; Okazaki, 2008), and seldom viewed as tourists. Lacson and Gozun (chapter "The Traveling Filipina in Periodicals (1898–1938)") inquired how the Filipina engaged in leisure travel during the colonial era, offering insights from the past which are somewhat relevant today. For instance, this latter chapter indicates that tourism is a leisure activity predominantly for the elite members of society. Although tourism today is becoming more accessible to the country's middle and working classes, it can be implied that tourism is still viewed as a luxury rather than a necessity for most Filipinos. Since this volume's call for chapters, a stream of work focusing on Filipino travel behaviour has emerged, with recent publications looking at Filipinos' future time perspectives during flight delays (De Guzman et al., 2019b) and their happiness during festival attendance and international group tour participation (De Guzman et al., 2019a; Mesana & De Guzman, 2022). There is a need to further examine Filipino travel behaviour, not only for marketing purposes but also to better unpack how such travel practices change in line with the evolution of culture and society in the Philippines (e.g., Ooi, 2019).

Apart from cultural and societal forces, macro-environmental factors that shape tourism are also changing. One unprecedented event that happened while this volume is being edited is the COVID-19 pandemic. This externality has greatly impacted host communities that are dependent on tourism in many countries (Gössling & Schweiggart, 2022), including those in the Philippines. Future studies should explore how Filipino host communities have adapted to the impacts of the pandemic and their prospects for livelihood recovery. Most importantly, researchers should analyze these communities' sentiments and support towards tourism given that the vulnerability of the industry to crises and disasters has been further exposed during this period (Gössling et al., 2021). Such analyses are expected to shed light on the role of tourism in a post-pandemic Philippines and beyond.

References

Alejandria-Gonzalez, M. C. P. (2016). Cultural tourism development in the Philippines: An analysis of challenges and orientations. *Journal of Quality Assurance in Hospitality & Tourism, 17*(4), 496–515. https://doi.org/10.1080/1528008X.2015.1127194

Aquino, R. S. (2020). *Understanding community change through tourism social entrepreneurship in the Philippines: Host community perspectives* [Unpublished doctoral thesis, Auckland University of Technology].

De Guzman, A. B., Cruz, T. M. C., Garchitorena, J. N. A., Gatus, J. K., & Hernandez, R. P. R. (2019a). Who says aging is lonely? A phenomenology of Filipino older adults' experiences of happiness when joining international group tours. *Educational Gerontology, 45*(6), 365–376. https://doi.org/10.1080/03601277.2019.1640836

De Guzman, A. B., Labrador, S. E. Z., & Rodil, F. A. (2019b). Understanding Filipino tourists' future time perspective and emotional experiences during delayed international flights through design triangulation. *International Journal of Tourism Sciences, 19*(4), 324–336. https://doi.org/10.1080/15980634.2019.1706127

Dela Santa, E., & Tiatco, S. A. (2019). Tourism, heritage and cultural performance: Developing a modality of heritage tourism. *Tourism Management Perspectives, 31*, 301–309. https://doi.org/10.1016/j.tmp.2019.06.001

Gier, L., Christie, P., & Amolo, R. (2017). Community perceptions of scuba dive tourism development in Bien Unido, Bohol Island, Philippines. *Journal of Coastal Conservation, 21*(1), 153–166.

Gössling, S., & Schweiggart, N. (2022). Two years of COVID-19 and tourism: What we learned, and what we should have learned. *Journal of Sustainable Tourism*, 1–17. https://doi.org/10.1080/09669582.2022.2029872

Gössling, S., Scott, D., & Hall, C. M. (2021). Pandemics, tourism and global change: A rapid assessment of COVID-19. *Journal of Sustainable Tourism, 29*(1), 1–20. https://doi.org/10.1080/09669582.2020.1758708

Mesana, J. C. B., & De Guzman, A. B. (2022). Happiology in community festivals: A case of Filipino repeat local participants. *Leisure Studies, 41*(1), 129–145. https://doi.org/10.1080/02614367.2021.1948594

Okazaki, E. (2008). A community-based tourism model: Its conception and use. *Journal of Sustainable Tourism, 16*(5), 511–529. https://doi.org/10.1080/09669580802159594

Ooi, C.-S. (2019). Asian tourists and cultural complexity: Implications for practice and the Asianisation of tourism scholarship. *Tourism Management Perspectives, 31*, 14–23. https://doi.org/10.1016/j.tmp.2019.03.007

Porter, B. A., Orams, M. B., & Lück, M. (2018). Sustainable entrepreneurship tourism: An alternative development approach for remote coastal communities where awareness of tourism is low. *Tourism Planning & Development, 15*(2), 149–165. https://doi.org/10.1080/21568316.2017.1312507

Richard S. Aquino is a Lecturer of Tourism and Marketing at the UC Business School, University of Canterbury in Christchurch, New Zealand. He holds a Doctor of Philosophy from the Auckland University of Technology in New Zealand, where he also obtained his master's degree in international tourism management, and a Bachelor of Science in Tourism from the University of Santo Tomas in Manila, Philippines. His doctoral research focused on how the adoption of social entrepreneurship through tourism changes host communities in the Philippines. His other research interests include sustainable tourism planning and development, geotourism, tourist behaviour, and recently, the decolonization of tourism knowledge production. Currently, he serves as the research notes editor of *Tourism in Marine Environments* and an editor of the *Advances in Southeast Asian Studies*. Apart from academic work, he has been actively involved in tourism planning consultancy projects in the Philippines and New Zealand.

Brooke A. Porter works in knowledge management as an instructional designer with international aid agencies. Brooke holds a Doctor of Philosophy from the Auckland University of Technology in New Zealand, a master's in education from Chaminade University in Honolulu, Hawai'i, and a bachelor of science in marine biology from the Florida Institute of Technology in Melbourne, Florida. Some of her current work investigates tourism as a development and conservation strategy as well as the role of gender. Her doctoral research explored marine tourism as a supplemental livelihood for fisheries-based communities in the Philippines. Brooke also serves as an Honorary Research Fellow at Auckland University of Technology in New Zealand, and as scientific adviser to The Coral Triangle Conservancy, an NGO in the Philippines.

CPSIA information can be obtained
at www.ICGtesting.com
Printed in the USA
LVHW080434310123
738223LV00005B/140

9 789811 940125